People, Fire and Forests

People, Fire and Forests

A Synthesis of Wildfire Social Science

edited by

Terry C. Daniel, Matt Carroll,
Cassandra Moseley, and Carol Raish

Oregon State University Press
Corvallis

Cite individual chapters by author or authors. Fictitious example:
Flame, W. W. 2007. Wildland Fire Events: Dealing with the
Consequences. In T. C. Daniel, M. S. Carroll, C. Moseley, and C. Raish
(eds.), *People, Fire, and Forests: A Synthesis of Wildfire Social Science.*
Corvallis: Oregon State University Press, Pp. 100-135.

*For permission to reproduce chapters of this book for class packets and
other uses, please contact the Oregon State University Press at the address
below, through our Web site, or at osu.press@oregonstate.edu*

The paper in this book meets the guidelines for permanence and durability
of the Committee on Production Guidelines for Book Longevity of the
Council on Library Resources and the minimum requirements of the
American National Standard for Permanence of Paper for Printed Library
Materials Z39.48-1984.

Library of Congress Cataloging-in-Publication Data
People, fire and forests : a synthesis of wildfire social science / edited by
Terry C. Daniel ... [et al.].
    p. cm.
  Includes bibliographical references and index.
  ISBN-13: 978-0-87071-184-8 (alk. paper)
  ISBN-10: 0-87071-184-9 (alk. paper)
  1. Wildfires--Social aspects--United States. 2. Fire ecology--United States.
3. Fire management--United States. 4. Wildfires--Prevention and control--
Social aspects--United States. I. Daniel, Terry C.
  SD421.3.P46 2007
  363.37'9--dc22

                                            2006039350

First published in 2007 by Oregon State University Press
Printed in the United States of America

Oregon State University Press
500 Kerr Administration
Corvallis OR 97331-2122
541-737-3166 • fax 541-737-3170
http://oregonstate.edu/dept/press

Table of Contents

Foreword: Synthesis and Collaboration

Hanna J. Cortner and Donald R. Field

Drought, forests under stress from years of fire exclusion, and continued residential development in high-fire-risk areas have combined to raise the prospects of wildland fire occurrences involving life and property. Fire has risen to a prominent place on the political agenda, prompting new public policy initiatives such as the National Fire Plan and the Healthy Forests Restoration Act of 2003 (HFRA). The National Fire Plan, developed after the 2000 fire season, addresses the need to respond to severe wildfire and its impacts on communities. The Healthy Forests Restoration Act, an outgrowth of President George W. Bush's Healthy Forests Initiative, authorizes $760 million a year for fuels reduction activity on 20 million acres of the nation's forests (half of the dollars must be spent for projects undertaken in wildland-urban interface areas). The act provides incentives for communities to prepare wildfire-protection plans and take proactive measures to encourage willing property owners to reduce fire risks on private property. The act also limits judicial review, and along with additional changes in administrative rules implemented under the Bush initiative, reduces the amount of environmental analysis required under the National Environmental Policy Act of 1969 in order to expedite timber harvesting associated with fuels reduction.

To be effective, these new policies will need to be informed by science. Science, for example, will play a role in HFRA's legislatively permitted all-party monitoring of "the positive and negative ecological and social effects of authorized fuel reduction projects." Science will also be needed to provide information to planners and managers about how individuals perceive fire hazards, how communities prepare for and respond to fire hazards, and how institutional arrangements facilitate or constrain alternative fire-management practices. Moreover, lessons learned from other hazards and how humans interact to prepare for and respond to them are also needed to inform future fire emergencies. Solving fire problems is not just about manipulating vegetation to reduce risk or about improving technical capabilities to fight fires; it is also about understanding social values, socioeconomic factors, demographic trends, and institutional arrangements, and about changing human behavior. Social science has an important, albeit often historically minimized, role to play in fire science.

During the 1980s and 1990s considerable work on public attitudes toward fire management, perceptions of fire risk, wildfire risk mitigation in the wildland-urban interface, and fire economics occurred (e.g., Cortner et al. 1990; Davis 1988; González-Caban and McKetta 1986; McCool and Stankey 1986; Taylor and Daniel 1984). Much of this work occurred about the time the wildland/urban interface as a fire problem gained a heightened national profile. This was once thought of as largely a southern California problem, but during the mid-1980s researchers began to realize that in varying degrees and in differing forms interface fire situations could be found in virtually every state as well as internationally. Multiple initiatives and partnerships were formed to focus discussion and resources on wildland/urban fire problems (USDA Forest Service et al. 1987), including efforts to define a research, development, and application agenda for fire-related social science research (Gale and Cortner 1987). Yet, this period was also marked by the skepticism of important managers who felt that "our best interests do not lie in sociological research." They argued that, while addressing "intellectually interesting" questions, such research did not serve any "practical purposes and would merely consume precious dollars that could be spent on more valuable research" (Bethea 1987, p. 8).

It is thus not surprising that sustaining interest in fire social science research proved problematic, and that there was a hiatus in the initiation of new fire social science during the early and mid-1990s. This changed, however, as the new millennium began to come into view. Very large, catastrophic fires captured media headlines and the attention of policy makers concerned about firefighter safety, loss of human life and property, and fiscal impacts on the national treasury. In addition to providing new dollars for fire-management activities and adopting new decision-making rules, the resulting policy changes included a new emphasis on fire research. The National Fire Plan, for example, outlined a cooperative long-term program of research and development to support efforts to reduce human and ecological losses from wildfire. The dollars provided through the National Fire Plan, and the Joint Fire Science Program—a partnership of six Department of Agriculture and Department of the Interior agencies authorized and funded by Congress in 1997—attracted a new generation of scholars to the fire research arena.

The early 2000s also saw other activities in support of fire social science, including the National Wildfire Coordinating Group's establishment of a social science research task group and sponsorship of Burning Questions, a social science research agenda on fire (Machlis et al. 2002). Social science also played a prominent role in a series of workshops co-sponsored by the National Fire Plan, Joint Fire Science Program, and USDA Forest Service to discuss priority research areas and identify characteristics of effective managerial and science partnerships (White 2004). Institutional support from the fire establishment for incorporating social science into the research mix has been increasing.

That new opportunities existed for social science researchers to explore the human dimensions of fire was clearly evident in June 2002 at the Eighth International Symposium on Society and Resource Management (ISSRM) in Bloomington, Indiana. Several sessions were devoted to fire (Jakes 2002), as well as a standing-room-only breakfast event organized by the Forest Service's North Central Research Station. A decade earlier at such meetings there would have been only a few isolated researchers working on fire-related issues. The participation and level of enthusiasm for fire social science demonstrated at the ISSRM symposium laid the foundation for the collaborative efforts leading to this volume.

While embracing this heightened research interest in fire, the two of us remained concerned that these new opportunities could be squandered if the resulting social science did not have direct and immediate application for fire managers and policy makers. Ecologically oriented fire researchers have had a much longer period of time to accumulate a body of knowledge, weave a potent story about the adverse ecological outcomes of past fire-exclusion policies, and build scientifically based arguments for the need to implement fuels reduction and ecological restoration programs. But what were the stories social scientists could cogently tell? What if we discovered, after all the new fire research dollars and infusion of researcher enthusiasm, the end result was a bunch of highly reductionist studies, which might be significant in their own right and contribute to the growth of social science theory, but have minimal cumulative impact or utility for managers and policy makers? Would there be another chance? Would the skeptics of the mid-1980s return to argue against the practicality of social science research? We agreed that there was a critical need to convene social scientists working on fire-related questions and to continue the networking and sharing, expanding upon the ideas identified at the ISSRM in 2002. Social scientists needed an opportunity to share research results, address explicitly the "so what" questions in terms of their research, identify further collaborative opportunities, focus on maximizing social science results on management and policy making, and have more time to talk to one another. We approached the Forest Service about organizing such a workshop. Pam Jakes of the North Central Research Station joined with us and provided Forest Service leadership in designing the workshop, the first event of what would evolve into a series of "Tucson Forums."

The resulting workshop, Tucson I, "Social Science Applied to Fire Management," was held January 26-28, 2003 (Cortner et al. 2003).

Workshop sponsors included the Ecological Restoration Institute at Northern Arizona University, the National Park Service Intermountain Region, the University of Wisconsin-Madison, USDA Forest Service North Central Research Station, and the Western Rural Development Center (Utah State University). Approximately forty participants from academic institutions, federal research and management agencies, and independent organizations attended the workshop. Because we realized that human/environment issues in fire are not bounded simply, and that there are multiple entry points for social science research, we made a number of tradeoffs in workshop design. For example, numerous areas of interest to social scientists broadly defined (e.g., historians, economists) were not covered. Instead we focused our discussions on five areas: individuals, communities, fire across the gradient, culture/ethnicity, and policy/institutions. Five brief papers addressing these themes were delivered. Each was designed to be thought provoking and integrative rather than an opportunity for presenting original research. We aimed at maximizing informal discussions around these topics as well as across perspectives and subject matter. Although several managers were invited and attended the workshop, in this forum we decided to primarily emphasize networking among researchers as a needed first step.

Importantly, researchers attending the workshop committed to several ongoing and collaborative activities to foster communication among themselves as well as to maximize the utility of social science research applied to fire management. A call for papers was issued for a special issue on humans, fire, and forests for the international journal Society and Natural Resources. The two of us served as guest editors, managing a process that yielded a surprisingly large number of submissions, far in excess of what had been anticipated. It became clear the journal could not plan for just a single issue. Consequently, special-issue papers eventually appeared in volumes 17(6), 17(8), and 18(4) of the journal (Cortner and Field 2004).

Another suggested follow-on and collaborative activity from Tucson I centered on the need for a better merging of science and management. In addition, researchers at the workshop agreed that it would be useful to develop a more structured framework or model that would facilitate synthesis as well as further the identification of where research gaps remained. A matrix integrating bio-physical, social-demographic and socio-cultural dimensions of the wildfire problem was proposed as an organizing mechanism to help accrete our collective knowledge and foster integrative discussions about what was known and not known across these multiple dimensions. Al Luloff (Pennsylvania State University), Courtney Flint (Pennsylvania State University), Rick Krannich (Utah State University), and Don Field agreed to take the lead developing such a matrix.

Finally, another committee (Terry Daniel and Barbara Morehouse of the University of Arizona and Dan Williams of the USDA Forest Service Rocky Mountain Research Station, along with Cortner, Field, Jakes, and Luloff) volunteered to take the next steps in furthering the ideas of synthesis, matrix application, and managerial applications. The committee met in May 2003 in St. Paul, Minnesota, and outlined a work plan to further the discussions from Tucson I, including the commissioning of a number of synthesis papers on an expanded—albeit again not inclusive—set of fire social science topics.

Preparation of a series of synthesis papers, the committee realized, would not be an easy task, for a number of reasons. First, the specific focus of those papers would be synthesis of what was already known, not original research. Scientists are often more comfortable focusing on new research. This comfort might be related to their inquisitive nature and desire to be at the forefront of new discovery. But it might also be related to the long-standing incentives in academe and in government research centers that reward original research more heavily than synthesis.

Second, a primary audience for the papers would be managers and policy makers. Federal, state, and local resource managers with responsibilities for making decisions prior to, during, or after wildfire events want their decisions to be informed by the best available science. And, as noted above, there is increased recognition of the importance of understanding the social values and social issues that affect, and are affected by, their decisions. Making the link between research and managerial action, however, is not as uncomplicated as it might sound. Social scientists, for example, are trained to embed their research topics and results in social science theory and methodologies. Furthering science and disciplinary development, they are frequently told, is more important than solving public policy problems (Ripley 1991). Scientists often discuss implications, but are reluctant to go beyond describing the consequences of alternative options to making outright managerial recommendations. In part, this is because of the incompleteness of all research, which entails continued uncertainty and a high chance of error. In part, it is because some are wary of moving beyond neutral science to advocacy. These factors often provide constraints on achieving practicality.

Finally, while managers might be a principal audience, the products would also have to be highly regarded and used by social science colleagues, including both government scientists, who have a responsibility to transfer scientific information to agency line officers, and university faculty involved in research and teaching. Finding the right balance between scientific rigor and managerial "friendliness" is a challenging conceptual and writing task.

Along with Barbara Morehouse we agreed to identify lead authors for the synthesis papers and assemble those authors for a pre-writing meeting in Tucson in January of 2004 (Tucson II). Cortner agreed to serve as manager/ treasurer for the project, which again received financial support from Pam Jakes' research project at the North Central Station.

At Tucson II, lead authors presented proposals for the synthesis papers that they and their chosen co-authors had agreed upon, and discussed related project activities. The lead authors made a number of significant decisions. In addition to agreeing to present their papers at a series of panels during the next ISSRM meeting in Keystone, Colorado, June 2-6, 2004, the authors agreed to assemble their papers for book publication. Terry Daniel, Matt Carroll (Washington State University), Cass Moseley (University of Oregon), and Carol Raish (USDA Forest Service Rocky Mountain Station) volunteered to lead this activity, and thus serve as editors of this book. In addition, the lead authors each agreed to prepare a five-page companion paper highlighting the essential managerial lessons learned from their syntheses. These lessons learned would be presented at a panel in Keystone and submitted for publication in a USDA Forest Service General Technical Report (GTR). Pam Jakes and Dan Williams agreed to serve as editors of the GTR. In essence, the GTR would be designed with the goal of maximizing managerial utility, collating the lessons in a form and format easily accessible by managers, while the synthesis papers would provide the detailed scientific backup for the findings presented in the GTR.

Not unexpectedly, much discussion during Tucson II focused on development and application of the matrix model. Although social scientists have long argued that focus on the biophysical and technical factors addresses just a small portion of most natural resource problems, discussion of the matrix also made it apparent that much existing social science research failed to relate adequately to the biophysical context. While social scientists may excel at correlating their principal variables to the age, gender, or political affiliation of their human subjects, many studies are separated from ecological context, as if it makes no difference whether the study is taking place in a ponderosa pine or Douglas fir forest. Consequently, the authors decided that, as a whole, the book would promote the matrix concept of multi-dimensionality, but given the existing body of research, not each and every chapter would be able to use the matrix effectively as an organizing framework. Consequently, a conscious decision was made to neither force rigorous adherence to the matrix model nor to insist that all chapters would equally apply it. Instead the concluding chapter of the volume would expand upon the matrix concept, illustrate how existing social science research could inform its development, and serve as a challenge for the body of future fire research to be more integrative and more attuned to fire's multiple dimensions—biophysical, socio-demographic, and socio-cultural.

A final decision made by the participants at Tucson II was to organize another forum, Tucson III. This time they agreed that it would be important to have a greater focus on managerial participation and dialogues. Morehouse agreed to take the lead in facilitating this meeting, assisted by Cortner, Carroll, Field, and Jonathan Taylor of the U.S. Geological Survey. Tucson III was held January 10-12, 2005and had extensive involvement by managers and community representatives, expanding the conversation to topics that had not been highlighted in previous forum activity, such as communication during fire events.

Like much public policy, the Tucson Forums developed incrementally. There was no overarching research proposal from the outset that set out a grand design enumerating all the products that eventually resulted. Without Forest Service financial support the process could not have proceeded. But even then, additional support was needed and pieced together from here and there, including Cortner's then-current employer, the Ecological Restoration Institute at Northern Arizona University, conference co-sponsors, the participants' own research projects, and personal pocketbooks. Much depended on the willingness of different individuals to step into a leadership role for different aspects of the project. As with other successful collaborations, there was not just one leader, but many leaders.

The data and information presented in this volume and through the other activities of the Tucson Forums collaboration, it is hoped, will lead to on-the-ground managerial actions that are ecologically sound, socially acceptable, economically efficient, and politically feasible. Given the fact that millions of acres of public lands are still at high risk for future catastrophic fire events, the issues highlighted by the recent fire seasons and discussed by the authors in this book are not likely to go away any time soon. As historian Steven Pyne has often eloquently reminded us, fire is not just a biophysical occurrence, it is also a cultural phenomenon, and humans are the "keepers of the flame" (Pyne 1982, 2001). Keeping that flame will necessarily involve original research and synthesis in the human dimensions arena as well as collaboration and integration among multiple disciplines across time and space.

REFERENCES

Bethea, J. M. 1987. "Role of social science: Remarks." In R. D. Gale and H. J. Cortner (eds.), People and Fire at the Wildland/Urban Interface: A Sourcebook. Washington, D.C.: USDA Forest Service.

Cortner, H. J., P. D. Gardner, and J. G. Taylor. 1990. "Fire hazards at the urban-wildland/interface: What the public expects." *Environmental Management*, 14:57-62.

———, D. R. Field, and J. D. Buthman (eds). 2003. Humans, fire, and forests— social science applied to fire management. Workshop summary. Flagstaff, Arizona: Ecological Restoration Institute.

———, and D. R. Field. 2004. "Introduction to the special issue: Humans, fire, and forests: The reemergence of research on human dimensions." *Society and Natural Resources* 17:473-75.

Davis, J. B. 1988. "The wildland-urban interface: What it is, where it is, and its fire management problems." In W. C. Fischer and S. F. Arno (compilers), Protecting people and homes from wild fire in the interior West: Proceedings of the symposium and workshop. General Technical Report INT-251, Ogden, Utah: USDA Forest Service Intermountain Research Station. pp. 160-65.

Gale, R. D., and H. J. Cortner. 1987. *People and Fire at the Wildland/Urban Interface: A Sourcebook.* Washington, D.C.: USDA Forest Service.

González-Caban, A., and C. W. McKetta. 1986. "Analyzing fuel treatment costs." *Western Journal of Applied Forestry*, 1:116-21.

Jakes, P. J. (compiler). 2002. Homeowners, communities and wildfire: Science findings from the National Fire Plan, Proceedings of the Ninth International Symposium on Society and Resource Management. General Technical Report NC-231, St Paul, Minnesota: USDA Forest Service North Central Research Station.

Machlis, G. E., A. B. Kaplan, S. P. Tuler, K. A. Bagby, and J. E. McKendry. 2002. Burning questions: A social science research plan for federal wildland fire management. Moscow, Idaho: University of Idaho, College of Natural Resources, Idaho Forest, Wildlife, and Range Experiment Station.

McCool, S., and G. Stankey. 1986. Visitor attitudes toward wilderness fire management policy, 1971-1984. Research paper INT-RP-357, Ogden, Utah: USDA Forest Service Intermountain Forest and Range Experiment Station.

Pyne, S. J. 1982. *Fire in America: A Cultural History of Wildland and Rural Fire.* Princeton, New Jersey: Princeton University Press. Reprinted in paperback 1997. Seattle: University of Washington Press.

———. 2001. "The fires this time, and next." *Science* 294: 1005-6.

Ripley, R. 1991. "Political science, policy studies, and practitioners: The possibilities of partnerships." *Policy Currents* (newsletter of the Public Policy Section of the American Political Science Association) 1(3): 1-3.

Taylor, J. G., and T. C. Daniel. 1984. "Prescribed fire: Public education and perception." *Journal of Forestry*, 82 (6): 361-65.

USDA Forest Service, National Fire Protection Association, and United States Fire Administration. 1987. Wildfire Strikes Home. Video cassette. Quincy, MA: National Fire Protection Association.

White, S. M. 2004. Bridging the worlds of fire managers and researchers: Lessons and opportunities from the wildland fire workshops. General Technical Report PNW 599, Portland, Oregon: USDA Forest Service Pacific Northwest Research Station.

Introduction

Terry C. Daniel, Matthew S. Carroll, Cassandra Moseley, and Carol Raish

People, Fire, and Forests provides a synthesis of existing social science research relevant to the management of wildfire risks. Like major wildfire episodes of the past, the record-setting fires that introduced the twenty-first century stimulated renewed public concern and political action. The primary focus has been the protection of human lives and of developments that have been rapidly expanding into the wildland-urban interface—and into the path of increasingly large and intense wildfires. Ecological restoration, especially of fire-adapted systems, has also been a concern, urged particularly by environmental managers and citizens' groups. The key premise of this volume is that understanding and effectively responding to wildfire risk requires recognition of the interrelated effects of the biophysical and sociodemographic features of at-risk environments and the socio-cultural characteristics and histories of the people exposed to that risk. The recent resurgence of social science research related to wildfire risk inspires this synthesis. The predictable decline as other concerns inevitably redirect public attention and the political agenda urges timely capture and documentation of what has been found about the critical human/social dimensions of the wildfire problem. The complementary goals of *People, Fire, and Forests* are to make relevant social science research more available and useful to wildfire risk managers and to encourage and guide further social science research into wildfire and related human-environment problems.

Dimensions of Wildfire Risk

The biophysical dimension of wildfire risk is the most obvious and has had the longest and most sustained research and management attention. Terrain, vegetation cover (fuel type and condition), climate, and weather have long been recognized to be among the most critical factors affecting the probability, extent, and intensity of a wildfire. These factors form the primary bases for fire-hazard warning systems, fire-protection planning, and

Terry C. Daniel, Dept. of Psychology, University of Arizona (tdaniel@U.Arizona. edu); Matthew S. Carroll, Dept. of Natural Resource Sciences, Washington State University; Cassandra Moseley, Ecosystem Workforce Program, University of Oregon; Carol B. Raish, USDA Forest Service, Rocky Mountain Research Station fire-suppression strategies. As human development has moved up to and intertwined with wildlands, human structures have added a new element to the fuel mix, and have complicated fire-behavior models and fire-suppression tactics.

Of course, wildfire is not solely or even primarily a biophysical problem. Structures are more than fuel for the fire. They are also homes, churches, hospitals, and schools, and the people who reside in, visit, and use these places add an essential social dimension to wildfire risk management. Wildfire is a problem because it disrupts human use of the landscape, threatens and negatively affects people's lives, and damages developments and natural environments that people value. A key motivation for early wildfire-suppression policies was to protect valuable timber resources. Now human developments pose by far the greatest economic risk, forcing a shift in focus for wildfire-management policies. But fire also has beneficial uses in the landscape. All over the world people historically have set fire to the land to improve and maintain pasture and agricultural fields, and to gain access to other environmental resources. Indeed, human use of fire has been so pervasive and of such long duration that much of what today we take to be natural landscapes was in fact created by primitive human land-management practices. It is now widely recognized by biologists and ecologists that fire is essential for sustaining many important natural ecosystems, necessitating modifications of fire-management policies, and complicating the messages about fire that managers and agencies send out to the public.

People have long been recognized as part of the wildfire problem, but primarily as sources of ignitions and targets for fire-prevention campaigns ("only YOU can prevent forest fires"). The rapid growth of the wildland-urban interface has meant that wildfire-suppression efforts are increasingly directed toward protection of structures and people, sometimes at the expense of actions that might have more effectively and quickly contained the fire. The people themselves can get in the way of fire-fighting activities, and communicating with, evacuating, and comforting affected people have become major components of managing a fire event. The number, distribution, and capabilities of the people threatened by a fire are a key concern in pre-fire planning and suppression strategies. Special attention must be given to children, the elderly, and others with limited mobility. Because of differing personal experiences or special situations, institutional constraints, or cultural backgrounds, people respond differently to pre-fire education and warnings, to emergency instructions during a fire, and to recovery and restoration efforts after a fire. Institutional conflicts among local, state, and federal agencies and private landowners can hamper protection efforts. Wildfire risk can be significantly reduced or exacerbated by the locations of homes and other structures in the landscape and by what building materials and designs are used. Knowing about the relevant sociodemographic characteristics of at-risk areas/populations and how they are distributed across a fire-threatened area can be as important to fire-protection planning and suppression strategies as knowing the amount, condition, and distribution of fuels.

While people are clearly part of the wildfire risk problem, people are also an essential part of the solution. As wildfire risk-management strategies have begun to emphasize pre-fire mitigation, the support and active participation of communities and individual property owners in at-risk areas have assumed growing importance. The large-scale fuel-reduction treatment programs proposed by the National Fire Plan and the Healthy Forests Restoration Act, and especially the necessary maintenance of these treatments into the future, cannot be effectively accomplished without very substantial cooperation and contributions from local communities and property owners. Sustained political support from the larger population of citizens is also required.

Public education and safety programs, such as Firewise and other disaster preparation and emergency response programs, recognize that well-prepared communities and individuals can facilitate fire-protection efforts by better taking care of themselves, and even by providing important information and assistance in the event of a fire. But effectively recruiting and maintaining needed public support and cooperation requires understanding how communities and individuals operate, how they become aware of and perceive wildfire risks, what motivates and constrains their responses to that risk, and how they might learn more effective responses and be persuaded to implement and maintain them. For example, research has shown that the source of fire-risk information must be considered credible and trustworthy, and that interactive face-to-face communication increases credibility and encourages adoption of risk-mitigation measures (Lindell and Perry 2000; Lindell and Whitney 2000). Just as no two forests (grasslands, chaparral, etc) are alike in their fire behavior, communities and individuals differ in their perception of and response to wildfire risks, and to efforts to recruit them to participate in risk-management programs. Still, as in the biophysical realm, the methods of science offer a means to understand common processes and to abstract basic principles that may be hidden in the complexity of differences. The social science research reviewed in *People, Fire, and Forests* provides important lessons and basic principles that can apply across different cultures, communities, and individuals. When properly applied by wildfire risk managers these lessons and principles can reduce risks before a fire, facilitate suppression efforts during a fire, and speed up and improve recovery and restoration efforts after a fire.

Managing Wildfire Risk

Wildfire risk management has historically most relied on two basic approaches—fire prevention and fire suppression. Considerable effort has been spent on public education campaigns to reduce wildfire starts, with the Smokey Bear campaign being among the most successful of all public relations programs. Similarly, improvements in fire-suppression technology and increased fire-fighting resources have successfully reduced the size of whatever fires do start. Public support for prevention and suppression programs has been relatively easy to attain. For protecting the forest (and the public) from wildfires, it is hard to argue with don't let fires start in the first place, and put them out as quickly as possible if they do start burning. But risk management founded on this simple logic has not worked out exactly as intended.

By most accounts, the frequency of very large wildfires has increased over the past two decades (Arno and Allison-Bunnell 2002), caused and/ or exacerbated by drought, fuel accumulations, insect outbreaks, and prior land-use practices, but particularly due to effective (perhaps too effective) fire prevention and suppression (USDA Forest Service 2003). The notable spike in damage to developed property in 2000 and again in 2003 is a strong signal that the trend toward more large fires will continue and that the exposure of people and property to wildfire risk will keep growing. Recent severe fires were widely covered by national news media and were featured dramatically on television. Public attention and alarm promoted political action and new risk-management policies, including the National Fire Plan and the Healthy Forests Restoration Act.

In addition to continuing fire prevention and suppression efforts, fuel reduction—by thinning of small-diameter trees, removal of brush, prescribed burning, and the creation of fire breaks—has been elevated to a major focus (McCarthy 2004; Western Governor's Association 2001). However, there has been considerable controversy about the motivations and the effectiveness of these measures in different ecological circumstances (Agee 2002; Hessburg and Agee 2003; Martinson et al. 2003). Moreover, the scale of the proposed fuel-reduction program may substantially exceed existing or achievable capabilities of responsible agencies, with 39 million acres in the interior west estimated as affected by excessive fuels (General Accounting Office 1999) and 126 million acres of public lands judged to be at high risk from wildfire (USDA Forest Service 2000).

A significant obstacle to fuel-reduction programs is cost. From the perspective of the responsible public agencies even the unprecedented billions of dollars appropriated for recent wildfire risk-reduction programs is barely sufficient to get the process started. Moreover, most of the National Fire Plan appropriations have been directed toward more traditional fire suppression and preparation, with limited funding for hazard reduction and other risk-management approaches (McCarthy 2004). Sharing costs with states and local communities, themselves strapped for money, is not likely to make up the shortfall. Finding ways to generate economic benefits to offset costs shows some promise, but is significantly hampered by the inaccessibility and low quality of the small-diameter materials that most need to be removed, and the subsequent lack of demand for the materials that most need to be removed. Moreover, fuel-reduction programs are perceived by many to be thinly disguised timber harvests that would otherwise not be allowed, paradoxically making economic success a political liability. In addition to financial costs, wildland-urban interface communities and individual property owners frequently perceive thinning and prescribed burning treatments as degrading scenic beauty, naturalness, ecosystem health, wildlife habitat, and other amenity values that brought them to these areas in the first place.

The perceived trade-off of immediate effort, costs, and degradation of desired amenities to achieve partial protection against damage from an uncertain, low-probability event in the future is understandably not attractive to many people. To make matters worse, to be effective fuel-reduction treatments have to be repeated on a regular basis in perpetuity, especially if no wildfire occurs. This makes these mitigation programs even more difficult to promote to at-risk communities and individuals, and to the national citizenry who must pay a large share of the financial costs. In short, the success of wildfire risk management hinges as much on the acceptance, support, and compliance of at-risk communities and individuals and the general public as on biophysical fire science and technology.

Wildfire Risk in Context

Wildfire has historically been rather low on the list of concerns for public safety and environmental risk-management agencies in the U.S. The observation of Gardner, Cortner, and Widaman (1987) that wildfire was not high on the list of risk concerns for the general public also remains largely true today. Wildfire has not attracted much attention from those charged with protecting the public against a wide range of hazards, and has essentially been ignored in the vast hazards and risk-management literature. Thus, it is appropriate to step back for a moment to consider where wildfire fits in the greater scheme of the many hazards and risks that modern humans face.

The National Weather Service monitors and annually reports on fatalities, injuries, and property damage from natural hazards in the U.S. A total of sixteen major hazards are covered, ranging from avalanches to winter storms. Compared to the death rates from health, crime, and technological hazards, which claim hundreds of thousands of lives each year, natural hazards altogether are not a major source of fatalities, typically numbering around five hundred per year. There are hundreds of wildfires every year, and hundreds of thousands of acres are burned, but wildfire has not historically affected large numbers of people even by the standards of natural hazards. Few people are killed and there has typically been relatively little damage to homes, businesses, and other properties that count most in hazard statistics. Wildfire is not included in the main list of natural hazards monitored by the National Weather Service. Instead, fire weather is found among the eleven "other" hazards, along with fog, rain, and dust storms.

Technical assessments and public concerns about hazards are strongly influenced by the number of fatalities and injuries to people. Wildfire has rarely achieved the levels of mortality caused by other natural hazards, on an annual or per event basis. Reported fatalities from wildfires were three for the year 2000 and five for 2001. This must be compared to about 160 fatalities per year for heat waves, and eighty per year for floods. Wildfires accounted for an average of less than 0.5% of natural-hazard fatalities between 2000 and 2004, and a little less than 2.5% of injuries, with the highest number being the 138 recorded for 2002. In contrast, tornados resulted in nearly one thousand injuries per year over these five years. The fact that most people injured and fatalities from wildfires have been firefighters, and not the general public, would further reduce public perception of risk. But property damage is another key factor in risk assessments, and it is here that the fires of 2000 and 2003 stand out. Wildfires typically contribute less than 5% of damage caused by natural hazards, but in 2000 fires accounted for over a third and in 2003 just less than a quarter of all property losses from natural hazards.

Wildfires have historically been a rural phenomenon, happening well away from and having little impact on developed population centers. But people and developments have been increasingly moving up to and into what were previously remote wildlands. Decades of fire-protection efforts that were well intended and reasonably justified in their time have set up these wildland-urban interface areas to have larger and more intense fires. The unprecedented fires that ushered in the twenty-first century dramatically signal the emergence of a new and far more dangerous context for wildfire, a context within which wildfire managers and policy must now contend.

People, Fire, and Forests

The following chapters present a synthesis of social science research that addresses the critical human-social dimensions of wildfire. The four chapters in the first section review work from the fields of natural hazards, diffusion of innovations, social acceptability, and risk perception and response, and examine how all of these aspects are influenced by larger social and cultural factors. These chapters focus on the effects of perceptions, values, and beliefs on individuals' responses to hazards and risks based on a large body of relevant social science research and on the smaller body of available research specifically addressing wildfire risk. The three chapters in the second section of the book review research on how local communities cope with wildfire risk, as a threat and as a reality. This section is organized around an event-driven model of wildfire risk, distinguishing between the responses required of communities and wildfire risk managers before, during, and after a wildfire event. The four chapters in the third section are focused on institutional and economic factors that influence how wildfire risk-management policy is made and how interrelationships between federal, state, and local agencies and private interests facilitate or hamper the effective implementation of those policies, and how the costs and benefits of wildfire risk-management options are distributed through society. The concluding chapter of the book is primarily addressed to social scientists who are or who might become involved in wildfire risk-management research. The key message of this chapter, and of the volume as a whole, is that to be most useful to management practice and to accumulating scientific understanding, wildfire risk research must be fit within a framework that recognizes the interrelationships and interdependencies among biophysical, sociodemographic, and socio-cultural dimensions of the problem.

Although *People, Fire, and Forests* is specifically focused on wildfire, the social science lessons and principles presented may readily be applied to a wide range of other environmental and natural resource management issues. All environmental problems have a substantial human-social component. Indeed, "environmental problem" is a misnomer, as it is not the environment, but humans and human societies that define and experience environmental change as a problem. Moreover, it is humans and their societies that create environmental problems for themselves. Thus, the success of wildfire risk management and of environmental management more generally depends very substantially on understanding and affecting the behavior of individuals, communities, institutions, and society. The authors of *People, Fire, and Forests* offer this synthesis of social science research relevant to wildfire risk management to increase environmental managers' understanding and appreciation of the importance of the human-social dimensions of their essential tasks, and to encourage social science colleagues to commit some of their intellect and research skills to expanding and refining the scientific basis for more effective environmental management.

REFERENCES

Agee, J. K. 2002. "The fallacy of passive management." *Conservation Biology in Practice* 3(1):18-25.

Arno, S. F., and S. Allison-Bunnel. 2002. *Flames in Our Forest: Disaster or Renewal?* Washington, D.C.: Island Press. 227 p.

Gardner, P. D., H. J. Cortner, and K. Widaman. 1987. "The risk perceptions and policy response toward wildland fire hazards by urban homeowners." *Landscape and Urban Planning* 14: 163-72.

General Accounting Office (GAO). 1999. "Western national forests: a cohesive strategy is needed to address catastrophic wildfire threats." Report to the subcommittee on forests and forest health, committee on resources, House of Representatives. GAO/RCED-99-65. Washington, D.C.: General Accounting Office.

Hessburg, P. F., and J. K. Agee. 2003. "An environmental narrative of inland northwest United States forests, 1800-2000." *Forest Ecology and Management* 178:23-59.

Lindell, M. K., and R. W. Perry. 2000. "Household adjustment to earthquake hazard: A review of research." *Environment and Behavior* 32:590-630.

——, and D. J. Whitney. 2000. "Correlates of seismic hazard adjustment adoption." *Risk Analysis* 20: 13-25.

Martinson, E., P. N. Omi, and W. Sheppard. 2003. "Effects of fuel treatments on fire severity." In R. T. Graham (ed.), Hayman fire case study, Fort Collins, Colorado: USDA Forest Service, Rocky Mountain Research Station.

McCarthy, L. F. 2004. Snapshot: The state of the National Fire Plan. The Forest Trust, April 2004 [cited May 25 2004]. Available from http://www.theforesttrust.org/images/forestprotection/Snapshot-Master.pdf.

National Weather Service, NOAA, Weather Hazard Statistics, http://www.nws.noaa.gov/om/hazstats.shtml#, accessed January 2005.

USDA Forest Service. 2000. Protecting people and sustaining resources in fire-adapted ecosystems–a cohesive strategy, the Forest Service management response to the General Accounting Office Report, GAO/RCED-99-65.

——. 2003. Wildfire statistics. http://www.nifc.gov/stats/wildfirestats.html. Accessed May 6, 2004.

Western Governor's Association. 2001. A collaborative approach for reducing wildland fire risks to communities and the environment. Western Governor's Association 2001. http://www.westgov.org/wga/initiatives/fire/final_fire_rpt.pdf.

Section I
Public Perceptions and Acceptance

Carol Raish

Understanding public perceptions and acceptance of programs and activities related to wildfire risk management requires information that has been gathered over the past several decades in a variety of disciplines. This section reviews pertinent work from research on natural hazards, diffusion of innovations, risk perceptions, and behavioral responses to hazard and risk. The ways in which beliefs, values, and perceptions affect public acceptance of fire-related management programs, as well as intercultural variations in perceptions and acceptance, round out the examination.

The first chapter, by McCaffrey and Kumagai, reviews social science theory relating to human responses to natural hazards, providing a useful background for the growing field of research on human response to wildfire. The chapter also draws on work concerning the diffusion of innovations that directly relates to public acceptance of fire-mitigation measures and other land-management agency initiatives. The authors discuss how awareness and perception of natural hazards and knowledge of the hazard translates into action. Based on these principles, they examine why at-risk communities have been slow to adopt wildfire-protection innovations like defensible space and fuels reduction.

Trigger events (such as a serious nearby fire or having to be evacuated), change agents (concerned community leaders, for example), and inter-personal networks can be useful in overcoming reluctance to adopt wildfire risk-mitigation actions. In concluding, McCaffrey and Kumagai observe that, taken together, natural hazards theory and studies of diffusion of innovations provide considerable insight into ways to increase wildfire risk-mitigation behaviors.

Shindler focuses on the social acceptability/public acceptance of fuel-reduction treatments, such as prescribed fire and mechanical thinning. His findings are similar to those of McCaffrey and Kumagai concerning acceptance and adoption of innovations; Shindler concludes that adoption and retention of resource-management programs depend on the extent to which the programs are physically possible (consistent with ecological

Carol B. Raish, USDA Forest Service, Rocky Mountain Research Station
(craish@fs.fed.us)

processes), economically feasible, and culturally adoptable. The chapter stresses the importance of knowledge of fire and fuels management as a primary factor in public acceptance of agency programs, but cautions that serious thought must be given to what it means to "educate" the public. Anonymous education messages, such as brochures, tend to produce low responses. People respond more positively to interactive forms of information exchange such as guided field trips, informal workshops, interpretive centers, and school programs. These types of efforts, in conjunction with citizen participation in the planning process and an agency focus on local concerns, economies, and places of interest, lead to the trust in agency personnel and decisions that is needed to foster public acceptance of fuels treatment projects. The chapter concludes that public trust in the agency and its personnel is the most significant predictor of agency effectiveness in managing fire and fire risk.

The chapter by Daniel addresses wildfire as a perceived risk drawing from the substantial literature on risk perception. Daniel finds that, although it has been essentially ignored in this literature, wildfire has a profile that is similar in important ways to the more commonly researched risk response situations. Thus, the general risk-perception literature can assist in developing a better understanding of individual wildfire risk perceptions and willingness to support programs and undertake actions designed to reduce that risk.

The limited research specifically addressing wildfire risk-management behaviors shows that acceptance is related to perception of the risk and of the trade-offs between risk-reduction costs and expected protection benefits. At-risk persons view costs from wildfires as related to aesthetic and convenience features associated with their homes and surroundings. The costs of mitigation measures, such as the nuisance and health effects of smoke from prescribed burns and the effort and expense of mechanical thinning, are seen as being immediate and certain. In contrast, the benefits of risk reduction are seen as less clear, far in the future, and highly uncertain. Thus, individual homeowners in fire-prone areas often appear to prefer accepting future wildfire risk to bearing immediate costs and sacrifices to mitigate that risk. The challenge for wildfire risk managers is to shift the balance in favor of homeowner acceptance of undertaking mitigation measures.

The previous chapters indicate that individual perceptions of and responses to wildfire risks are influenced by a variety of community and personal experiences, perceptions, and knowledge of risks. The chapter by Raish et al. explores the idea presented in historical and anthropological research that both variation and similarity exist in perceptions and practices concerning fire use and management among different cultural/ethnic groups, and between subgroups within the larger designations. Variations in fire use and management views among diverse Native American tribes are examples. These types of differences often have not been discussed with practitioners or taken into consideration by agency managers when planning fire and fuels management activities. Evidence indicates that the body of traditional knowledge seen in past resource-management practices may affect contemporary attitudes, producing positive views toward mechanical thinning and prescribed burning among groups with prior traditions of active forest management. The important point for agency managers is that these views may be locally specific. Echoing Shindler's discussion of successful fire and fuels programs that address the needs and concerns of the local population and include them in the planning process, the chapter emphasizes that public land managers must understand that significant cultural variation exists and integrate it into their consideration of the various management scenarios.

This section of *People, Fire, and Forests* demonstrates that research on natural hazards, diffusion of innovations, social acceptability, and risk perceptions contributes to understanding how people comprehend and respond to hazardous fire situations and how risky and relevant they perceive those situations to be. Studies of community and individual attitudes, values, and behavior expose factors that can be expected to affect public acceptance or distrust of agency wildfire risk-management programs. Research from history and anthropology adds understanding of the differing perceptions of diverse cultural, ethnic, and racial groups, providing a more comprehensive understanding of human response to wildfire risk.

No Need to Reinvent the Wheel: Applying Existing Social Science Theories to Wildfire

Sarah McCaffrey and Yoshitaka Kumagai

Introduction

Social science research on fire has only recently begun to gain critical mass under the sponsorship of the National Fire Plan. Previous to that, there were only a handful of studies on the topic in the 1980s and the 1990s. However, there is no need to completely reinvent the scientific wheel to begin to understand social wildfire dynamics. There is much that can be learned from existing disciplines. Natural hazards research can provide insight into the dynamics of mitigation and key variables that may influence mitigation decisions and responses to an actual event such as risk perception, past experience, and post-fire blaming tendencies. The field of Diffusion of Innovations in turn suggests reasons why wildfire mitigation efforts, particularly the creation of defensible space as a preventive practice, might be adopted only slowly, while also suggesting the usefulness of trigger events, change agents, and interpersonal networks in overcoming the inherent difficulties. Taken together, these two fields can provide context and a starting framework in which to place current wildfire issues and offer insight into ways to increase wildfire mitigation.

This chapter will examine the general theories that have developed to understand human responses to natural hazards and to the adoption of mitigation measures and new technologies. Information on these topics is also presented in chapters by Shindler and Daniel in this volume. The first section will focus on the natural hazards research field and how it informs understanding of human response to wildfires. The second section will discuss components of the Diffusion of Innovations field that shed light on factors that foster or inhibit adoption of mitigation measures. The final section discusses how these two seemingly distinct areas are actually quite connected.

Sarah McCaffrey, USDA Forest Service,, North Central Research Station (smccaffrey@fs.fed.us); Yoshitaka Kumagai, Regional Sustainability Research Institute, Akita International University

Natural Hazards Research

Social science research on other natural hazards has been going on since before World War II. Decades of research on earthquakes, hurricanes, floods, and other hazards have identified a broad framework of dynamics and variables that play a role in shaping human response to a hazard. Because an integral part of the current fire problem is the human–hazard interaction, much from this work can provide insights. Understanding human response to destruction is a broad and diffuse area of study. Research has examined different parts of the disaster process (from long-term prognostication to aftermath) from the perspective of a variety of disciplines and theories, from physics to sociology, and from mathematical calculations to psychological tests. Although the natural hazards field is used for the primary framework of this chapter, research in numerous fields has relevance for understanding social response to natural hazards. Two of these related fields of study—disaster research and risk analysis—merit a brief discussion. Although each field emerged from different disciplines and with a different focus, increasing convergence with natural hazards has meant that clear lines of distinction between the three fields can be hard to draw.

Disaster research grew out of sociology and military funding and examines the recovery process after a disaster. Originating from the study of a 1917 munitions explosion in Halifax, Nova Scotia, most disaster research studies looked at human response to human-caused hazards and were done by sociologists and political scientists (O'Riordan 1986). The field came into its own after World War II when the military, seeking to understand social response under stressful conditions, funded a great deal of research into potential public responses to wartime disasters. Basic methodology was developed in the early 1950s by the National Opinion Research Council with a focus on use of theories of collective behavior and social organization (O'Riordan 1986; Quarantelli 1994 [1988][1]). Over time, increasing emphasis was given to natural hazards, although the emphasis remained not on how to change or decrease exposure to a natural disaster but only on how to respond to one once it had occurred (Cook 1997).

Risk analysis grew primarily out of engineering and the need to establish reliability and safety standards for new technologies such as nuclear reactors. The initial heavy emphasis in the field on probability theory (Kasperson et al. 1994 [1988]; Kirby 1990) proved problematic, as results of such probability-based risk analyses often did not match the more contingent, experiential risk assessment of the public. As a result, risk analysis broadened its area of study in the 1980s to include notions of communications and perception theory, social/political embeddedness, and ethics (Kasperson et al. 1994 [1988]; Plough and Krimsky 1990 [1987]). This brought the field into closer alignment with natural hazards research as more work began to be done to understand what influenced lay people's risk assessment (Plough and Krimsky 1990 [1987]).

Natural hazards research came out of geography with a focus on understanding human adjustments to natural hazards. Developed from an effort to understand a practical problem—why flood damage continued to rise despite all the dams and levees that were built under the 1936 Flood Control Act—the field has maintained a strong bent on finding practical means and appropriate public policy to mitigate the damage caused by natural hazards (Mitchell 1993). Rather than understanding organizational response to a disaster or calculating risk, natural hazards research takes a behavioral approach to understanding individual adaptation (O'Riordan 1986). Fundamentally, the field attempts to understand why certain adjustments are favored over others and to explain the mechanisms that affect adoption of mitigation measures and policies (Mileti 1994 [1989]; Mitchell 1993).

Over time, perception became the primary variable to explain the difference between theoretical and actual adjustments (Whyte 1986). By examining how individuals perceived hazards and potential adjustments differently and identifying which factors influenced differences in perception and choice, researchers hoped to shed light on behavior that had previously been seen merely as maladaptive (Palm 1990; White 1994 [1973]). Two categories were identified that most influenced how an individual responded to natural hazards: factors that affected an individual's awareness and perception of the hazard, such as how long they had lived in the area and past personal experience with the hazard; and factors that influenced how that knowledge translated into action, such as availability of adequate resources to act, sense of control, and the salience of the hazard in comparison with other daily concerns (Burton et al. 1993 [1978]; Palm 1990). Despite the expanded list of explanatory variables to consider, the questions initially asked in the early flood analyses have remained central to current hazards research. These are to identify: 1) the nature of the physical hazard; 2) the type of adjustments already made; 3) the theoretical range of available adjustments; 4) reasons for the differences in adjustments that are chosen; and 5) how changing public policy influences choice of adjustments (Mitchell 1993; White 1994 [1973]). In its own way, natural hazards work for several decades has been using the model for wildfire social science research proposed in this book: incorporating biophysical, sociocultural, and sociodemographic variables as part of its base list of questions.

COPING STAGES—The defining book of traditional natural hazards theory, *The Environment as Hazard* (Burton et al. 1993 [1978]), identifies four, generally sequential, societal stages of coping with hazards: loss absorption, acceptance, reduction, and change. Movement from one stage of coping occurs when a threshold has been crossed. The first stage, loss absorption, takes place when the effect of a hazard is small enough to impose few costs to society and adaptations are unconsciously made to absorb any costs. Once the effect of a hazard begins to exceed a society's natural absorptive capacity, an awareness threshold is reached and the affected group begins to accept the natural event as a hazard and to make conscious adjustments. At first these are fairly passive; the hazard is recognized but little is done to alter it other than devising ways of spreading the costs (often referred to as bear and share). At this point, bearing the cost is preferable to the effort and uncertainty of trying to make any changes. When the costs of the hazard become too large, the action threshold is crossed and efforts are made to actively reduce the costs by modifying the hazard or changing human behavior. Such action to reduce human vulnerability to a hazard is commonly referred to as mitigation. The final coping method occurs only in extreme cases when the cost of the hazard has become so extreme, despite mitigation efforts, that complete change, of land use or living methods, is required; e.g., prohibiting development of floodplains or buying out property in such areas. Most cultures and societies, particularly highly developed ones, are resistant to such large-scale change and to occur it is generally necessary to have a concurrent institutional or societal change (Burton et al. 1993 [1978]).

MITIGATION—The tools for mitigation are diverse and can be broken into four, generally sequential, categories: redistribution, engineering and technology, regulation and policy, and culture (Mileti 1994 [1989]). Redistribution efforts do not try to change the hazard but work to increase ability to both absorb the losses—through the creation of reserve funds and of disaster-assistance organizations such as the Red Cross—and to redistribute the cost across a population larger than that directly affected, through insurance and governmental and charity disaster relief. Once damage levels reach an action threshold, more active measures directed toward minimizing hazard damage come into play, although this shift by no means eliminates the need for or use of redistributional mechanisms. Usually the first active mechanisms are structural: larger-scale engineering and technological efforts to prevent or diminish the effect of the hazard by shifting its location, its timing, or the process that creates it. These can be directed toward changing the nature of the hazard in some manner (dams, levees, fuel load reduction) or toward preventing or reducing potential loss (warning systems, building material improvements, retrofitting). In the United States, such measures, until fairly recently, have been the preferred means of trying to mitigate a hazard.

Over time, environmental modification alone has generally been found to be insufficient to mitigate hazards, usually for two reasons. First, structural solutions often actually exacerbate the problem by encouraging settlement of hazardous areas, such as floodplains and high fire-hazard areas, as they become seen by the public as "protected" (Mileti 1994 [1989]). Second, structures do not completely eliminate a hazard but often merely raise the hazard threshold—there may be fewer hazardous events overall, but when they do occur it will be because they overwhelm the safeguards, so they will be bigger and more damaging (Rossi et al.1982). Fire suppression can be seen as an example of a large-scale government attempt to modify the environment to minimize a hazard. Similar to the construction of dams and levees for floods, fire suppression has, rather than reducing the problem, only served to raise the bar by creating a higher fuel load and lowering the sense of risk for individuals who build structures in fire-prone areas (Beebe and Omi 1993).

Once the limits of such structural fixes are recognized, efforts move toward nonstructural efforts to modify human behavior to avoid the hazard and reduce vulnerability. Nonstructural tools include direct use of policy incentives; regulatory mandates such as land use planning, building codes, and local ordinances; and more indirect efforts to shift cultural norms and rules. Land use planning is used to redirect or control development in hazardous areas, such as flood-plain zoning or requiring subdivision plans to include adequate fire service access. Building codes help increase ability to withstand a hazard and include structural (e.g., nail spacing—particularly relevant for hurricanes and earthquakes) and material (such as fire-resistant roofs) requirements. Local regulations can help control activities, such as vegetation clearance ordinances, that may contribute to a hazard (Burby et al. 1999; Mileti 1994 [1989]; Sorensen and Mileti 1987).

Cultural norms and rules are more nebulous to describe and certainly harder to control, but can have a significant influence on both the creation and mitigation of hazards. In the case of the wildfire hazard, cultural norms often thought to be important include societal perceptions of fire as the enemy, different views of acceptable resource-management practices, what a "natural" landscape looks like, and notions of individual choice, private property, and responsibility.

While the structural and nonstructural categories provide a neat division, in reality the two are not as easily separated. For instance, defensible space is a combination of both types of mitigation. Changing building and vegetation characteristics (roof material, enclosed porches, fire-resistant vegetation) are both, in essence, modifications to the environment and so might be considered structural. However, to occur on a meaningful scale they also require changes in human behavior, both to actively manage the vegetation and to accept what might initially be considered less aesthetically pleasing characteristics (non-wood shingle roofs, more open vegetation).

Natural hazards studies have identified several key variables and dynamics that are often important in understanding how people respond to a natural hazard before, during, and after an event. The following section will provide a brief discussion of several of these variables and how they may apply to wildfire; more detailed discussion of many of them can be found in subsequent chapters.

SALIENCE—Part of the difficulty in changing human behavior lies in the fact that modern lives are complicated and natural hazards generally have low salience compared to other concerns (Neil 1989); doing anything about a hazard tends to be relegated to the "I'll think about it tomorrow" category. Daniel (this volume) discusses the low salience of wildfire and other natural hazards as public concerns, citing their relatively low fatality rate when compared to health, technological, and other hazards, such as automobile accidents. Low placement of wildfire on the list of hazards is also discussed by Shindler (this volume). Palm (1994 [1981]) found that knowledge that a person was buying a home within one-eighth of a mile (.20 km) of California's Hayward Fault had no consistent effect on either the decision to buy or on the purchase price; other factors, such as other location considerations and style of house, were more important. These findings are also reflective of the fact discussed further by Daniel (this volume) that individuals balance both the perceived risk and benefit of where they live, and the higher the perceived benefit the greater the risk tolerance (Slovic et al. 1987).

KNOWLEDGE AND INFORMATION—Access to information is clearly important in shaping response to a hazard. Inadequate, inaccurate, or incomplete information can inhibit ability to develop a clear understanding of a hazard and alternative ways of limiting its impact. Studies have shown that as scientific knowledge increases the accuracy of probability estimation also rises (Mileti 1994 [1989]). Several recent fire studies show that the more accurate the understanding of the causes of the fire hazard and of the ecological impacts of different fuels treatments the more acceptable the associated mitigation practice (Blanchard 2003; McCaffrey 2002; Shindler et al. 2003). However, provision of information, while necessary, is by no means sufficient in decisions to mitigate as other important factors, such as risk perception, come into play (McCaffrey 2004).

RISK PERCEPTION—Perceived risk is how serious the threat is deemed to be coupled with the "subjective probability of experiencing a damaging environmental extreme" (Mileti 1994 [1989]). Although important, it is a particularly difficult variable because it is extremely subjective, with level of perceived risk influenced by a variety of considerations. For instance, how people calculate the likelihood of an event can be shaped by mental strategies used to make the hazard feel more manageable, such as denying the risk outright ("it won't happen to me"), or assuming that a structural adjustment, such as levees or fire breaks, provides complete rather than partial protection (McCaffrey 2004; Mileti 1994 [1989]; Mileti and Sorensen 1987; Slovic et al. 1990 [1979]). Gender, ethnicity, education, income, and political preference have all been found to influence risk perceptions, with the group with the lowest risk-perception scores made up of better-educated, white males with high incomes and conservative leanings (Slovic 1999). Raish et al. (this volume) describe differences in fire knowledge, use, and concerns based on cultural, ethnic, and racial variations. Studies also have found links between worldviews (fatalistic, hierarchical, individualistic, etc) and risk perception (Slovic 1999). While it seems logical that higher risk perception would be closely tied to increased mitigation, studies of other hazards have not found a consistent relationship between the two; in some cases there is a significant positive relationship and in others there is no relationship. Within fire studies the effect of risk perception is equally mixed (McCaffrey 2004).

Studies have also shown that certain qualitative characteristics of the hazard itself may factor into an individual's risk estimation. A grouping of characteristics labeled "Dread Risk" (controllability, catastrophic potential, and fatal consequences) was found to be fairly predictive of level of perceived risk. A second grouping labeled "Unknown Risk" (degree to which hazard is unknown, unobservable, has delayed harm, and is new) was found to have less effect (Slovic 1997). Other qualitative characteristics shown to have influence are the voluntariness of exposure to the hazard and the number of people exposed. Collectively known as the psychometric paradigm, the usefulness of these sets of variables in understanding hazard response is disputed, with some researchers arguing that it explains only a small portion of the variance of perceived risk and that affect[2] is more influential (Sjoberg 2000), while others have field tested the paradigm and found it to provide useful insight (Trumbo 1996). Certainly on the surface the model gives some idea why wildfire, a historically controllable phenomenon that affects a discrete area and kills relatively few people, with fairly low dread and unknown characteristics, does not seem to inspire a large sense of risk for those who live in its potential path (McCaffrey 2004).

(See Daniel [this volume] for more detailed discussion of this paradigm and of risk perception.)

EXPERIENCE—It is often thought that at least those who have experienced a disaster will be more likely to take mitigation steps, but natural-hazards work has not always found experience to have a constant or predictable effect. Studies indicate that, while experience can sometimes increase risk perception and mitigation efforts, its influence generally only lasts for a relatively short period immediately following the event (Sims and Bauman 1983). In some cases, experience may also have a negative effect as individuals decide to do nothing because "lightning doesn't strike twice in the same place" or out of a sense of fatalism about whether their efforts can make a difference. The few relevant fire studies show a similarly mixed result (McCaffrey 2004).

MITIGATION EVALUATION—Once enough factors align to lead an individual to investigate alternatives, various factors then influence the process of choosing and implementing mitigation adjustments. After a range of adjustments has been identified, individuals often engage in two general types of evaluation—cost-benefit and implementation feasibility. The cost-benefit analysis includes consideration of the financial cost of adjustments and their estimated return over a relevant time frame, as well as sociocultural and personal considerations, such as how well the adjustment conforms with personal beliefs and societal traditions, mores, and laws (Kates 1994 [1971]).

Implementation capacity includes consideration of the environmental and technical feasibility of an adjustment; how well it fits with the site and current land use; and the availability of necessary skills, tools, and materials (Kates 1994 [1971]). Wealth is a consistent consideration: in general it has been found that relatively high levels of resource wealth are necessary for mitigation programs to be initiated at either an individual or a societal level (Tierney 1993). Less material wealth is believed to lower the awareness threshold (as there is less absorptive capacity) but to increase the action threshold (as there are fewer resources to invest in mitigation). Greater material wealth, however, means the mitigation action threshold is lowered rather than raised as there is less tolerance for loss. Greater wealth also means this stage is quite persistent as there are the resources to maintain the mitigation measures and the cost of the next stage, radical change, is generally quite high (Burton et al. 1993 [1978]).

Finally, larger-scale social, political, and power issues that may affect the decision maker's implementation capacity will also come under consideration (Mileti 1994 [1989]). Often a key variable is the presence of external incentives to act. This generally takes the form of government policy and regulations that either encourage or discourage adoption of mitigation measures. At the local level many items, such as education and transportation, are much higher on the agenda than working to minimize potential damage from a potential hazard and, in fact, local planners often have good incentives, such as increased revenue from property taxes, to encourage intensive development in high-hazard areas. Nor does the federal government's tendency to provide substantial post-disaster assistance provide local governments with a positive incentive to be active in mitigation planning (Burby et al. 1999). Certainly the historic federal policy of fire suppression has enabled local governments to effectively ignore wildfire as a hazard needing any mitigation-planning consideration. State governments, for their part, can be important players as they have enough hazard exposure to have the incentive to do something, the ability to provide leadership, and the mandates that are often necessary for local communities and individuals to put hazard issues on their planning radar screen (Berke 1998).

EVACUATION—Evacuation during natural disasters is a rather drastic experience for people who may encounter potentially life-threatening risks. Evacuation orders are usually made by law-enforcement personnel and can be either mandatory or voluntary, depending on how imminent the threat. Several studies have identified circumstances where people are more likely to evacuate (Fischer et al. 1995). In general, people tend to evacuate when they are told to do so by emergency officials, when they are contacted frequently by proper officials, when past warnings or evacuation orders were accurate, when affected people have children at home, and if evacuation messages are specific or clearly disseminated. Perry (1979) found that people who have survived past disasters are less likely to evacuate. It was also found that people living in urban areas are more likely to evacuate than those in rural areas (Fischer et al. 1995).

SOCIAL COHESION—Social cohesion often emerges during and immediately after a natural disaster (Kaniasty and Norris 1995; Siegel et al. 1999). A natural disaster can lead to the disappearance of social barriers among people or groups in the community, generating social solidarity (Barton 1970). This cohesion can help a stricken community to effectively tackle issues during the disaster and later enhance community recovery efforts. It is reported, however, that participation in social cohesiveness varies with a combination of factors: ethnicity, educational level, personal networks, and the extent of damage (Kaniasty and Norris 1995). It has also been found that social cohesion is usually observed during or in the wake of disaster; it disappears once social structures return to the form that existed before the disaster struck (Siegel et al. 1999; Sweet 1998). This phenomenon was also found during a preliminary analysis of a study on the social impacts of the

2000 and 2001 wildfires in the western U.S. (See chapters in this volume by Carroll and Cohen and by Burchfield.)

BLAMING AND SOCIAL DISINTEGRATION—Blaming behavior is often observed among victims after natural disaster. Although the primary agents of natural disaster are natural forces, victims are likely to disregard those elements. Instead, they often blame a government entity for the damage. Rochford and Blocker (1991) point out that victims of the Tulsa (Oklahoma) flood (1986) blamed the Army Corps of Engineers for the flood damage. Carroll et al. (2004) found that homeowners who incurred property damage during the Butte Complex fires in California (1999) attributed the damage to a backfire started by the California Department of Forestry and Fire Protection in spite of the fact that there was no record of such a backfire. These cases suggest that victims need to find human agents so that they can assign responsibility to their damage. Blame and/or responsibility is often placed on government institutions in natural disasters because governments are expected to protect the public from any disaster (Hans 1990; Hans and Ermann 1989; Nigg and Tierney 1993).

Blaming behavior may increase a sense of fatalism about the effect of individual mitigation efforts in decreasing future damage, as victims shift their attention from their own efforts to governmental responsibility. In relation to wildfire, such a shift could have a long-term impact on fire mitigation efforts, given the importance of local cooperation and of homeowners maintaining adequate defensible space (Cohen and Saveland 1997).

Blaming behavior can lead to several post-disaster problems. It may lead to hostility and decreased trust in the relevant government entity. It may also lead to social disintegration, hindering community recovery. The Buffalo Creek flood (West Virginia) in 1972 disrupted the local social fabric, traumatized the community, fragmented social cohesiveness, and generated enduring changes in the community (Erikson 1994). Often a seed of disintegration existed within a community before the disaster; in such circumstances, there is disagreement on the interpretation of the disaster and the proper role of local residents and organizations in responding to it (Couch and Kroll-Smith 1985; Kroll-Smith and Couch 1990). Victims are motivated to sue the people or organizations perceived to have caused the disaster (Couch and Kroll-Smith 1985; Picou and Rosebrook 1993). The ensuing dispute over who is responsible for the damage, what should have been done to prevent it, and who should pay for compensation often triggers the emergence of disparate groups and coalitions within the impacted community (Aronoff and Gunter 1992). Social disintegration tends to occur in reaction to hazards where damages emerge gradually or sporadically, with spatially different impacts thus providing little focal point for community identity (Couch and Kroll-Smith 1985; Soliman 1996).

Social disintegration also affects a community's quality of life. The effect may be temporary or permanent. Dyer et al. (1992) found that the Exxon Valdez oil spill disrupted established earning patterns, increased psychological stress, and led to a decline in social support systems and subsistence activities, such as fishing; understandably, those directly connected with fishing business suffered the most psychological distress (Dyer 1993). Ultimately, it was found that people suffered more from social and cultural disruption than from immediate financial loss (Dyer 1993; Dyer et al. 1992; Picou 1990). Thus, there appear to be links among blaming behavior, social disintegration, and quality of life. There is little reason to think that people who are impacted by wildfire will not bear similar negative affects. (For more detailed discussion see Carroll and Cohen [this volume]).

RECOVERY—How a disaster-stricken community recovers may depend on that community's preexisting assets and capacities—social, physical (Patterson 1999), and human. Arnoff and Gunter (1992) found that factors such as homogeneous population, pre-disaster cooperative atmosphere, and capacity to negotiate through the existing political system enabled people to recover from disaster effectively. Patterson (1999) points out that the greater the extent of a community's vertical networks—access to external support and connections with state or federal governments—the greater likelihood of a quick recovery. In addition, effective disaster recovery may require agencies to penetrate communities and accurately communicate with local people (Kulis 1981). These findings highlight the importance not only of educating the public about risk and mitigation of wildfire, but also of encouraging them to enhance their community's social and human capital. (For more detailed discussion see Jakes and Nelson [this volume.])

DEVELOPING NEW LEGISLATION AND CHANGING POWER STRUCTURE—Severe disaster damage often stimulates demand for the passage of new legislation. For example, after a series of earthquakes in Southern California, new legislation that required strict building codes for homeowners was passed to prepare for future earthquakes (Alesch and Petak 1986). Similarly the Healthy Forest Restoration Act was rapidly passed by Congress immediately after the 2003 Southern California fires, despite the fact that much of the land burned was chaparral and so will not be directly affected by the Act.

Disasters can also change power structures within a stricken community. Severe damage brought about by Hurricane Agnes in Wilkes-Barre, Pennsylvania, instigated the reorganization of local governments and changed the local power structure and flood-mitigation policies (Wolensky

1983). Residents who were impacted by the Three Mile Island nuclear accident became politically active in the wake of the accident (Goldsteen and Schorr 1991; Schorr 1982; Walsh 1981). Because of the emergence of new political coalitions, local power structures became more pluralistic, making the community more politically diversified (Goldsteen and Schorr 1991).

EVOLVING NATURAL HAZARDS PERSPECTIVES: VULNERABILITY—In the early 1980s, political economists began to criticize the natural hazards field for ignoring the social, political, economic, and historical context within which an individual makes a decision. Hazards were seen to be less a result of individual choice than of the "ongoing organizational values of society and its institutions" (Mitchell 1993:197). This political economy critique led to the development of the "vulnerability thesis" (Hewitt 1997; O'Riordan 1986). The thesis contends that most natural hazards are a result of structural inequalities that push less powerful people into marginal, more environmentally sensitive areas where, in order to meet subsistence demands, they overuse the land, straining the system's resiliency and contributing to more frequent and severe natural hazard events (Hewitt 1997; Mitchell 1993; O'Riordan 1986; Palm 1990). This view argues that as those most affected are also those with the least ability to make adjustments and decisions that affect their safety, trying to understand individual response does little to resolve the problem (Hewitt 1997; O'Riordan 1986). Instead, the most effective actions to minimize the danger of a natural disaster need to be directed toward modifying the context of the situation (Hewitt 1997).

Although developed mostly in a Third World context, partial support for the model's applicability in the United States can be found in the higher death rates amongst the old and poor during heatwaves as well as the difficulties these groups have in large-scale evacuations. How useful vulnerability is in thinking about the wildfire hazard is uncertain, given that in some areas it is not the poor and marginal who are being forced to live in high-hazard areas but more well-to-do people who are choosing to live there.[3] Rodrigue (1993) suggests that the problem lies in the conflation of vulnerability (capacity to evade, withstand, or recover from a disastrous event) and risk (actual exposure to hazard damage). In the Third World context this causes little confusion, because those most exposed to the hazard are also the most vulnerable. When looking at homes built in Southern California or the Oakland hills, however, the conflation is problematic: it is those best able to withstand and recover from a wildfire that are, voluntarily, the most exposed to risk. In these areas, Rodrigue argues, vulnerability is diffused throughout society through insurance and government emergency services; in effect the costs are "broadly socialized" while the benefits, such as views and natural setting, are narrowly "privatized." Rodrigue's separation of vulnerability and risk seems apt, given that hazards work done in developed countries emphasizes the notion of risk perception rather than that of vulnerability.

The political economy/vulnerability critique adds the valuable recognition of the need to examine the social and historical influences underlying the natural hazard and potential mitigation activities. However, its emphasis on the macro-level concerns tends to discount the role individuals have in shaping structures (Palm 1990). Ironically, the vulnerability thesis, while arguing to protect the vulnerable, also tends to treat individual humans as pathetic and weak and reinforces the need for experts, although this time experts in empowerment rather than technology (Hewitt 1997).

Another difficulty with the political economy perspective in relation to wildfire is its tendency toward focusing on larger-level institutional structures as the central problem. This is no doubt a useful focus in Third World countries where government structures often significantly affect an individual's access to basic livelihood resources. However, in developed nations with their more-developed resource base, institutional structures are less central to hazard creation and are also rarely the primary factor inhibiting mitigation. For instance, studies in the U.S. have found that mitigation efforts are not limited for lack of federal and state level interest and support (Rossi et al. 1982). Rather it is behavior at the local level—government and individual—that has the most effect on whether or not mitigation takes place. Rossi et al. (1982) found that local decision makers' concern for natural hazards was low, as they preferred to rely on traditional responses where the federal government primarily bore the cost through structural mitigation and post-disaster relief. Certainly a large part of resolving the fire problem will require the active involvement of local communities and individuals, from homeowners to planners. However, larger-level institutional structures cannot be discounted; congressional funding issues and conflicting internal and interagency priorities are an important part of the wildfire story.

More recently, hazards researchers have begun to explore ways of integrating the traditional focus on individual behavior with the political economy emphasis on societal level issues (Mitchell 1993). Two of the frameworks proposed are quite similar. Hewitt (1997) calls his integrative model the "human ecology of disaster." Along with the traditional focus on physical factors and individual risk adjustments and the political economy focus on vulnerability and structural context, Hewitt adds a middle level of intervening or contingent variables that are not directly related to the hazard. These are important because "both institutional and cultural phenomena may buffer or focus damage, without being tied to specific vulnerabilities or agents of damage" (Hewitt 1997:29). This idea, that a hazard may result from actions that have nothing to do with the hazard, is an important point. As Pyne (1997) notes, the original policy of fire suppression was not exclusively shaped by a desire to protect life and property but also by a desire to protect timber resources for production purposes and to legitimate the agency's existence. More recently, community access to National Fire Plan funds for mitigation has been shaped by the intervening variable of the state government and how it has decided to administer the funds. As a result, some states may be better prepared for a wildfire as communities with better access to funds are expected to have stronger ability to mitigate the wildfire hazard (Steelman et al. 2004).

Palm (1990) also integrates the two approaches by starting with the individual and the household (which he terms the micro level) and then embedding that within the societal structure (macro level). Interactions between the two levels are then identified (meso level) to understand how structural factors influence individual actions, what dynamics either constrain or enable individual actions. One relevant meso-level factor Palm discusses is the notion of gatekeepers, individuals (such as a planner or fire marshal) who as a result of their position have the ability to make decisions that either constrain or enable an individual's adjustment choices.

Both authors present their framework in the context of looking at a web of relations. For Hewitt (1997) a natural hazard occurs as a result of a breakdown in the web of relations linking society and nature. For Palm, in emphasizing linkages between micro and macro "more attention is given to the 'web' within which individuals and collectivities live, and the impacts of this web on individual choice" (Palm 1990:156). This imagery is a useful visual acknowledgment of the complex interrelationships that influence human response to wildfire.

Diffusion of Innovations

Palm's reference to the notion of gatekeepers suggests a link with another relevant field of study: "Diffusion of Innovations." This field works to understand the process by which a new idea or technology is communicated and adopted. Primarily developed in rural sociology to understand why agricultural innovations were or were not adopted (Rogers 2003 [1983, 1995]), over time its rubric has been used to examine different points of the process—such as earliness of knowledge of an innovation, individual traits amenable to adoption, and network analysis—through the lenses of a spectrum of disciplines including rural sociology, education, public health, and marketing (Rogers 2003 [1983, 1995]). Rogers' book, Diffusion of Innovations, is the primary work that brings together studies in these diverse areas in an effort to establish some level of general theory for the field. The book is credited with shaping and institutionalizing diffusion research in its current mode and has become an accepted base reference for the field (Fliegel 1993). Five areas will be briefly discussed here to illustrate how this broad field can inform our wildfire understanding: attributes of the innovation that influence adoption, the role of change agents, adopter traits and categories (innovativeness), stages of adoption, and communication.

An innovation's attributes are important because, by definition, an innovation is something new and so the risks and benefits of its adoption are unclear. Several characteristics of the innovation itself contribute to how much uncertainty is involved in the cost-benefit calculation surrounding its adoption. Rogers identifies five characteristics of the innovation itself that play a role in its adoption rate:[4] relative advantage, compatibility, trialability, complexity of the innovation, and observability of its effect (Rogers 2003 [1983, 1995]). Relative advantage, which has been found to be the best predictor of adoption rates, is essentially a cost-benefit analysis—the degree to which an innovation is seen as superior to the old idea. This can mean some type of economic or social advantage due to improved status (Fleigel 1993; Rogers 2003 [1983, 1995]). Compatibility refers to the degree that the innovation is consistent with the needs, experience, lifestyle, and previous values and ideas of the adopter (Rogers 2003 [1983, 1995]). Trialability, or divisibility for trial, is the degree to which the innovation can be tested on a limited basis. A successful trial increases likelihood of full-scale adoption as it decreases the uncertainty regarding its effectiveness (Rogers 2003 [1983, 1995]). Distributing free samples of a new product is a mass-marketing application of this notion (Fliegel 1993). Complexity is how difficult the innovation is to understand and use; innovations that are simple and easy to understand are usually more readily adopted (Fliegel 1993; Rogers 2003 [1983, 1995]). Observability is how apparent the benefits of the innovation are to others and reflects the finding that innovations generally are adopted less as a result of any type of formal or scientific information than of seeing the results of adoption by peers (Rogers 1987). Often these characteristics are interlinked; a successful trial will not only encourage adoption by the individual who did the test but also by others, as it increases the observability of the innovation's effectiveness. In general, relative advantage, compatibility, trialability, and observability are positively related to an innovation's adoption rate, whereas complexity is negatively related.

Based on these characteristics it is not all that surprising that wildfire's protective innovations, such as defensible space, have been slow to catch on, as they have few of the characteristics associated with rapid adoption. The goal of defensible space is for a structure to survive if a fire does occur.

However, structural survival might easily be attributed to chance rather than mitigation and makes proving the relative advantage of mitigation difficult. Similarly, short of starting a fire near your house and watching what happens, trialability is problematic. Defensible space also falls short in terms of compatibility on several counts. Many individuals hold norms that see a thick forest of trees as natural and desirable; removing any vegetation to create defensible space would go against these norms. Further, prescribed fire and salvage logging do not fit into many individuals' ideas of acceptable management practices. Finally, fire mitigation ranks high on the complexity scale. While on a certain level fire is a simple phenomenon, in the end how to successfully reduce its danger is a complex story involving several different management practices and cooperation of many individuals and agencies.

Change agents are often an important ingredient in successful innovation adoption and might well fit into Palm's gatekeeper category. Rogers describes a change agent as someone who provides "a communication link between a resource system with some kind of expertise and a client system" (2003:368). This description is almost tailor-made to describe the position of a fire chief active in promoting defensible space or community-wide fire planning and mitigation efforts. The role of the change agent is both to provide information and to create interest in and eventual adoption of an innovation by a specific population. In effect, a change agent is a gatekeeper of information on the innovation, and the type of information and manner of provision they choose to use can all influence an individual's perception of adjustment choices. While often professionally trained and affiliated with the change agency, change agents may also have less formal training. Several factors have been identified that facilitate a change agent's effectiveness. These include: frequency of contact with clients; whether the change agent's attitude and the innovation itself are oriented to meeting clients' needs not just the agency's; and whether the agent is of the same peer group as the clients, is credible, and encourages the client's ability to understand and evaluate innovations (Rogers 2003 [1983, 1995]).

Diffusion studies have emphasized defining the differences between those who adopt first and those who adopt later, tending to combine personality indicators of adoption into one trait to study innovativeness (Fleigel 1993). Defined as "the degree to which an individual or other unit of adoption is willing to adopt new ideas before other members of a social system do so" (Rogers 1987), innovativeness became the main dependent variable of diffusion research. This emphasis reflects finding that once a threshold of people using the innovation is achieved, a take-off or critical mass point is reached and societal pressures will take over and less active encouragement will be needed (Rogers 1995:340). Sociodemographically, those who are more likely to adopt early tend to have a higher education and social status. In terms of personality characteristics, rationality, intelligence, abstract thinking ability, and positive attitudes towards education, science, uncertainty, and change are all positively related with innovativeness (Rogers 2003 [1983, 1995]). In terms of communication style, early adoption is positively related with social participation, exposure to mass media, and local interpersonal channels, active information seeking, and change-agent contact (Buttel et al. 1990; Rogers 2003 [1983, 1995]).

The innovation-adoption decision process has five generally sequential stages: knowledge, persuasion, decision, implementation, and confirmation (Rogers 2003 [1983, 1995]). The knowledge stage is where information is disseminated to increase awareness of the innovation. The persuasion stage is the point where individuals form a favorable or unfavorable opinion of the innovation. At the decision stage, an individual makes an active decision to adopt or reject the innovation. This is the point where characteristics of the innovation are most relevant as issues of trialability and relative advantage begin to be considered. It is at this point where trial by others and demonstrations "can be quite effective in influencing adoption by individuals, especially if the demonstrator is an opinion leader" (Rogers 1983:171). When the decision has been made and individuals enter the implementation stage, they begin seeking a great deal of information on the innovation, including how and why it will work. Finally, actual adoption is not the end of the process, as individuals seek confirmation that their decision to adopt was the right one. Without such confirmation discontinuance of use of the innovation is not uncommon.

How information is communicated is another important area affecting adoption rates. Different media channels are influential at different stages of the adoption process; using the wrong communication channel at the wrong stage has been associated with later adoption (Rogers 2003 [1983, 1995]). During the awareness stage, mass media is the most effective communication channel. However, once the persuasion stage has been reached, interpersonal communication channels, particularly with expert information sources, become the most influential method. Such two-way communication is most effective in reducing the inherent uncertainty of adopting a new innovation, as it allows for discussion and clarification. Not surprisingly, interpersonal communication is particularly important for complex innovations or ones that require continual monitoring (Fliegel 1993; Rogers 1987).

A key element in the communication process and how information "diffuses" is to what degree the individuals involved are similar (homophilous) or dissimilar (heterophilous) for one or more characteristics such as beliefs, values, status, occupation, and other demographic factors. Generally, ideas spread easily through a homophilous group but when there are different levels of communication involved due to differences in social position, education, and/or technical training it is more likely that the new idea will be ignored, misunderstood, or considered suspect (Rogers 2003 [1983, 1995]). However, some level of heterophilous communication is necessary for innovations to truly spread (Rogers 2003 [1983, 1995]). This is particularly relevant when considering the change agent. If the change agent belongs to a different social group than the one he or she is working with (which has often been the case with college-trained agricultural extension workers) communication may be inhibited. In fact, change agent success is positively correlated with homophily with clients (Rogers 2003 [1983, 1995]).

This correlation is due in part to the finding that a change agent's effectiveness is directly related to their credibility. There are two types of credibility: competence and safety. The first is associated with level of expertise and knowledge regarding the innovation and the second with perceived trustworthiness. In general, heterophilous sources are seen as having competence credibility, whereas those from a similar background will be seen as trustworthy. This creates a rather fine line for a change agent to tread.

"An ideal change agent would have a balance of competence and safety credibility. A change agent might be homophilous with his or her clients in social characteristics (such as socioeconomic status, ethnicity, and the like) but heterophilous in regard to technical competence about the innovations being diffused" (Rogers 2003:385). This means that to some degree the change agent is also heterophilous with both groups, creating the potential for role conflicts and communication problems at one end or the other. This information is relevant for fire-management organizations to take into consideration when working with homeowners to encourage use of defensible space.

Preventive Innovations: Diffusion of Fire-mitigation Efforts

Both natural hazards and Diffusion of Innovations fields and their variants have important points to consider for studying wildfire. While there is little evidence of any hazards studies that have explicitly used Diffusion of Innovations, articles on how to encourage mitigation work often implicitly invoke the paradigm when they provide a list of steps that parallel those that the diffusion model has found to be most effective in encouraging adoption of innovations. In fact there are many congruities between Diffusion of Innovations and natural hazards theory. Perhaps most relevant to wildfire is that both models address decision making in the face of uncertainty. Diffusion of Innovations has been described as "an uncertainty-reduction process" (Rogers 2003 [1983, 1995]) and hazards work focuses on understanding how individuals interpret and respond to the uncertainty created by a potential hazard event. Both also emphasize the importance of understanding how perceptions influence the process. "In other words, perceptions count. The individuals' perceptions of the attributes of an innovation, not the attributes as classified objectively by experts or change agents, affect its rate of adoption." (Rogers 2003:223)

In certain ways, much of traditional natural hazards work might be considered a subset of Diffusion of Innovations. Hazard mitigation is a particular type of innovation, one adopted to avert something most people would rather not think about. It is usually not something adopted due to its potential to improve one's life through increased income, knowledge, or comfort but rather to potentially protect one's current lifestyle. This fits into a specific Diffusion of Innovation category, that of a preventive innovation. The difficulty with this type of innovation is that it does little to decrease uncertainty and so tends to have a very slow adoption rate: "the undesired event may, or may not, occur if the innovation is not adopted. So the desired consequences of a preventive innovation are uncertain. Under such circumstances, the individual's motivation to adopt are rather weak" (Rogers 1983:171).

When considered in this light, it is not hard to see why fire-mitigation behavior has proven difficult to firmly establish. Preventive innovations generally have few of the innovation characteristics associated with rapid adoption rates. Relative advantage and observability are difficult to calculate because both are factors based on an uncertain future event (Rogers 1987). Yet preventive innovations are too important to be written off as too difficult to encourage. In this light, Rogers (1987) drew from the small proportion of diffusion studies on preventive innovations to identify factors that might increase likelihood of adoption of preventive innovations. The role of a trigger event, a cue-to-action that "crystallizes a favorable attitude into overt behavior change," appears to be particularly important in shifting an individual into adopting a preventive innovation (Rogers 2003 [1983, 1995]). Having a relative die in a car accident may push someone to finally start using their seatbelt routinely or, in the case of natural hazards, a flood may lead an individual to finally raise their house above normal flood levels.

But for the trigger event to have the desired effect, there first needs to be knowledge of the innovation. For this, the mass media has been found to play an important role in creating awareness of the problem and needed skills (Rogers 1987). With wildfires this may be problematic as a fire consuming houses makes for a better story and more likely coverage than a piece on defensible space and associated concepts of vegetation modification. For preventive innovations, interpersonal communication networks, important in any diffusion process, are particularly critical in creating localized incentives—supportive and peer pressure—to adopt (Rogers 1987). One study used mass media to recruit at-risk individuals into smaller instructional groups, which can provide the peer reinforcement that has been found most effective in changing behavior (Rogers 1987; Rogers 2003 [1983, 1995]). The study also found audience segmentation increased adoption by allowing use of messages tailored to the interests of the targeted group. In essence this is ensuring that the information is received by a homogeneous group, thereby facilitating its diffusion. Segmentation also allows the most effective message to be created to highlight the innovation's relative advantage to the target group, a key barrier to overcome with preventive innovations (Rogers 2003 [1983, 1995]).

Credibility of the information source or message provider is also particularly important with preventive innovations. If the source is seen to have ulterior motives or to be contradicting past practices it is likely to be given short shrift. During the energy crisis of the 1970s, the public paid little heed to efforts of power utilities and oil companies to encourage energy conservation, as they were seen to only profit from higher energy prices and to be contradicting previous efforts to encourage energy use (Rogers 1987). Certainly, this description sounds familiar when considering the current dilemma of federal agencies in trying to encourage support for a policy of letting wildfires burn under certain conditions and for the use of prescribed burning, given their historic singular emphasis on suppression.

Finally, while individuals likely have few immediate benefits or personal gain in adopting preventive innovations, many organizations often have strong incentives to discourage any innovation that changes public behavior (Rogers 1987). An obvious example is the long battle tobacco companies fought against anti-smoking campaigns. With wildfire an example can be seen in the loud and often effective resistance by the roofing industry to efforts by planning and fire agencies to ban wood shingle roofs. In addition, the internal "training, rewards, and professional values in many fields discourage prevention" (Rogers 1987:92). For example, the potential negative career impact of an escape provides little incentive to fire managers to increase their use of prescribed fire.

Conclusion

There is thus much that can be learned from existing disciplines in understanding current social wildfire issues. Natural hazards theory, with its concepts of sequential coping stages, action thresholds, and two phases of the reduction stage, technological and human behavior change, provides insight into why fire mitigation may be taking hold slowly. It also provides insights into key variables that influence individual mitigation decisions and responses to an actual event. Diffusion of Innovations in turn suggests reasons why wildfire mitigation efforts, especially defensible space as a preventive innovation, might be adopted only slowly, while also suggesting the usefulness of trigger events, change agents, and interpersonal networks in overcoming the inherent difficulties. Taken together, these two fields provide a great deal of insight into ways to increase wildfire mitigation.

NOTES

1. For several books that feature reprints of key natural hazards articles, we have chosen to include both dates, with original publication date in brackets, as both are indicative of the article's enduring importance.
2. Affect: "a positive (like) or negative (dislike) evaluative feeling toward an external stimulus" (Slovic 1999:694).
3. It is important to note that not all individuals living in the residential wildland intermix (RWI) are wealthy. According to the Program for Watershed and Community Health, three to five million of the ten to fifteen million people living in the RWI do not have enough resources to meet basic economic needs (Lynn 2003).
4. Throughout his book, Rogers proposes such characteristics as general rules of thumb gleaned from examining dozens of diffusion studies. He openly acknowledges that they are by no means universal and, in the 1983 edition, for each generalization enumerates how many studies supported and how many did not support the generalization.

REFERENCES

Alesch, D. J., and W. J. Petak. 1986. The politics and economics of earthquake hazard mitigation: Unreinforced masonry buildings in Southern California. Boulder, Colorado: Institute of Behavioral Science, University of Colorado.

Aronoff, M., and V. Gunter. 1992. "Defining disaster: Local constructions for recovery in the aftermath of chemical contamination." *Social Problems* 394: 345-65.

Barton, A. H. 1970. *Communities in Disaster.* Garden City, New York: Anchor Books.

Beebe, G. S., and P. N. Omi. 1993. "Wildland burning: The perception of risk." *Journal of Forestry* 91(9): 19-24.

Berke, P. 1998. "Reducing natural hazard risks through state growth management." *Journal of the American Planning Association* 64(1): 75-87.

Blanchard, B. P. 2003. Community perceptions of wildland fire risk and fire hazard reduction strategies at the wildland-urban interface in the Northeastern United States. Amherst, Massachusetts: University of Massachusetts. Masters Thesis.

Burby, R., T. Beatley, P. Berke, R. Deyle, S. French, D. Godschalk, E. Kaiser, J. Kartez, P. May, R. Olshansky, R. Paterson, and R. Platt. 1999. "Unleashing the power of planning to create disaster-resistant communities." *Journal of the American Planning Association* 65(1): 247-58.

Burton, I., R., W. Kates, and G. F. White. 1993 [1978]. *The Environment as Hazard*. New York: The Guilford Press.

Buttel, F. H., O. F. Larson, and G. W. Gillespie Jr. 1990. *The Sociology of Agriculture*. New York: Greenwood Press.

Carroll, M. S., Y. Kumagai, S. Daniels, M. Carroll, J. Bliss, and J. Edwards. 2004. "Causal reasoning processes of people affected by wildfire: implications for agency-community interactions and communication strategies." *Western Journal of Applied Forestry* 19(3): 184-94.

Cohen, J., and J. Saveland. 1997. "Structure ignition assessment can help reduce fire damage in the WUI." *Fire Management Notes* 57(4): 19-23.

Cook, S. 1997. "Wildfire adapted ecosystems meet man's development." *Australian Journal of Emergency Management* 12(2): 24-31.

Couch, S. R., and S. J. Kroll-Smith. 1985. "The chronic technical disaster: Toward a social scientific perspective." *Social Science Quarterly* 663: 564-75.

Dyer, C. L. 1993. "Tradition loss as secondary disaster: Long-term cultural impacts of the Exxon Valdez oil spill." *Sociological Spectrum* 131: 65-88.

———, G. A. Duane, and S. J. Picou. 1992. "Social disruption and the Valdez oil spill: Alaskan natives in a natural resource community." *Sociological Spectrum* 12: 105-26.

Erikson, K. T. 1994. *A New Species of Trouble: Explorations in Disaster, Trauma, and Community*. New York: W.W. Norton & Co.

Fischer, H. W. III., G. F. Stine, B. L. Stoker, M. L. Trowbridge, and E. M. Drain. 1995. "Evacuation behavior: Why do some evacuate, while others do not? A case study of the Ephrata, Pennsylvania, USA evacuation." *Disaster Prevention Management* 44: 30-36.

Fliegel, F. C. 1993. *Diffusion Research in Rural Sociology: The Record and Prospects for the Future*. Westport, Connecticut: Greenwood Press.

Goldsteen, R., and J. K. Schorr. 1991. *Demanding Democracy after Three Mile Island*. Gainesville: University of Florida Press.

Hans, V. P. 1990. "Attitude toward corporate responsibility: A psychological perspective." *Nebraska Law Review* 69: 158-89.

———, and D. M. Ermann. 1989. "Response to corporate versus individual wrongdoing." *Law and Human Behavior* 13: 151-66.

Hewitt, K. 1997. "Regions of risk: A geographical introduction to disasters." In: B. Mitchell (ed.), *Themes in Resource Management*. Singapore: Longman Singapore Publishers Ltd.

Kaniasty, K., and F. H. Norris. 1995. "In search of altruistic community: Patterns of social support mobilization following Hurricane Hugo." *American Journal of Community Psychology* 234: 447-77.

Kasperson, R. E., O. Renn, P. Slovic, H. S. Brown, J. Emel, R. Goble, J. X. Kasperson, and S. Ratick. 1994 [1988]. "The social amplification of risk: A conceptual framework." In: S. L. Cutter (ed.), *Environmental Risks and Hazards*. Englewood Cliffs, New Jersey: Prentice-Hall.

Kates, R. W. 1994 [1971]. "Natural hazard in human ecological perspective: Hypotheses and models." In: S. L. Cutter (ed.) *Environmental Risks and Hazards*. Englewood Cliffs, New Jersey: Prentice-Hall.

Kirby, A. 1990. *Nothing to Fear: Risks and Hazards in American Society*. Tucson: University of Arizona Press.

Kroll-Smith, S. J., and S. R. Couch. 1990. *The Real Disaster is Above Ground: A Mine Fire and Social Conflict*. Lexington: University of Kentucky Press.

Kulis, S. 1981. "Primary groups in disaster: The importance of shared functions." Annual Meeting of the American Sociological Association, Toronto, August.

Lynn, K. 2003. "Wildfire and rural poverty: Disastrous connections." Natural Hazards Observer. 28(2). Available at: http://www.colorado.edu/hazards/o/novo03/novo03da.html.

McCaffrey, S. M. 2002. For want of defensible space a forest is lost: Homeowners and the wildfire hazard and mitigation in the residential wildland intermix at Incline Village, Nevada. Berkeley: University of California. Ph.D. dissertation.

———. 2004. "Thinking of wildfire as a hazard." *Society and Natural Resources* 17: 1-8.

Mileti, D. 1994 [1989]. "Human adjustment to the risk of environmental extremes." In: S. L. Cutter (ed.), *Environmental Risks and Hazards*. Englewood Cliffs, New Jersey: Prentice-Hall.

———, and J. H. Sorensen. 1987. "Natural hazards and precautionary behavior." In: N. Weinstein (ed.), *Taking Care: Understanding and Encouraging Self-protective Behavior*. Cambridge, England: Cambridge University Press.

Mitchell, B. 1993. *Geography and Resource Analysis*. 2nd ed. Singapore: Longman Group UK Limited.

Neil, R. B. 1989. "Community attitudes to natural hazard insurance: What are the salient issues?" In: J. Oliver and N. R. Britton (eds.), *Natural Hazards and Reinsurance*. Australia: Lilyfield Printing Pty. Ltd.

Nigg, J. M., and K. J. Tierney. 1993. "Disasters and social change: Consequence for community construct and affect." Paper presented at the Annual Meeting of the American Sociological Association, Miami, Florida, August 13-17.

O'Riordan, T. 1986. "Coping with environmental hazards." In: R. W. Kates and I. Burton (eds.), *Geography, Resources, and Environment: Themes from the Work of Gilbert F. White*. Vol. II. Chicago, Illinois: University of Chicago Press.

Palm, R. 1990. *Natural Hazards: An Integrative Framework for Research and Planning*. Baltimore, Maryland: The Johns Hopkins University Press.

———. 1994 [1981] "Public response to earthquake hazard information." In: S. L. Cutter (ed.), *Environmental Risks and Hazards*. Englewood Cliffs, New Jersey: Prentice-Hall.

Patterson, J. 1999. "A review of the literature and programs on local recovery from disaster." Natural Hazards Research Working Paper #102, Natural Hazards Research and Applications Information Center, Institute of Behavioral Science, University of Colorado, Boulder.

Perry, R. W. 1979. "Evacuation decision-making in natural disasters." *Mass Emergencies* 4(1): 25-38.

Picou S. 1990. Social disruption and psychological stress in an Alaskan fishing community: The impact of the Exxon Valdez oil spill. Boulder: University of Colorado Natural Hazards Center.

———, and D. D. Rosebrook. 1993. "Technological accident, community class-action litigation, and scientific damage assessment: a case study of court-ordered research." *Sociological Spectrum* 131: 117-38.

Plough, A., and S. Krimsky. 1990 [1987]. "The emergence of risk communication studies: Social and political context." In: T. S. Glickman and M. Gough (eds.), *Readings in Risk*. Washington D.C.: Resources for the Future.

Pyne, S. J. 1982. *Fire in America: A Cultural History of Wildland and Rural Fire*. Princeton, New Jersey: Princeton University Press. Reprinted in paperback 1997. Seattle: University of Washington Press.

Quarantelli, E. L. 1994 [1988]. "Disaster studies: An analysis of the social historical factors affecting the development of research in the area." In: S. L. Cutter (ed.), *Environmental Risks and Hazards*. Englewood Cliffs, New Jersey: Prentice-Hall.

Rochford, B. E. Jr., and J. R. Blocker. 1991. "Coping with 'natural' hazards as stressors: The predictors of activism in a flood disaster." *Environment and Behavior* 23(2): 171-94.

Rodrigue, C. M. 1993. "Home with a view: Chaparral fire hazard and the social geographies of risk and vulnerability." *California Geographical Society* 33: 29-42.

Rogers, E. M. 1987. "The Diffusion of Innovations perspective." In: N. Weinstein (ed.), *Taking Care: Understanding and Encouraging Self-protective Behavior*. Cambridge, England: Cambridge University Press.

―――. 2003 [1983, 1995]. *Diffusion of Innovations*. Fifth ed. New York: The Free Press.

Rossi, P. H., J. D. Wright, and E. Weber-Burdin. 1982. "Natural hazards and public choice: The state and local politics of hazard mitigation." In: P. H. Rossi (ed.), *Quantitative Studies in Social Relations*. New York: Academic Press.

Schorr, J. K. 1982. "The long-term impact of a man-made disaster: An examination of a small town in the aftermath of the Three Mile Island nuclear reactor accident." *Disasters* 333: 50-59.

Shindler, B., J. Leahy, and E. Toman. 2003. Public acceptance of forest conditions and fuel reduction practices: A survey of citizens in communities adjacent to National Forests in Minnesota, Wisconsin, and Michigan. Report to North Central Research Station, USDA Forest Service and the Joint Fire Science Program.

Siegel, J. M., L. B. Bourque, and K. I. Shoaf. 1999. "Victimization after a natural disaster: Social disorganization or community cohesion?" *International Journal of Mass Emergencies and Disasters* 17(3): 265-94.

Sims, J. H., and D. D. Baumann. 1983. "Educational programs and human response to natural hazards." *Environment and Behavior* 15(2): 165-89.

Sjoberg, L. 2000. "Consequences matter, 'risk' is marginal." *Journal of Risk Research* 3(3): 287-95.

Slovic, P. 1997. "Risk perception and trust." In: V. Molak (ed.), *Fundamentals of Risk Analysis and Risk Management*. Boca Raton, Louisiana: CRC Press Inc.

―――. 1999. "Trust, emotion, sex, politics, and science: Surveying the risk-assessment battlefield." *Risk Analysis* 19(4): 689-701.

―――., B. Fischhoff, and S. Lichtenstein. 1987. "Behavioral decision theory perspectives on protective behavior." In: N. Weinstein (ed.), *Taking Care: Understanding and Encouraging Self-protective Behavior*. Cambridge, England: Cambridge University Press.

―――, B. Fischhoff, and S. Lichenstein. 1990 [1979]. "Rating the risks." In: T. S. Glickman and M. Gough (eds.), *Readings in Risk*. Washington D.C.: Resources for the Future.

Soliman, H. H. 1996. "Community responses to chronic technological disaster: The case of the Pigeon River." *Journal of Social Service Research* 461: 89-107.

Sorensen, J. H., and D. S. Mileti. 1987. "Programs that encourage the adoption of precautions against natural hazards: Review and evaluation." In: N. Weinstein (ed.), *Taking Care: Understanding and Encouraging Self-protective Behavior*. Cambridge, England: Cambridge University Press.

Steelman, T. A., G. Kunkel, and D. Bell. 2004. "Federal and State influence on community responses to wildfire threats: Arizona, Colorado, and New Mexico." *Journal of Forestry* 102(6): 21-27.

Sweet, S. 1998. "The effects of a natural disaster on social cohesion: A longitudinal study." *International Journal of Mass Emergencies and Disasters* 163: 321-31.

Tierney, K. J. 1993. Socio-economic aspects of hazard mitigation. Preliminary paper #190 ed. University of Delaware, Disaster Research Center.

Trumbo, C. W. 1996. "Examining psychometrics and polarization in a single-risk case study." *Risk Analysis* 16(3): 423-32.

Walsh, E. J. 1981. "Resource mobilization and citizen protest in communities around Three Mile Island." *Social Problems* 303:1-21.

White, G. F. 1994 [1973]. "Natural hazards research." In: S. L. Cutter (ed.), *Environmental Risks and Hazards*. Englewood Cliffs, New Jersey: Prentice-Hall.

Whyte, A. V. T. 1986. "From hazard perception to human ecology." In: R. W. Kates and I. Burton (eds.), *Geography, Resources, and Environment: Themes from the Work of Gilbert F. White*. Vol. II. Chicago, Illinois: University of Chicago Press.

Wolensky, R. P. 1983. "Power structure and group mobilization following disaster: A case study." *Social Science Quarterly* 64(1): 97-110.

Public Acceptance of Wildland Fire Conditions and Fuel Reduction Practices: Challenges for Federal Forest Managers

Bruce Shindler

Federal forest managers today are faced with unprecedented, complex challenges. Risks to our national forests, affected by years of fire suppression, drought, increased stand density, insect outbreaks, and human population growth at the wildland-urban interface present a technical challenge perhaps greater than any other confronted by our natural resource agencies (Grote 2000). Furthermore, the last two decades of forest management have been fraught with legal challenges and public protests, reflecting serious problems with public acceptance, a critical element to successful implementation of any action on the ground. Most recently, major wildfire events have attracted national media coverage, which can raise public awareness but also tend to exaggerate risks and distort information. Fire professionals in the western U.S. are experiencing this dilemma as they attempt to determine appropriate levels of salvage operations and rehabilitation in the aftermath of large fires in 2002, 2003, and 2005. Throughout all this, resource professionals are increasingly called on to manage forest ecosystems in ways that simultaneously sustain biophysical, economic, and social aspects of those systems (Clark 1999; Dombeck 1996).

Public acceptance has always been a major factor in the ability of federal agencies to effectively manage forests (Shindler et al. 2002), and is especially important now that the National Fire Plan (NFP) and the Healthy Forest Restoration Act (HFRA) have directed personnel to improve forest conditions through fuel-reduction activities. However, the stated goal of improving forest conditions is often debated and of some controversy. In the current sociopolitical climate the scrutiny of bureaucratic actions runs high and questions of trust and credibility are the subject of each decision. Over the last two decades (but particularly since Joint Fire Science Program and NFP initiatives), a substantial amount of research has been conducted

Bruce Shindler, Dept. of Forest Resources, Oregon State University
(bruce.shindler@oregonstate.edu)

to advance our understanding of public concerns, knowledge, and attitudes about fire-management activities. Raish et al. (this volume) provide the review of research on variations among cultural/ethnic/racial groups concerning these topics. Drawing from research on public concerns, knowledge, and attitudes, this chapter outlines the social acceptability concept and describes a set of common but specific challenges to agency fuel-reduction efforts. The analysis aims to contribute to more durable decisions by helping structure management's response for gaining public acceptance and support.

The Importance of Social Acceptability

The concept of social acceptability in natural resource management can be traced to the work of Firey (1960) and Clawson (1975), who sought to understand why certain policies and practices persisted in society over time. They concluded that adoption and retention of any resource program depends on the extent to which it is physically possible (consistent with ecological processes), economically feasible (practices generate revenue or benefits in excess of costs), and culturally adoptable (consistent with prevailing social customs and norms). Much emphasis has been placed on increasing knowledge and developing practices that meet the first two criteria; however, until recently research on the third component has been sparse. Yet practices lacking this criterion—societal acceptance and approval—will ultimately fail regardless of their technical or economic merit (Firey 1960; Vaske et al. 2001). See McCaffrey and Kumagai (this volume) for a related discussion of factors affecting acceptance of wildfire risk-mitigation measures.

Shindler et al. (2002) delineated several specific reasons why attention needs to be paid to social acceptability of public forest management. First, values play a role in decisions. Though technical and economic information is important, few management decisions are limited to "objective science." Science alone cannot tell us what ought to be or how to balance difficult tradeoffs. To gain public acceptance, decisions must also account for public values. This requires involving citizens and understanding their interests. Second, people have a right to participate in decisions that affect them. American citizens are the ultimate owners of public forests; residents of the wildland-urban interface bordering forests, in particular, have legitimate concerns and thus, a stake in forest management. Finally, in a democracy, it is a simple fact that social acceptability matters. Power ultimately rests with citizens. In the case of federal forest management, it has been delegated to agencies like the Forest Service and the Bureau of Land Management. If policies are inconsistent with public values, over time this delegated power will be taken away by citizens who work to modify, postpone, or prevent the implementation of plans. They can circumvent agency authority through the courts, their legislators, and the media (Shindler et al. 1993). The results can include higher management costs, inability to implement projects, and frustration among all parties involved.

Citizen support is an essential component of effective fire-management programs, particularly fuel-reduction activities that typically occur at the wildland-urban interface. Whether it is over the use of prescribed fire or thinning treatments, the public has legitimate concerns about practices that occur close to their homes or other places they care deeply about. What else could we expect? Most citizens grew up being told repeatedly by Smokey Bear that suppressing all forest fires is good and is a normal part of forest management. More recently, what many have heard about the use of prescribed fire has come from high-profile escapes that destroy homes such as the Cerro Grande Fire in Los Alamos in 2000 (Grote 2000). As for thinning, much of the public is unable to distinguish this treatment from harvesting—an unpopular activity in many places (Shouse 2002). Other fuel-reduction practices exist (e.g., mowing, livestock grazing, chaining, herbicides) but their application is relatively limited or they are considered too contentious for most settings.

Social acceptability can be difficult to understand and to gain. For example, numerous factors play a role in judgments regarding fire and fuel reduction, including: beliefs regarding the outcome of an activity, values, knowledge, emotions, issue importance, context, trust, personal experience, perception of risk, and visual quality (Bright et al. 2002; McCool and Stankey 1986; Wagner and Flynn 1998; Winter et al. 2002). Moreover, the process of arriving at a decision is as important as the decision itself. Further complicating social acceptability is its dynamic nature; it is a continuing process, not an outcome or end result (Shindler et al. 2002). As scientists, managers, and citizens learn more, or factors change, judgments also can change (Shindler and Toman 2003). Because citizens will continue to judge the implementation of actions, managers must continue to pay attention to public acceptance.

Challenges to Building Public Acceptance

In light of the critical role citizens play in an agency's ability to implement fuel-reduction practices, improving our understanding of the factors that contribute to public acceptance seems essential. This chapter relies on primary research to examine common challenges to fuel managers across the country. Although each situation may stem from a unique set of biophysical and sociodemographic circumstances, the nature of public responses about fire management suggests they can be organized and subjected to critical thinking. For example, locations where agencies have been able to move forward with treatments are typically in communities where residents are fairly sophisticated in their knowledge of fire issues and where personnel have built trustworthy relations (Shindler and Toman 2003; Winter et al. 2002). Raish et al. (this volume) present information on this topic concerning the role of knowledge and past experience with using fire as a management tool as a factor in the willingness of some Native American groups to accept agency prescribed fire and other forest management practices. One of the difficult choices managers face is which "public" to pay attention to; local, regional, and national publics often have different perspectives about natural resources problems (Brunson and Steel 1996). When a forest practice occurs "somewhere else," it may be a non-issue or at least have little impact on people's lives. This appears to be the case for fuel reduction, where recent research shows that urban publics seem less concerned about the threat of wildfire and have a low level of awareness of treatments compared to rural residents (Kneeshaw et al. 2004a; Shindler and Brunson 2002). An initial implication in this synthesis is that individuals more directly affected by fire will be the first to judge management actions. This is congruent with legislative directives (i.e., NFP and HFRA) that place importance on community-based approaches and encourage partnerships with local citizens. Therefore, this analysis focuses primarily on the community level where fuel-reduction practices are planned and implemented. The purpose is to encourage thoughtful consideration of these challenges as they both constrain and facilitate acceptance of fire-management programs.

Public understanding and management context

Since the shift in federal forest policy from suppression of all fires to using fire as a management tool some twenty-five years ago, citizens have generally come to understand that fire is a natural, normal part of ecosystems. For example, in a national survey of the general population more than 60% recognized the benefits of wildfire or the role that wildfire plays in our forests (Shindler and Brunson 2002). At the same time, media coverage of large fires has also broadened public awareness of risks. But a confounding factor is that the relevancy of forest fire and fuel reduction is not evenly distributed. Fire-management issues are a low-level concern for many citizens, particularly urban residents, who may give the topic little consideration and put little effort into understanding fire-related issues (Shindler and Brunson 2002; Shindler and Wilton 2002). The low level of wildfire on the list of public safety issues is discussed in greater detail in Daniel (this volume). Achieving widespread understanding of associated problems and support for fuel-reduction programs is hindered by this imbalance. For instance, Shindler and Brunson (2002) also found that more than a quarter of the general public believe that that all fires should be put out, regardless of their origin, and most of these individuals reside in urban areas. Thus, the importance of an issue in peoples' lives plays a role in acceptability (Bright and Manfredo 1996, 1997). Judgments about fire management can be strong, especially in rural forest communities where fire has become an important issue and is personalized by proximity and the likelihood that outcomes will affect a valued place or individual livelihoods (Kneeshaw et al. 2004b).

Although knowledge of fire in general is growing, people still understand little about the management practices intended to reduce forest fuels and maintain healthy conditions. It follows then that the ability of fire professionals to specify conditions, outline treatment alternatives, and engage citizens in discussion about the nature of the options is essential. But the trend in forest management has been towards large-scale, one-size-fits-all management solutions. Citizens may have difficulty identifying with large landscapes or a regional fire plan; instead, they identify with places that have personal meaning (Stankey and Shindler 1997). Citizens are acutely aware of the local context in which decisions are made; that is, the unique characteristics of places, how places have evolved over time, and what expectations they (or their community) have for local resources (Williams and Stewart 1998). At this level citizens may not readily support new (or different) forest practices such as prescribed fire because they do not have much personal experience by which to judge them (Shindler et al. 1996). Expectations play a role in acceptance of practices. When citizens believe there will be positive outcomes, they are more likely to have positive attitudes towards restoration and fuel treatments (Bright et al. 2002; Winter et al. 2002).

Although wildfire hazard reduction is a universally accepted goal, researchers have found geographic variations in citizens' concerns about the use of specific treatments (Kneeshaw et al. 2004a; Winter et al. 2002). For example, in a four-state study Brunson and Shindler (2004) found the use of prescribed fire and thinning to be highly acceptable in Oregon but much less so in Utah, where livestock grazing was the preferred treatment. In a separate study, Shindler and Toman (2003) noted that residents in Oregon understood significantly more about the effects of thinning than they did about prescribed fire. Taylor and Daniel (1984) observed that educational information about prescribed fire led to public support of the practice, but did not alter the public's perceptions of scenic quality or recreation use of affected areas. Researchers have noted that differences in acceptance are largely about how the goal is achieved and if it reflects public sentiment

(Kneeshaw et al. 2004a). Thus, paying particular attention to community conditions and helping residents understand how potential impacts will affect personal property, local economies, and valued places is important. Citizens may be generally accepting of fuel reduction practices, but tend to sit up and take notice—often becoming vocal for the first time—when it involves identifiable places and resources. Specific attention at this level makes sense because local residents are directly and disproportionately affected by fuel-reduction treatments applied at the interface. Planning for local circumstances can often mean the difference between public acceptance and resentment of management policies (Shindler et al. 2002; Steelman and Kunkel 2004).

Knowledge and information delivery

Knowledge of fire and fuel management is a primary factor in public acceptance of agency programs. Numerous studies in the last twenty-five years provide evidence of a link between knowledge and acceptance of fuel-management activities (e.g., Cortner et al. 1990; Gardner et al. 1987; Parkinson et al. 2003). For example, Manfredo et al. (1990) noted a correlation between knowledge of fire and fire policy and support for prescribed burning. Loomis et al. (2001) saw positive effects from introducing educational materials; respondents became more knowledgeable about and tolerant of prescribed fire and more confident that prescribed fire would reduce wildfire risk. They also perceived a reduction in risk and potential problems from smoke. A related contribution comes from Bright and Manfredo (1997), who found that information influenced the strength of existing attitudes (believers became more positive), but not necessarily the direction of the attitudes (change people's minds).

It is easy for such findings to lead to a management attitude of "if people just understood the facts, they would approve of our actions" followed by attempts to "educate" the public. Unfortunately, this idea oversimplifies the role and nature of knowledge. Certainly technical information is useful to citizens, but information alone is rarely enough to change people's opinions or their behaviors (Stankey 1995). Essential elements in information delivery and the credibility of the information provider are often overlooked. How and where people get information matters greatly; facts do not speak for themselves. They must be appreciated and interpreted by individuals (Jamieson 1994).

Serious thought must be given to what it means to "educate" the public about fire management and fuel reduction. People tend to respond to meaningful examples in recognizable places, instead of anonymous information that comes from brochures, newspaper articles, written plans, and so forth. For example, studies of citizen-agency interactions (e.g., Cortner et al. 1998; Shindler and Neburka 1997) show that people do not react favorably to traditional one-way forms of communication such as agency meetings for scoping purposes commonly used to satisfy National Environmental Policy Act requirements. Such approaches provide for little genuine participation by citizens and little commitment in either the fire plans or the process by which they were developed (Stankey and Shindler 1997). Citizens prefer more interactive forms of information exchange (Daniels et al. 1996; Parkinson et al. 2003). In recent surveys, citizens rated interactive approaches, such as guided field trips, small informal workshops, interpretive centers, and school programs as the most useful in understanding fuel-reduction problems (Shindler and Toman 2003; Toman et al. 2006).

Because context is important, the public also requires information specific to their situation. In a three-state study by Winter et al. (2002) the size of fuel treatments, planning (whether treatments were part of larger plans), cost-effectiveness, staff qualifications, and treatment locations were all important to citizens. Similarly Shelby and Speaker (1990) posited that providing specific information about the reasons for and location, time, and effects of a prescribed burn resulted in greater acceptance. Expanding the issue to forest restoration, Hull and Gobster (2000) argued the discussion could be elevated if restoration goals were articulated and if people understood the consequences of specific actions. They recommended that managers spell out the benefits of restoration in terms of human health and enhancements to communities. Indeed, McCool and Stankey (1986) concluded that those who favored a prescribed-fire policy saw specific benefits to the ecological resource. In sum, Daniels et al. (1996) stressed that people need a common base of knowledge about fire management to effectively participate in decision making.

Finally, information about fire management needs to come from a credible source and be scientifically sound (Shelby and Speaker 1990). There are discouraging longitudinal data that citizens are paying less attention to Forest Service fire information than they did several years ago (Shindler and Toman 2003); one reason is that few people agree that the agency contributes to public understanding of the costs and benefits of fuel reduction or does a good job of providing information about its fire-management activities. In contrast, the most positive public responses typically come from situations where resource managers are able to articulate in clear terms the purpose of a particular practice, including the ecological basis for it (Shindler and Neburka 1997). In these cases citizens can engage in genuine discussion about fuel-reduction strategies and determine for themselves which treatments are most appropriate for local problems. Also, these settings often are places where decision makers (e.g., district rangers) have some visible presence in the deliberations; participants view this as legitimizing their own efforts and time spent. Effectively reaching citizens depends not only on how they interpret information, but also on how they feel about the information providers and the methods used to communicate it.

Decision-making processes

Concerns about public acceptance of fire-management and fuel-reduction activities often focus on final decisions and their "objective" quality. The rationale has often been that if a decision is technically sound and economically feasible—and if citizens are allowed to review and comment or attend a public meeting—then it should be socially acceptable. However, research throughout the last decade has repeatedly shown that the public's idea of a legitimate management plan corresponds to the quality of decision-making procedures used (e.g., Lawrence et al. 1997; Shindler et al. 2002; Winter et al. 2002). Of particular importance in forest communities is the opportunity for citizens to participate in each phase of the planning process, especially when practices such as prescribed fire and thinning operations are viewed with uncertainty or skepticism. In the southwestern U.S., Steelman and Kunkel (2004) observed that the decision process provides a useful framework for evaluating how structural responses (e.g., building codes, fuel programs, buffer zones) and social responses (e.g., management and planning techniques) work together in a community's response to the threat of wildfire.

Today most forest agencies are attempting some form of "collaborative planning" for fire management. The Healthy Forest Restoration Act even ties certain types of funding to community-based fire plans. The upshot is that many management units are struggling with collaborative approaches because personnel are so familiar with the highly mechanistic, impersonalized NEPA scoping format used in most forest planning. This traditional form is often denigrated by participants as an ineffective, sterile, rule-bound, one-way exchange (Cortner et al. 1998; Shindler et al. 2002).

Thus, along with questions about how large an area to treat and which treatment to use, fire managers also should be asking questions about their local constituents. For example, who should be included in the planning discussion, what is the public's role in this project, and what do people need to know to participate? This approach reflects a more thoughtful strategy and can help structure the planning process in advance (Delli Priscoli and Homenuck 1990). Only after agency managers first deliberate and agree on planning objectives, how decisions will be made, and who the public is for a given project, should a particular planning process be initiated. These deliberative steps help avoid costly problems later on. They also make it easier to engage the public by forcing the planning team to discuss their expectations about the public's involvement, help determine which team members are best suited for the public contact role, and help develop buy-in on the eventual process.

It is clear that citizen participation in planning is most useful when people have an understanding of the consequences of the choices. Gaining public acceptance often relies on the ability of fire managers to frame options in clear and meaningful terms, usually through personal contact. Managers have had success using forums such as meetings and field tours with homeowner associations, "friends" groups, and local watershed councils (Shindler and Toman 2003; Winter et al. 2002). In these settings, people can actively engage one another to talk through their concerns, actually walk the particular landscape to be treated, examine the risks and consequences of various choices, and work out acceptable strategies to unique local problems—all with the likelihood that greater trust will be built among those involved.

Trust building

Trust in public agencies to carry out fire-management and fuel-reduction practices is a central requirement of effective programs. As noted above, there is new evidence that trust in agencies like the Forest Service to implement a responsible fuel-management program may be eroding (Shindler and Toman 2003; Shindler et al. 2003). However, these studies also suggest citizens' negative feelings frequently stem from frustration with the federal bureaucracy in general and not necessarily with personnel on local management units. These feelings often are attributable to the tension over adherence to agency policies set at the national (or regional) level and the public's view about the need to manage forest conditions at the community level. Successful plans will require visible administrative leadership to structure the organizational approach for improving citizen-agency interactions (Shindler et al. 2002). Trust in agency personnel is most apparent when they focus on specific local concerns. Trust is the most significant predictor of agency effectiveness for managing fire and fire risk (Winter and Cvetkovich 2003).

Across forest communities, Winter et al. (2002) identified several aspects of citizens' trust in land management agencies. First, people are concerned with the professional skill of land managers, including experience, education, and training. In other words, people want assurance that fuel treatments will be carried out by professionals who "know what they are doing." Beebe and Omi (1993) also found that citizens want competent professionals to manage (or eliminate) risk. Second, many people question managers' ability to control wildfire, which in turn influences their attitudes toward prescribed fire. Beebe and Omi (1993:20) pointed out that high-profile wildfire events remind people that "fire persistently confounds attempts at control or containment."

Another important trust factor is how residents view an agency's efforts to communicate about fuel treatments (Winter and Cvetkovich 2003; Winter et al. 2002). For example, a majority of Georgia residents surveyed preferred that nearby residents be warned before a prescribed fire was lit, rather than forgoing notification to take full advantage of good weather (Gilbert and Brunson 2002). Yet most had never been contacted before a prescribed fire. Oregon residents who agreed that the Forest Service provided good information about management activities were more likely to be supportive of prescribed fire (Shindler and Toman 2003). In an extensive examination of citizen-agency interactions Shindler and Aldred-Cheek (1999) concluded that effective trusting relations could be organized around six common factors: 1) inclusiveness, 2) sincere leadership, 3) innovative and flexible communication, 4) early commitment and continuity, 5) sound planning skills, and 6) efforts that result in action.

Forest agencies should recognize that managers need better tools for engaging the public; by any standard, the existing "tool kit" is antiquated (Shindler et al. 2002). At the same time, field personnel must be given adequate authority to lead at the community level. An organizational commitment to multi-partner cooperation is prerequisite to improving relations and building public trust. This concept should be no stretch for fire-management organizations; county, state, and federal agencies cooperate with one another all the time.   The final link involves citizen partners. Success will depend on whether the leadership on federal forests is serious about genuine involvement of stakeholders and how well the actions of fire-management and outreach personnel reflect this philosophy. Currently, most collaborative efforts and trust building remain the job of personnel at the lowest organizational levels, where relationships are established and face-to-face interactions can make a difference in communities. Thus far, success can usually be traced to single individuals with strong interpersonal skills and a commitment to communication (Yaffee and Wondolleck 1997). These individuals seem to know that "trust is built by leaning forward when we listen, not when we speak" (Putnam 2001:48). Broad-scale progress will occur in a meaningful way only when agencies promote these ideas and support personnel in their outreach efforts.

Visual quality and perceptions of "natural conditions"

Citizens' concerns about fire-management and fuel-reduction activities are often studied and expressed in terms of values, risk, smoke and air quality, and so on. But aesthetics may be the first and one of the few pieces of information by which citizens judge management activities. A central problem is that many of our forests now encompass different age classes, stocking levels, and stand densities than those professional foresters believe are healthy, but they are considered "natural" by the public (Brunson and Reiter 1996). While the initial basis for personal judgments of forest conditions is visual, it is clear that a more comprehensive, holistic form of public evaluation is needed.

A management approach based on visual quality seems limiting, largely because many other contextual (e.g., ecological) factors are not accounted for (Gobster 1996; Shindler et al. 2002). A preferable approach would be one that encourages people to look beyond the scenic to the ecological perspective (Hull and Gobster 2000). Yet, changing the public's mind about what they observe will be difficult. For example, participants involved in on-the-ground evaluations of prescribed fire and thinning treatments in Oregon felt the most important consideration was the visual impact and not the information they received about the treatment (Toman et al. 2004). However, once these visitors spent time on a treated site, they also considered the extent to which managers had accomplished their fuel-management objectives. In other cases, positive aesthetic judgments were linked with information about the scientific basis for practices (Ribe 1999) and the extent to which practices met community objectives for economic benefits or recreation uses (Bliss et al. 1994). Therefore, one approach is to help citizens evaluate forest settings not only by what is there, but also why it is there (Shindler et al. 2002). Fire managers can provide opportunities to raise awareness of fuel objectives and show people what treatment outcomes look like, both initially and over time.

One challenge will be to further delineate the goal—prominent among forest management agencies today—of achieving "natural" conditions. After 250 years of manipulation, what Americans perceive to be "natural" about their forests is not necessarily what is natural. Fire suppression has changed forests in all western states, creating severe consequences for forest health and fire conditions. But while Smokey Bear's message decreed that any forest fire should be suppressed, fire managers now tell people that they need to intervene to return "the balance of nature" (Shindler et al. 2002). Forestry professionals attempt to mimic truly natural conditions; sometimes this involves reintroducing fires that reflect historic patterns or using silvicultural treatments that look like small, natural disturbances or to create open, park-like stands in ponderosa pine forests. Although preliminary research indicates public reaction to such treatments is generally favorable (Brunson and Shelby 1992; Toman et al. 2004), not everyone accepts these approaches. Some groups see thinning as a contrived excuse to commercially harvest forests while other individuals are concerned about prescribed fire creating smoke or risk to property.

Thus, legitimate questions arise about what natural conditions are, how they are perceived, and how we should achieve them. The answers may vary from one setting to another, but reaching agreement on them must include citizens. To start, Daniel (2003:13) says simply "fire managers should get their story straight." We can expect public resistance when current conditions are perceived, accurately or not, as "natural." After all, we are asking people to accept the premise that forests require active manipulation by managers to restore natural conditions. This may also require admitting that prior manipulations (including years of fire suppression) have created something other than natural, healthy forests.

Risk and Uncertainty

Fuel-reduction programs are largely about reducing risk—risk of wildfire, risk to natural systems, risk to life and property. But fuel management also involves much uncertainty about how forests work as well as how they will respond to practices intended to achieve certain conditions. In general, there is a correlation between risk perception and the acceptability of forest management activities (Kneeshaw et al. 2004b; Wagner and Flynn 1998). In the case of prescribed fire, Shindler and Brunson (2002) found in their national survey that citizens were most concerned about damage to private property, loss of wildlife habitat, increased smoke, and effects on their water supply. As might be assumed, acceptance was higher for prescribed fire away from homes and private property. Additional concerns involve the perceived risk of an escaped, catastrophic fire (Winter et al. 2002). In areas where residents have previously experienced a wildfire, the perceived risk of a prescribed fire going out of control can be much higher (Shindler et al. 2003; Winter and Fried 2000). Also, hazards that are communicated in the media can seem more threatening than they actually might be (Beebe and Omi 1993). Dramatic fire events attract a high level of media coverage, reinforcing the public's tendency to overestimate risks.

Although fuel-reduction activities are often associated with risk, the real concern can stem from the uncertainty surrounding them. Citizens may associate new management activities with risk because they are unfamiliar with (and uncertain about) the outcomes. Most notable are concerns about thinning and the ecological effects on the forest ecosystem (Bliss 2000). For many, the risk here is often associated with allowing (trusting) managers to harvest trees in the name of fuel reduction. While prescribed fire may be viewed as a short-term risk because the fire is out quickly, smoke dissipates, and green-up occurs soon thereafter, thinning can be considered a longer-term question (Shindler et al. 2002). Simply, the final results of a harvest operation may not be known for years.

Findings about the risk of natural hazards (e.g., floods, earthquakes, and so on) by McCaffrey and Kumagai (this volume) and McCaffrey (2004) are particularly interesting for how they put concerns about fire into social context. As hazards go, the risk of wildfire failed to score high with the public because 1) years of fire suppression have created a feeling of control, 2) the extent of most wildfires is reasonably limited; most people do not live near an area prone to wildfire, 3) there is generally enough warning for evacuation to avoid fatalities, and 4) outright denial ("it won't happen to me"). Wildland-urban interface residents are aware of wildfire risks, but are often willing to trade off these risks for the benefits and values they derive from living there (McCaffrey 2004; Winter and Fried 2000). "Public reaction to wildfire suggests that many Americans want competent professionals to manage fire flawlessly, reducing the risk to life, property, and public lands to nil" (Beebe and Omi 1993:24).

Fire managers face a difficult conundrum. On the one hand, there is a need to sensitize people to wildfire risks so that they take actions to minimize losses (e.g., creating a defensible space). On the other hand, overemphasizing fire risks could lead to public hostility towards fire, even the use of prescribed fire (Beebe and Omi 1993). Winter and Cvetkovich (2003) described this as a gap between expert knowledge and public understanding. Kumagai et al. (2004) warned that such misunderstanding between managers and citizens puts property owners in fire-prone areas at risk. Bridging the gap requires explanations that take into account public concerns, different levels of understanding, and presenting the logic behind choices as opposed to standard messages that merely gloss over detail and treat all audiences the same (Winter and Cvetkovich 2003). Ehrenhaldt (1994) recognized that for people to make a rational choice about a policy they have to understand the consequences of the choices. To the degree that managers can tell them, people want to know specifics about what is likely to happen, where it will happen, who will be affected, and how uncertain we are about the outcomes (Shindler et al. 2002). Currently, few forums exist where discussions occur to help citizens understand the risks, allow them to weigh the trade-offs, and thus increase the acceptability of fuel-reduction activities.

Conclusions

These challenges represent a growing body of knowledge about the relationship between federal forest managers and public acceptance of fuel-reduction programs. The role that fire-management personnel are being asked to play today is much different from that of the past, when citizen participation was minimal and technical expertise was foremost. This suggests that, in this new role, managers can achieve greater public acceptance by being responsive to the suite of ecological and social factors affecting fuel management (Shindler et al. 2002). The ability of fire-management professionals to engage citizens in discussion about the nature of the options will be just as important as providing technical details. Expectations are high because fire management often becomes very personalized for citizens. Our communications should reflect that we understand their concerns and are committed to a long-term relationship in forest communities.

While this chapter has pointed out specific challenges to help focus management responses to gaining public acceptance, it also recognizes that these are integrated problems that are frequently embedded within one another. Thus, five basic strategies emerge from this analysis to help guide resource professionals and citizens toward more integrated solutions. First, we need to treat the goal of public acceptance as a process that cultivates understanding through the deliberation of ideas and the evaluation of alternatives. This approach recognizes that acceptance is more likely to evolve from an informed public. Because it is a process, acceptance is always provisional. Conditions that are acceptable now can become unacceptable in time based on the specific context of the problem and relationship of the players involved.

Second, it will be important to develop the capacity within fire agencies to respond to public concerns. This can best be achieved through an organizational plan for multi-partner relationships with conviction at both the local and regional level. Such a plan must recognize the skills necessary to conduct the public outreach job and then enable motivated personnel to develop them. This will also mean providing greater flexibility for personnel to take risks, experiment with new ideas, and involve citizens in the process. If this is to be successful, the clarification of roles is essential. The agencies must define their relationship with the public as well as the role they are willing to let citizens play in planning fuel-reduction programs.

Third, fire managers must approach trust building as the central, long-term goal of public communication and outreach. No matter how brilliant a plan of action may be, nothing is validated unless the people involved trust one another. Building trust takes great patience, requires many opportunities for parties to interact, and is a continual process of adjustment.

The fourth strategy involves focusing on the contextual conditions of fire management and forest communities. How fire practices affect specific sites and familiar settings greatly influences public acceptance. Thus, personnel may need to improve their understanding of the range of contextual factors present including the importance of local places, public perceptions of the uncertainty and risk of different management alternatives, and the concerns shared by citizens for the biological, social, and economic conditions of their community.

Finally, stable leadership is essential for developing a shared understanding of forest conditions and fire-management practices. Citizens are looking for agencies to play a stronger leadership role and to establish a strategy for communities to work together (Stankey and Shindler 1997). Good leaders are needed to help structure the public conversation and build a common understanding of the consequences of choices; this could include scenarios depicting what changes in forest conditions will look like and how soon they might occur, as well as the ramifications of non-action. For citizens to have a real ability to participate in fire planning, they must possess a capacity for participation. The discussion is much more useful when they understand ecological processes, the relevant economics, and the interests that are at stake. As people come to understand the trade-offs, there will be broader public acceptance of more liberal fire management policies.

REFERENCES

Beebe, G., and P. Omi. 1993. "Wildland burning: The perception of risk." *Journal of Forestry* 93(9):19-24.

Bliss, J. C. 2000. "Public perceptions of clearcutting." *Journal of Forestry* 98(12):4-9.

———, S. Nepal, R. Brooks, and M. Larsen. 1994. "Forestry community or granfalloon?" *Journal of Forestry* 92(9):6-10.

Bright, A. D., and M. Manfredo. 1996. "A conceptual model of attitudes toward natural resource issues: A case study of wolf reintroduction." *Human Dimensions of Wildlife* 1(1):1-21.

———, and M. Manfredo. 1997. "The influence of balanced information on attitudes toward natural resources." *Society and Natural Resources* 10(5):469-83.

———, S. Barro, and R. Burtz. 2002. "Public attitudes toward ecological restoration in the Chicago Metropolitan Region." *Society and Natural Resources* 15:763-85.

Brunson, M.W. and B. Shelby. 1992. "Assessing recreational and scenic quality: how does "new forestry" rate?" *Journal of Forestry* 90(7):37-41.

———, and D. Reiter. 1996. "Effects of ecological information on judgments about scenic impacts of timber harvests." *Journal of Environmental Management* 46:31-41.

———, and B. Steel. 1996. "Sources of variation in attitudes and beliefs about federal rangeland management." *Journal of Range Management* 49:69-75.

———, and B. Shindler. 2004. "Geographic variation in social acceptability of wildland fuels management in the western U.S." *Society and Natural Resources* 17(8):1-18.

Clark, J. R. 1999. "The ecosystem approach from a practical point of view." *Conservation Biology* 13:679-81.

Clawson, M. 1975. *Forests for Whom and for What?* Baltimore, Maryland: Johns Hopkins University Press.

Cortner, H., P. Gardner, and J. Taylor. 1990. "Fire hazards at the urban-wildland interface: What the public expects." *Environmental Management* 14(3):209-22.

———, M. Wallace, S. Burke, and M. Moote. 1998. "Institutions matter: The need to address the institutional challenges of ecosystem management." *Landscape and Urban Planning* 40:159-66.

Daniel, T. C. 2003. "Social science of wildfire risk management: Individual level of analysis." In: Humans, Fires, and Forests—Social Science Applied to Fire Management. Ecological Restoration Institute Workshop Proceedings, Northern Arizona University, Flagstaff, Arizona: 9-16.

Daniels, S. E., G. Walker, M. Carroll, and K. Blatner. 1996. "Using collaborative learning in fire recovery planning." *Journal of Forestry* 94(8):4-9.

Delli Priscolli, J., and P. Homenuck. 1990. "Consulting the publics." In: R. Lang (ed.), *Integrated Approaches to Resource Planning and Management*. Banff, Alberta: The Banff Centre School for Management: 67-79.

Dombeck, M. 1996. "Thinking like a mountain: BLM's approach to ecosystem management." *Ecological Applications* 6:699-702.

Ehrenhaldt, A. 1994. "Let the people decide between spinach and broccoli." *Governing* 7(10):6-7.

Firey, W. 1960. *Man, Mind, and Land.* Glencoe, Illinois: The Free Press. 256 pp.

Gardner, P., H. Cortner, and K. Widaman. 1987. "The risk perceptions and policy response toward wildland fire hazards by urban homeowners." *Landscape and Urban Planning* 14(2):163-72.

Gilbert, L., and M. W. Brunson. 2002. A qualitative study of homeowner attitudes toward messages about prescribed fire in central Georgia. Joint Fire Science Program Project Report. Utah State University, Logan, Utah.

Gobster, P. H. 1996. "Forest aesthetics, biodiversity, and the perceived appropriateness of ecosystem management practices." In: M. Brunson, L. Kruger, C. Tyler, and S. Schroeder (eds.), Defining social acceptability in ecosystem management: A workshop proceedings. Gen. Tech. Rep. PNW-GTR-369. Portland, Oregon: USDA Forest Service, PNW Research Station: 77-97.

Grote, R. W. 2000. Forest fire protection. CRS Report for Congress RL 30755. Congressional Research Service, The Library of Congress. Dec. 5.

Hull, B. R., and P. Gobster. 2000. "Restoring forest ecosystems: The human dimension." *Journal of Forestry* 98(8):32-36.

Jamieson, D. 1994. "Problems and prospects for a Forest Service program in the human dimensions of global change." In: K. Geyer and B. Shindler (eds.), Breaking the mold: Global change, social responsibility, and natural resource management. USDA Forest Service Research Report. Portland, Oregon: PNW Research Station: 23-28.

Kneeshaw, K., J.Vaske, A. Bright, and J. Absher. 2004a. "Acceptability norms toward fire management in three national forests." *Environment and Behavior* 36:1-21.

————, J.Vaske, A. Bright, and J. Absher. 2004b. "Situational influences of acceptable wildland fire management actions." *Society and Natural Resources* 17(6):477-90.

Kumagai, Y., J. Bliss, S. Daniels, and M. Carroll. 2004. "Research on causal attribution of wildfire: An exploratory multiple-methods approach." *Society and Natural Resources* 17:113-27.

Lawrence, R., S. Daniels, and G. Stankey. 1997. "Procedural justice and public involvement in natural resources decision making." *Society and Natural Resources* 10(6):577-89.

Loomis, J. B., L. Bair, and A. Gonzalez-Caban. 2001. "Prescribed fire and public support: Knowledge gained, attitudes changed in Florida." *Journal of Forestry* 99(11):18-22.

McCaffrey, S. 2004. "Thinking of wildfire as a natural hazard." *Society and Natural Resources* 17(6):509-16.

McCool, S. F., and G. Stankey. 1986. Visitor attitudes toward wilderness fire management policy—1971-Research Paper INT-357. Ogden, Utah: USDA Forest Service, Intermountain Research Station. 7 pp.

Manfredo, M. J., M. Fishbein, G. Haas, and A. Watson. 1990. "Attitudes toward prescribed fire policies." *Journal of Forestry* 88(7):19-23.

Parkinson, T. M., J. E. Force, and J. Kapler Smith. 2003. "Hands-on learning: Its effectiveness in teaching the public about wildland fire." *Journal of Forestry* 10:21-26.

Putnam, N. 2001. "Sustainability on the ground." *Journal of Forestry* 99(8):48.

Ribe, R. G. 1999. "The aesthetics of forestry: What has empirical preference research taught us?" *Environmental Management* 13:55-74.

Shelby, B., and R. Speaker. 1990. "Public attitudes and perceptions about prescribed burning." In: J. Walstad, S. Radosevich, D. Sandberg (eds.), *Natural and Prescribed Fire in Pacific Northwest Forests*. Corvallis: Oregon State University Press: 253-60.

Shindler, B., P. List, and B. Steel. 1993. "Managing federal forests: Public attitudes in Oregon and nationwide." *Journal of Forestry* 91(7)17-19.

————, B. Steel, and P. List. 1996. "Public judgments of adaptive management: A response from forest communities." *Journal of Forestry* 94(6)4-12.

————, and J. Neburka. 1997. "Public participation in forest planning: Eight attributes of success." *Journal of Forestry* 91(7):17-19.

————, and K. Aldred-Cheek. 1999. "Integrating citizens in adaptive management: A propositional analysis." *Journal of Conservation Ecology* 3(1):13-23.

————, and M. Brunson. 2002. Wildland fire study: A national survey of citizens. Joint Fire Science Program Project Report. Oregon State University, Corvallis.

————, M. Brunson, and G. Stankey. 2002. Social acceptability of forest conditions and management practices: A problem analysis. General Technical Report PNW-GTR-537. Portland, Oregon: USDA Forest Service, Pacific Northwest Research Station. 68 pp.

————, and J. Wilton. 2002. A social assessment of ecosystem health: public perspectives on PacificNorthwest Forests. USDA Forest Service Pacific Northwest Research Station Research Report. 110 pp.

————, J. Leahy, and E. Toman. 2003. Public acceptance of forest conditions and fuel reduction practices: A survey of citizens in communities adjacent to national forests in Minnesota, Wisconsin, and Michigan. USDA Forest Service North Central Research Station Research Report. 51 pages.

————, and E. Toman. 2003. "Fuel reduction strategies in forest communities: A longitudinal analysis of public support." *Journal of Forestry* 101(6):8-15.

Shouse, B. 2002. "Bush's forest plan under fire." *Science Now*, October 10:6-7.
Stankey, G. H. 1995. "The pursuit of sustainability: Joining science and public choice." *The George Wright Forum* 12(3):11-18.
——, and B. Shindler 1997. Adaptive Management Areas: Achieving the promise, avoiding the peril. General Technical Report PNW-GTR-394. Portland, Oregon: USDA Forest Service, Pacific Northwest Research Station. 21 pp.
Steelman, T. A,. and G. Kunkel. 2004. "Effective community responses to wildfire threats: Lessons from New Mexico." *Society and Natural Resources* 17(8):679-699.
Taylor, J. G., and T. Daniel. 1984. "Prescribed fire: Public education and perception." *Journal of Forestry* 82:361-65.
Toman, E., B. Shindler, and M. Reed. 2004. "Prescribed fire: The influence of site visits on citizen attitudes." *Journal of Environmental Education* 35(3):13-17.
——, B. Shindler, and M. Brunson. 2006. "Fire and fuel management communication strategies: Citizen evaluations of agency outreach activities." *Society and Natural Resources* 19: 321-336.
Vaske, J. J., M. Donnelly, D. Williams, and S. Jonker. 2001. "Demographic influences on environmental value orientations and normative beliefs about national forest management." *Society and Natural Resources* 14:761-776.
Wagner, R. G., and J. Flynn. 1998. "Public perceptions of risk and acceptability of forest vegetation management alternatives in Ontario." *The Forestry Chronicle* 74(5):720-27.
Williams, D., and S. Stewart. 1998. "Sense of place: An elusive concept that is finding a home in ecosystem management." *Journal of Forestry* 96(5):16-23.
Winter, G, and J. Fried. 2000. "Homeowner perspectives on fire hazard, responsibility, and management strategies at the wildland-urban interface." *Society and Natural Resources* 13:33-49.
——, C. Vogt, and J. Fried. 2002. "Fuel treatments at the wildland-urban interface: Common concerns in diverse regions." *Journal of Forestry* 100(1):15-21.
Winter, P. L., and G. Cvetkovich. 2003. A study of southwesterner's opinions on the management of wildland and wilderness fires. Research Report, USDA Forest Service, Pacific Southwest Research Station, Riverside, California. 30 pp.
Yaffee, S. L., and J. Wondolleck, 1997. "Building bridges across agency boundaries." In: J. Franklin and K.Kohm (eds.), *Creating a Forestry for the 21st Century*. Washington, D.C.: Island Press: 381-96.

Perceptions of Wildfire Risk

Terry C. Daniel

Wildfire risk managers often start with the assumption that wildfire is an important hazard that demands mitigation. But a review of literature reveals that wildfire has generally not been high on the list of concerns for the public, nor has it attracted much attention from those charged with protecting the public against the wide range of hazards modern people face. Wildfire has essentially been ignored in the substantial risk-perception research literature. Wildfire may in fact not be among the most serious hazards for modern humans, especially for the largest numbers who live in highly developed urban areas. Moreover, even for those who live in higher-risk areas the objective probability of a wildfire causing serious damage to any particular individual property can be quite small. To mitigate the low-probability risk of uncertain amounts of damage from wildfire in the future people are asked immediately and in perpetuity to exert effort, pay costs, and accept sacrifices in return for uncertain and incomplete protection. Faced with such unattractive trade-offs, it is not surprising that many individuals who are at risk from wildfire fail to fully embrace and implement recommended fuels reduction, defensible space, and other mitigation programs. To be successful, wildfire risk-management programs must be designed and presented with greater appreciation of the perspectives of at-risk individuals, for whom fire risk must compete with an array of more salient and more pressing concerns, and whose commitment to wildfire risk-mitigation efforts can be expected to be limited.

Wildfire as Hazard

The National Weather Service reports annually on sixteen major natural hazards, ranging from avalanches to winter storms. Compared to the hundreds of thousands of lives claimed each year in the U.S. by health, technological, and other hazards (e.g., automobile accidents, smoking, pollution), natural hazards altogether are not a major source of fatalities, typically numbering around five hundred per year. Wildfire is not listed as a hazard. Instead, fire weather is included in a secondary list among eleven

Terry C. Daniel, Dept. of Psychology, University of Arizona
(tdaniel@U.Arizona.edu)

other hazards, along with fog, rain, and dust storms. On average wildfire (fire weather) accounted for less than 0.5% of natural hazard fatalities in the last five years reported (1999 to 2004) and it has never ranked in the top half of the twenty-seven hazards monitored. Similarly, wildfires accounted for a little less than 2.5% of injuries in the same period. Moreover, most people injured or killed in wildfires have been firefighters, and not the general public, a fact likely to reduce further both professional and public concerns.

Hazard statistics typically include damage to agricultural crops, and damage to potentially merchantable timber was an early motivation for wildfire-management programs, but damage to homes and infrastructure has become the greatest concern. Dramatic increases in losses to developed property have been the key factors driving recent risk-management policy changes. Both fatality and damage statistics have strong effects on professional risk assessments and on national risk- and emergency-management policy, but such objective statistics typically play a much smaller role in public perception of hazards. Technical assessments of risks are frequently different from the perceptions of individuals who are at risk, and whose acceptance, support, and compliance are critical to the success of risk-management programs.

Several decades of hazard perception, risk analysis, and decision research have identified a number of important factors that affect the perceptions, understandings, intuitions, feelings, and actions of people who are at risk (see the compilation by Slovic 2000). Little of this research has addressed natural hazards, and virtually none has specifically addressed wildfire hazard. However, wildfire does present a profile that is similar in important ways to more studied risks. The purpose of this chapter is to draw upon the more general risk-perception research to develop a better understanding of individuals' perceptions of wildfire risk and their willingness to support programs and to comply with recommended actions intended to reduce that risk. While a compelling case can be made that ecological impacts are the most important consequences of wildfire, both the risk-perception research literature and national risk-management policy, have been concerned almost entirely with direct damage to people and developed property. This synthesis will thus be focused on the direct risks that wildfire poses to people and developments.

Responses to Wildfire Risk

Individuals' responses to wildfire risk do not occur in a vacuum. Perceptions and reactions differ depending upon the biophysical and social-demographic settings in which wildfire risk is encountered. Individual response is also influenced by the sociocultural background of the person who is exposed. A simple model of individual response to wildfire risk is shown in Figure 1.

The biophysical setting includes climate, topography, vegetation cover (fuel type, amount, distribution, and fire regime), and other features that affect the persisting objective risk of wildfire and constrain risk-management options in an area. These are the features that have been emphasized in traditional fire-hazard warning systems. Contemporary emphasis on fuel reduction to mitigate risk in fire-prone settings emphasizes the biophysical dimension. Relevant features of the social-demographic setting may include the spatial distribution and construction features of developments, mobility of the resident population, availability of fire-protection resources, governmental regulations, and less formal relationships shared among neighbors. Institutional aspects of the social-demographic setting, such as requirements for fire-retardant construction materials, burning restrictions, and the deployment of fire-suppression resources have long played a central role in hazard management, as noted in McCaffrey and Kumagai (this volume). More recently, community-awareness and action programs have been directed at encouraging and reinforcing adoption and maintenance of risk-reducing behaviors on individual properties, such as defensible space designs (see Jakes and Nelson, this volume). Individual responses to biophysical and social-demographic setting factors are moderated by the person's sociocultural background, including personal and cultural

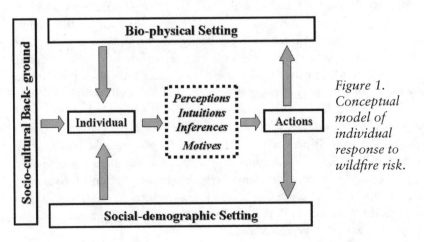

Figure 1. Conceptual model of individual response to wildfire risk.

experiences with fire (extensively discussed in Raish et al., this volume), attitudes toward risk in general and wildfire in particular, and relevant social prohibitions and incentives. Understanding and affecting individual perceptions of wildfire hazard and the level of support for and compliance with risk-management programs requires consideration of the joint effects of all three contextual factors.

Perceiving Risks

Hazards are typically defined technically in terms of biophysical (e.g., physical or chemical compositions, dispersal characteristics,) and social-demographic (e.g., exposed populations, physical/physiological vulnerability) factors. Technical risk assessments are based on estimates of the amount of potential harm/damage and the number of people and/or properties that might be exposed (e.g., Rohrmann 1998; Rohrmann and Renn 2000). The severity of a risk is calculated as the magnitude of the consequences multiplied by the probability of occurrence, i.e., as the expected (negative) value. The risk-perception literature has addressed an array of risks, ranging from alcoholic beverages to X-rays (e.g., Fischhoff et al. 1978; Slovic et al. 1979). This body of work shows that there are consistent patterns in the public's perceptions of risk, and that these patterns often do not correspond well to the parameters emphasized by technical risk assessments (e.g., Slovic 1987, 2000).

Public risk perceptions are more closely related to psychological characteristics of hazards, especially dread, familiarity (the unknown), and exposure (McCaffery and Kumagai, this volume, Slovic et al. 1980). The hazards perceived to have the most dreaded consequences are those that are potentially catastrophic in scale, usually fatal; exposure to which is involuntary and inequitable; and the consequences of which are threatening both to future generations and specifically to the individual rating the hazard. Nuclear weapons, nerve gas, and terrorism are high in dread, while sunbathing, hair dyes, and home gas furnaces are low. More familiar (less unknown) hazards have consequences that are well known and have immediate effects that are readily observable. At the high end of familiarity are handguns, motor vehicles, and alcoholic beverages. Unknown risks include food irradiation and nuclear power. To a somewhat lesser extent the perceived severity of a hazard depends on the number of people who are potentially exposed, with alcoholic beverages and caffeine having high exposure and space exploration having low exposure. Interestingly, greater exposure leads to technical assessments of more severe risk, but often has the opposite effect on perceived risk.

Expert assessments of risks are also affected by psychological factors, but they are much more strongly associated with mortality, morbidity, and economic-damage statistics than are lay risk perceptions (Lichtenstein et al. 1978). When directly asked to estimate the number of deaths from different hazards, people tend to underestimate deaths from common causes and overestimate deaths from rare causes. In their summary of results from a number of studies, Slovic et al. (1979) concluded that for "... lethal events whose frequencies were most poorly judged ... overestimated items were dramatic and sensational whereas underestimated items tended to be unspectacular events which claim one victim at a time and are common in non-fatal form" (reprinted in Slovic 2000, p 107).

Risk-perception research has focused mostly on technological hazards. Slovic et al. (1980), for example, studied ninety risks, only a few of which might be construed as natural hazards, such as hunting (ranked forty-sixth), mountain climbing (sixty-fourth), downhill skiing (seventy-third), and mushroom hunting (seventy-ninth). Sunbathing (eighty-eighth) has been included in several studies, and might also be construed as a natural hazard. In general, natural hazards tend to score lower as perceived risks than technological hazards. For example, Flynn et al. (1999) found that earthquakes and windstorms were ranked fifth and sixth, and flood was eleventh when they were the only natural hazards in a set of fifteen risks evaluated. Crime was the highest-ranked risk, followed closely by cancer and automobile accidents, with a substantial drop in risk rating means for the remaining hazards. The substantially lower ratings for natural hazards would probably be in line with technical assessments for the population of predominantly urban Portland, Oregon, residents represented in the study.

Perceiving Wildfire Risk

Very few comparative studies of risks have specifically included wildfire. An important exception is the cross-cultural study reported by Rohrmann (Renn and Rohrmann 2000) which compared twenty-five hazards, among them seven natural hazards, including (living in) fire areas. For the Australian respondents, fire areas ranked eleventh and was rated 6.4 on a 10-point risk-magnitude scale, compared to 8.8 for the highest-rated hazard, smoking, and 3.8 for the lowest, giving up your job. Ratings for other natural hazards ranged from 7.7 for sunbathing to 5.5 for unhealthy climate. Because there has been so little research directly on wildfire risk, extrapolations from general risk-perception research may be somewhat hazardous. McCaffrey (2004) nonetheless braved the following: "In relation to the three key characteristics [dread, unknown and exposure], wildfire fails to score high:

Years of successful fire suppression contribute to a feeling of control; the extent of most wildfires is reasonably limited; and there is generally enough warning to be able to evacuate, thereby avoiding fatalities. Wildfire also rates quite low on the second risk factor of 'unknown' as fire is an age-old and well-known danger whose effects are immediate and easily seen." (p 511)

Somewhat contrary to McCaffrey's suggestion about control, Winter and Fried (2000) found a significant tendency in their Michigan focus groups for participants who had directly or indirectly experienced a large fire in their residential area to view wildfire as erratic and impossible to control. Still, wildfire might be perceived as relatively controllable by the majority of individuals who have little wildfire experience. Recent efforts to portray fire as a natural and beneficial force in the forest may further reduce scores on the dread and the unknown factors, making it less likely that people would view wildfire as a major risk.

Extrapolations about the exposure factor are somewhat more problematic. The majority of people reside in urban areas and well-developed suburbs, and spend relatively little time in wild areas. At the same time, the number of people living in the wildland-urban interface is rapidly growing (Cortner and Gale 1990) and the level of exposure to wildfire hazard is likely to be getting higher. The USDA Forest Service (USDA/USDI 2000) estimated that over 89 million acres of national forest were at severe or moderately severe risk from wildfire, and over twenty thousand nearby communities were rated to be at significant risk (National Academy of Public Administration 2001). However, even for those individuals who live in the designated risk zones, the objective probability of any individual experiencing a damaging wildfire is likely to be very low. Moreover, risk-perception research indicates that the effect of greater exposure might be moderated by the fact that living in fire-prone areas is generally perceived to be voluntary, and voluntary risks are typically rated as more acceptable than risks that are imposed involuntarily (Slovic et al. 1980).

It is reasonable to expect that, as exposure increases, more people will experience wildfire, affecting perception of the risk. However, Gardner et al., (1987) reported that residents of communities that had recently experienced wildfires actually judged their exposure to be reduced, which the authors attributed either to the belief that "lightning doesn't strike twice" or that the recent fire had removed fuels and lessened their vulnerability. Even when direct experience of a hazard does increase awareness and concern, the effect is generally found to fade quite quickly (e.g., Chilton et al. 2002), a pattern also found for wildfires (Cortner et al. 1990; Gardner et al. 1987). Thus, objective increases in exposure to, and even direct experience of wildfire may not translate into greater perceived risk.

Accepting Risk-management Programs

Willingness to bear costs, make sacrifices, and take actions to protect against risk is related to the perception of the severity of the risk—but this relationship is not direct. Willingness to accept, support, or comply with risk-reduction programs depends upon a complex of interacting factors (e.g., Gregory 2002; Rohrmann 1998; Slovic 2000), with one of the key factors being the perceived trade-off between risks and benefits. All risky situations are associated with some benefits, or else they would simply be avoided altogether. To the extent that the benefits are assessed as outweighing the risks, an individual is likely to remain in a risky situation. For example, people may persist in living in flood-prone areas because real estate is cheaper there.

Technical assessments generally find a positive correlation between benefits and risks; that is, people tend to accept higher risks where the associated benefits are also high (e.g., Slovic et al. 1980). For example, sea breezes and scenic views may induce people to live on beaches in areas that have a high threat of hurricanes. Locations with lower benefits tend to be accepted only if the risks are also low. In contrast to technical assessments, benefits and risks tend to be negatively correlated in people's perceptions (e.g., Alhakami and Slovic 1994; Slovic et al. 1980). Beach dwellers who perceive high benefits from sea breezes and views tend to perceive risks from hurricanes to be lower than do people who do not appreciate these benefits as much. This psychological adjustment of the risk-benefit trade-off tends to make people underestimate the severity of risks in situations where benefits are perceived to be high, which may lead them to accept greater risks and to be less inclined to take actions to reduce those risks.

If the perceived costs of the actions required to reduce a recognized risk are high in resources, effort, or sacrifice of other values, people are less likely to accept, support, or comply with programs to reduce that risk (Fischhoff et al. 1979; Shindler, this volume). People have been found to be unwilling to bear even low costs (as in insurance premiums) to protect against low-probability risks, even if these risks have the potential for catastrophic consequences. When the likelihood of the risk event is perceived to be very small, people seem to treat it as effectively impossible and are unwilling to commit even very small amounts of effort or sacrifice to protect against the risk (Kunreuther et al. 2001; Kunreuther and Pauly 2004). A related factor is people's reluctance to treat mitigation actions, such as purchasing insurance, as an investment (Kleindorfer & Kunreuther 1999); people appear to assume that should the threatened risk not occur they will have wasted the cost and effort of mitigation. This may explain in part why people are more likely to buy and to pay disproportionately more for insurance against small, more probable risks (e.g., appliance service contracts) than for larger, less probable risks (e.g., earthquakes), even when the latter have substantially higher expected (negative) values (Kunreuther et al. 2001; Slovic et al. 1977).

While uncertainty is clearly an important feature of protection/risk trade-offs, even risks accepted as relatively certain, such as getting the 'flu or needing money for retirement, may not motivate protective actions when the risk consequence is perceived to be far in the future (e.g., Chapman et al. 2001). The effects of "time preference" or "discount rate" are well known in economics, but they do not always have the expected effects in risk analyses (Kleindorfer and Kunreuther 1999). Moreover, time preferences can be different depending upon the domain for the risk/decision, as in financial investments versus preventative health behaviors (Chapman et al. 2001). In general, however, risk-reduction programs that require immediate efforts and sacrifices in the interest of reducing risks that are far in the future are unlikely to be supported, especially if the risk is perceived as having very low probability.

Decisions to take actions to protect against a risk also depend upon a set of supporting beliefs about the risk and the actions required to reduce it. The individual must believe that the risks are real, that the mitigation actions required are plausible and appropriate, and can be successfully accomplished, and that the promised reductions in risk are reasonably certain to be attained (e.g., Chilton et al. 2002; O'Connor et al. 1999). A caveat to this quite logical pattern of contingencies is that the supporting data are largely based on one form or another of verbal survey. The consistent logical relations that are typically observed among verbally expressed beliefs, benefit/risk perceptions, and stated behavioral intentions may not always be revealed in actual behavior. Chapman et al. (2001), for example, found internally consistent and logical correspondences between reported beliefs, time preferences, and risk perceptions and stated intentions to take actions to reduce health and financial risks. However, observed actions by the same respondents, such as getting vaccinations, taking preventative medications, or investing in retirement programs were essentially unrelated to the expressed behavioral intentions. Chilton et al. (2002) expressed concern that much of the logical consistency they found in expressed intentions to take personal actions to reduce train, auto, and house fire risks may have been artifacts of the hypothetical scenarios and focus-group discussion procedures used in their study. They worried that these factors may have induced participants to try to appear more deliberate and reasoned in their judgments than they might be in more realistic circumstances. Recent research and theory recognizes that risk perceptions and decision making depend considerably on affective/emotional processes (Finucane et al. 2000; Kahneman 2003; Slovic et al. 2004) and there is growing evidence that emotional and cognitive processes are psychologically and neurologically substantially independent (e.g., Damasio 1994; LeDoux 1996; Zajonc 1980). This combination provides some basis for expecting that verbally expressed reactions to verbally represented risks might not always match direct reactions to real-world risks, where affective responses are more salient.

Risk-reduction programs that are to be implemented by others (neighbors, community, government) are generally more attractive to individuals than are programs that require personal costs and effort. Flynn et al. (1999) found that the most preferred means for mitigating earthquake risk were government programs to strengthen public buildings and infrastructure. Support for programs requiring strengthening of private buildings was split, with more people against than for such a program. The tendency to pass off risk-reduction costs to others is consistent with the observed tendency for people to perceive others as more exposed than they to just about any risk. Morton and Duck (2001), for example, found that Australian college students each judged their classmates to be significantly more vulnerable to skin cancer risk than themselves. These interrelated risk phenomena might also help to account for the fact that education programs are among the most preferred risk-mitigation options, even if they are not always the most widely subscribed to when offered. If it is others who are perceived to be most at risk and who are most responsible for implementing mitigation actions, then it is also those others who most need education about the risk.

Accepting Wildfire Risk-management Programs

The limited research on acceptance of wildfire risk-management options appears largely consistent with the more general risk literature. Individual acceptance of mitigation/protection programs is related to the perceived risk, but a number of other factors are also involved (e.g., Rohrmann and Renn 2000). Willingness to support and comply with wildfire risk-management programs depends upon perceived trade-offs between the costs and expected protection benefits of risk reduction. In the context of wildfire risks to residences the principle costs of mitigation as perceived by at-risk individuals are related to aesthetic and convenience features associated with their homes and surroundings, and for prescribed fire treatments, the nuisance and health effects of smoke (Gardner et al. 1987; Winter and Fried 2000; Winter et al. 2002). The perceived benefits of risk reduction are less clear, and much less certain. The objective probability of a severe, damaging fire for any given at-risk property is difficult to compute, but is likely to be very low, even for people living in a high-hazard area. Added to the low probability, none of the contending mitigation programs can promise complete protection if a fire were to occur.

A mail survey by Manfredo et al. (1990) is typical in finding the general public divided in their expressed support of wildfire mitigation programs. In this case a regional sample (Montana-Wyoming) slightly favored prescribed burning (55% for versus 41% against) while support from a national sample was even more closely divided (48 for versus 45% against). A survey reported by Shindler (1997) also found that people generally expressed support for fuel-reduction treatments, substantially preferring mechanical thinning to prescribed fire strategies, but the respondents were not necessarily indicating support for applying these treatments to their own properties. In spite of expressed awareness of fire risks and belief in at least the partial effectiveness of treatments, residents in hazardous areas have shown reluctance to allow or to perform fuel-reduction activities on their immediate properties. In the study by Winter and Fried (2000), participants acknowledged their responsibility and expressed intentions to "fireproof" their residences, but many also reported that they had not actually gotten around to doing so. Some rationalized this lack of compliance by arguing that the home insurance for which they were already paying was adequate and appropriate protection (see Holmes et al., this volume, for more on this tendency). Others expressed general pessimism about any mitigation or protection efforts based on the belief that a significant wildfire would be uncontrollable and damage would be capricious in any event.

Consistent with the preference for having others pay the costs of risk-reduction treatments, the respondents in Gardner et al. (1987) were more supportive of having the government apply fuel-reduction treatments and fire breaks on public lands around their properties. Winter and Fried (2000) also found higher levels of expressed support for the creation of fire-breaks and planting of less fire-prone tree species on adjacent public lands. Related to the desire to place the responsibility and costs for risk management on others, fire-safety education programs have consistently been among the most popular options in surveys of wildfire risk-management preferences (Cortner et al. 1990; Gardner et al. 1987). Focus group participants in

Winter and Fried's (2000) study most preferred the use of strictly enforced restrictions against campfires and burning, especially by "down-staters," who were perceived to be careless and inexperienced. Participants also strongly supported fire-safety education campaigns, presumably directed at the same foolish people perceived to be the primary source of wildfire threat. Interestingly, the study authors noted that fire-protection agency statistics showed that it was the residents themselves who were the most frequent cause of fires in the area, usually from inappropriate burning of trash and litter on their properties. Similar projection-of-responsibility factors may be behind the findings of Kumagai et al. (2004) that people who suffered property damage in a wildfire were inclined to blame the fire-protection agency for starting the fire (a backfire) that did the damage, even though it was widely known that the fire in question was started by lightning.

The reluctance of residents in fire-prone areas to implement fuel-reduction activities on their own properties is especially unfortunate given that this is the mitigation activity most likely to actually protect their homes (Cohen 1999; Wilson and Ferguson, 1986; 1984). Daniel et al. (2003) found evidence that reducing fire hazard by fuel reduction may not always require the sacrifice of aesthetic and naturalness values. Ratings of perceived scenic beauty and perceived fire hazard were found to be negatively correlated for a visualized set of hypothetical ponderosa pine forest homesites. These data are consistent with the repeated finding that scenic beauty of forest landscapes is highest for more open stands, featuring well-spaced large trees and relatively low (below eye-level) understories with clean, smooth ground covers (e.g., Brown and Daniel 1986; Daniel and Boster 1976; Ribe 1989). Fire hazard ratings by the untrained respondents showed substantial positive correlations with hazard indices based on an appropriate fire-behavior model, and the forest configuration judged least hazardous was consistent with most fuel-reduction prescriptions for wildfire hazard mitigation. Thus, people apparently can be expected to recognize wildfire hazard when they see it. Moreover, the most preferred conditions (taking both aesthetic and safety factors into account) fit very well with most descriptions of ecologically healthy conditions for southwestern pine forests (e.g., Conard et al. 2001; Covington 2000). As Keely and Fotheringham (2001) point out, however, the happy coincidence of aesthetics, ecology, and fire safety in the pine forest may not apply in other forest ecosystems, such as the boreal forest. Thus in many cases implementation of fuel-reduction programs will require difficult trade-offs. Residents in fire-prone areas will be asked to bear costs, exert effort, and sacrifice aesthetic and other benefits in the immediate-term in favor of uncertain increases in protection against low probability, but potentially catastrophic wildfires in the future. The findings from risk-perception research in general and the smaller literature specifically on wildfire risk concur that this combination creates a very challenging situation for wildfire risk-mitigation programs.

Implications

Wildfire is not perceived to be among the most important risks faced by modern humans and it has largely been ignored in risk-perception research. Better understanding is needed of what the general public and those specifically at risk know and feel about wildfire risk, and about risk-management alternatives. There are few direct data in this regard, and virtually all are based on verbal surveys or focus group discussions. Recent research and theory acknowledges the importance of emotional factors in risk perception and risk response, and there is growing consensus in basic psychology that cognitive-verbal and affective-emotional processes may be significantly dissociated. There is reason then for concern about the current over-reliance on verbal survey methods in wildfire risk-perception research.

Individual perceptions of wildfire risk and compliance with risk-management programs depend upon complex interactions between biophysical and social-demographic features of the setting in which the risk is encountered, and are also influenced by factors in the responding individual's sociocultural background. Whatever the objective status of wildfire in the array of technological and natural hazards that modern humans face, a growing number of individuals who live in high fire-hazard wildland/urban interface areas are coming to recognize that there are risks. Whether they fully and accurately comprehend the nature of the risk, the probability, and the magnitude of effects of a severe wildfire, remains an unanswered question. Efforts to present fire as a natural and mostly beneficial agent in the forest have probably further complicated public perception of the risks. Wildfire risk has recently achieved higher priority in the national risk-management arena, but expert assessments of wildfire risk at the level of the individual property are not yet well developed, nor widely publicized. Technical risk assessments generally do not correspond well with public perceptions, nor do they accurately predict public response. However, clearly defining and communicating wildfire risk on a site- and even person-specific basis could help to garner more effective support for and compliance with mitigation efforts, and should be viewed as a professional responsibility for wildfire risk managers.

As with any risk, a person's willingness to support and participate in efforts to reduce wildfire risk depends upon how s/he perceives the trade-offs between the immediate costs of mitigation against future, uncertain safety benefits. Whatever the objective risk, individual residents in fire-threatened areas appear to perceive the benefit/risk trade-off equation as tipped more toward accepting future wildfire risk than toward bearing immediate costs and sacrifices to mitigate that risk. This tendency is likely to be psychologically buttressed by underestimating wildfire risk and perhaps by overestimating the costs of mitigation. The challenge for wildfire risk managers is to shift the balance in the trade-off equation more in favor of accepting and performing mitigation actions. In addition to communicating and making more concrete the risks from wildfire, managers must also strive to make the effects of mitigation more palatable. This might be accomplished in part by an aggressive public relations campaign to emphasize the potential for harm and destruction. But a more sustainable and more ethical approach might be to work harder to design effective, even if less than optimal, fuel reduction and other mitigation/protection options that have less objectionable effects on aesthetic and other forest values.

ACKNOWLEDGMENTS

The author is indebted to Dr. Bernd Rohrmann, University of Melbourne, Australia, and to Dr. Tom Brown, USDA Forest Service, Rocky Mountain Research Station, for their insightful and very helpful reviews of earlier drafts of this chapter.

REFERENCES

Alhakami, A. S., and P. Slovic. 1994. "A psychological study of the inverse relationship between perceived risk and perceived benefit." *Risk Analysis* 14(6): 1085-96.

Brown, T. C., and T. C. Daniel. 1986. "Predicting scenic beauty of timber stands." *Forest Science* 32(2): 471-87.

Chapman, G. B., N. T. Brewer, E. J. Coups, S. Brownlee, H. Leventhal, and E. A. Leventhal. 2001. "Value for the future and preventative health behavior." *Journal of Experimental Psychology: Applied* 7(3): 235-50.

Chilton, S., J. Covey, L. Hopkins, M. Jones-Lee, G. Loomes, N. Pidgeon, and A. Spencer. 2002. "Public perceptions of risk and preference-based values of safety." *Journal of Risk and Uncertainty* 25(3): 211-32.

Cohen, J. D. 1999. Reducing the wildland fire threat to homes: Where and how much? Available at http://www.firewise.org/siam/papers.htm.

Conard, S. G., T. Hartzel, M. W. Hilbruner, and G. T. Zimmerman. 2001. "Changing fuel management strategies—the challenge of meeting new information and analysis needs." *International Journal of Wildland Fire* 10: 267-75.

Cortner, H. J., and R. D. Gale. 1990. "People, fire, and wildland environments." *Population and Environment* 11(4): 245-58.

———, P. D. Gardner, and J. G. Taylor. 1990. "Fire hazards at the urban-wildland interface: What the public expects." *Environmental Management* 14(1): 57-62.

Covington, W. W. 2000. "Commentary." *Nature* 408: 135-36.

Damasio, A. R. 1994. *Descarte's Error: Emotion, Reason, and the Human Brain.* New York: Avon.

Daniel, T. C. and R. S. Boster. 1976. Measuring landscape Aesthetics: The Scenic Beauty Estimation Method. Fort Collins, Colorado, USDA Forest Service Research Paper RM-167: 66p.

Daniel, T. C., E. Weidemann, and D. Hines. 2003. "Assessing public tradeoffs between fire hazard and scenic beauty in the wildland-urban interface." In P. Jakes (compiler), Homeowners, communities, and wildfire: Science findings from the national fire plan. St Paul, Minnesota, USDA Forest Service. General Technical Report NC-231: 36-44.

Finucane, M. L., A. Alhakami, P. Slovic, and S. M. Johnson. 2000. "The affect heuristic in judgments of risks and benefits." *Journal of Behavioral Decision Making* 13: 1-17.

Fischhoff, B., P. Slovic, S. Lichtenstein, S. Read, and B. Combs. 1978. "How safe is safe enough? A psychometric study of attitudes toward technological risks and benefits." *Policy Sciences* 9: 127-52.

———, P. Slovic, and S. Lichtenstein. 1979. "Weighing the risks: Which are acceptable?" *Environment* 2(4): 17-20.

Flynn, J., P. Slovic, C. K. Mertz, and C. Carlisle. 1999. "Public support for earthquake risk mitigation in Portland, Oregon." *Risk Analysis* 19: 205-16.

Gardner, P. D., H. J. Cortner, and K. Widaman. 1987. "The risk perceptions and policy response toward wildland fire hazards by urban home-owners." *Landscape and Urban Planning* 14(2): 163-72.

Gregory, R. 2002. "Incorporating value tradeoffs into community-based environmental risk decisions." *Environmental Values* 11: 461-88.

Kahneman, D. 2003. "A perspective on judgment and choice: Mapping bounded rationality." *American Psychologist* 58(9): 697-720.

Keeley, J. E., and C. J. Fotheringham. 2001. "History and management of crown-fire ecosystems: A summary and response." *Conservation Biology* 15(6): 1561-67.

Kleindorfer, P. R., and H. Kunreuther. 1999. "The complementary roles of mitigation and insurance in managing catastrophic risks." *Risk Analysis* 19(4): 727-38.

Kumagai, Y., J. C. Bliss, S. E. Daniels, and M. S. Carroll. 2004. "Research on causal attribution of wildfire: An exploratory multiple-methods approach." *Society and Natural Resources* 17: 113-27.

Kunreuther, H., N. Novemsky, and D. Kahneman. 2001. "Making low probabilities useful." *Journal of Risk and Uncertainty* 23(2): 103-20.

———, and M. Pauly. 2004. "Neglecting disaster: Why don't people insure against large losses?" *Journal of Risk and Uncertainty* 28(1): 5 -21.

LeDoux, J. 1996. *The Emotional Brain.* New York: Simon & Schuster.

Lichtenstein, S., P. Slovic, B. Fischhoff, M. Layman, and B. Combs. 1978. "Judged frequency of lethal events." *Journal of Experimental Psychology: Human Learning and Memory* 4: 551-78.

Manfredo, M. J., M. Fishbein, G. H. Haas, and A. E. Watson. 1990. "Attitudes toward prescribed fire policies: The public is widely divided in its support." *Journal of Forestry* 88(7): 19-23.

McCaffrey, S. 2004. "Thinking of wildfire as a natural hazard." *Society and Natural Resources* 17: 509-16.

Morton, T. A., and J. M. Duck. 2001. "Communication and health beliefs: Mass and interpersonal influences on perceptions of risk to self and others." *Communication Research* 28 (5), 602-26.

National Academy of Public Administration (NAPA). 2001. Managing wildland fire: Enhancing capacity to implement the federal interagency fire policy. Washington, D.C.: National Academy of Public Administration.

O'Connor, R. E., R. J. Bord, and A. Fisher. 1999. "Risk perceptions, general environmental beliefs, and willingness to address climate change." *Risk Analysis* 19(3): 461-71.

Renn, O., and B. Rohrmann. 2000. *Cross-cultural Risk Perception Research.* Dordrecht, The Netherlands: Kluwer.

Ribe, R. G. 1989. "The aesthetics of forestry: What has empirical preference research taught us?" *Environmental Management* 13(1): 55-74.

Rohrmann, B. 1998. "The risk notion - epistemological and empirical considerati ons." In: M.G. Stewart and R.E. Melchers (eds.), *Integrative Risk Assessment.* Rotterdam, The Netherlands: Balkema.

———, and O. Renn. 2000. "Risk perception research - An introduction." In O. Renn and B. Rohrmann, *Cross-cultural Risk Perception Research.* Dordrecht, The Netherlands: Kluwer.

Shindler, B. 1997. "Public perspectives on prescribed fire and mechanical thinning." Technical Notes from the Blue Mountains Natural Resources Institute, BMNRI-TN-9, pp 4.

Slovic, P. 1987. "Perception of risk." *Science* 236: 280-85.

———. 2000. *The Perception of Risk.* London, England: Earthscan Publications, Ltd.

———, B. Fischhoff, S. Lichtenstein, B. Corrigan, and B. Combs. 1977. "Preferences for insuring against small losses: Insurance implications." *Journal of Risk and Insurance* 44(2): 237-57.

———, B. Fischhoff, and S. Lichtenstein. 1979. "Rating the risks." *Environment* 2(3): 36-39.

———, B. Fischhoff, and S. Lichtenstein. 1980. "Facts and fears: Understanding perceived risk." In R. C. S. W. A. Albers (ed.), *Societal Risk Assessment: How Safe is Safe Enough?* New York: Plenum Press.

———, M. L. Finucane, E. Peters, and D. G. MacGregor. 2004. "Risk as analysis and risk as feelings: Some thoughts about affect, reason, risk and rationality." *Risk Analysis* 24(2): 311-22.

USDA Forest Service and USDI Department of the Interior. 2000. Managing the impact of wildfires on communities and the environment: A report to the president in response to the wildfires of 2000, September 8. U.S. Department of the Interior, Washington, D.C.

Wilson, A. A. G., and I. S. Ferguson. 1984. "Fight or flee? A case study of the Mount Macedon bushfire." *Australian Forestry* 47(4): 230-36.

———, and I. S. Ferguson. 1986. "Predicting the probability of house survival during bushfires." *Journal of Environmental Management* 23: 259-70.

Winter, G., and J. S. Fried. 2000. "Homeowner perspectives on fire hazard, responsibility, and management strategies at the wildland-urban interface." *Society and Natural Resources* 13(1): 33-50.

———, C. Vogt, and J. S. Fried. 2002. "Fuel treatments at the wildland-urban interface: Common concerns in diverse regions." *Journal of Forestry* 100(1): 15-22.

Zajonc, R. B. 1980. "Feeling and thinking: Preferences need no inferences." *American Psychologist* 35: 151-75.

Cultural Variation in Public Perceptions Concerning Fire Use and Management

Carol Raish, Armando González-Cabán,
Wade Martin, Ingrid Martin and Holly Bender

Much fire research in the social sciences has used the questionable assumption that diverse cultural groups have homogeneous perceptions and practices concerning fire use and management. Review of the available literature indicates that both variation and similarity exist with regard to fire and fire-related issues among cultural groups as well as among subgroups within larger designations, such as Native Americans. There is more information on these topics for some groups than for others, with considerable research on historic fire use among certain Native American groups and among rural Southern farmers and forest users, for example. There is considerably less information on fire use practices among Asian Americans. The information on Native American fire management practices seems to show greater preference for burning as a management tool among groups with active past and present burning traditions. Groups with less-active burning programs are less supportive and more concerned about possible negative effects of prescribed burning.

Sociocultural characteristics, including attitudes toward the biophysical environment and histories of natural resource use, are reflected in group perceptions and practices concerning fire. Regional and local biophysical characteristics of the environment related to vegetation type, fire history, and fire regime also affect the fire-use patterns and practices of resident cultural groups. In addition, socioeconomic and demographic factors, especially population size/density and the level of local and regional industrialization, influence burning practices and attitudes toward fire. Land and vegetation, socioeconomic structures, and population levels have all affected the burning practices and perceptions of culturally diverse human groups across time and space.

Carol Raish, USDA Forest Service, Rocky Mountain Research Station (craish@fs.fed.us); Armando González-Cabán, USDA Forest Service, Pacific Southwest Research Station; Wade Martin, California State University, Long Beach; Ingrid Martin, California State University, Long Beach; Holly Bender, Integrated Resource Solutions, Boulder, Colorado

Current United States demographic information indicates that racial and ethnic minority populations are increasing more rapidly than the non-minority population. National Forest visitation and use are likely to reflect this increasing diversity, with forest management solely for traditional user groups no longer adequate (Li et al. 2003; U. S. Bureau of the Census 2000). Growing recommendations for greater stakeholder involvement in land-management agency decision making, including actual co-management in the case of some Native American groups, underscore the importance of understanding the variation and similarities within and between the various cultural groups (and subgroups) concerning natural resource management (McAvoy et al. 2001, 2003). The contentious nature of the issue and potential for differing opinions concerning fire and fuels-management decisions make intercultural understanding in this area especially important.

As examples, the relationship between the Hispanic community in northern New Mexico and the land is very different from that of the Hispanic community in southern California; thus, desired treatment options for fuels management may differ. Some Native American groups (the Mescalero Apache, for example) have very active commercial logging and land management programs, while others are more conservative in what they endorse in terms of fuels management and prescribed fire. Tribal forest management often differs from federal and private forest management in that management for economic return on timber and non-timber forest products is not the only priority on tribal lands. Equal emphasis may be given to managing the forests to provide food, medicines, and materials for artistic expression, household use, and transportation. In addition, tribal forest lands serve as sanctuaries for worship, contemplation, and inspiration (Indian Forest Management Assessment Team [IFMAT] 1993; Morishima 1997 discussed in Kimmerer 2000). As public-land managers evaluate various treatment options for managing wildfire risks they need to consider the preferences of a variety of stakeholder groups (also discussed in Shindler, this volume). It is essential that managers understand that significant cultural variation exists and that this variation is integrated into their consideration of the various management scenarios.

This discussion reviews and synthesizes information on cultural variation and similarity in perceptions and practices concerning both managed fire and wildfire. It focuses on Native Americans but also presents information on other cultural/ethnic and racial groups including rural Southern forest users, Hispanics/Latinos, and Blacks/African Americans. Those selected reflect the availability of literature on group practices and perceptions concerning fire. For example, although there are studies on Asian American resource use (Anderson et al. 2000; Richards and Creasy 1996), there is little actual information on views concerning fire use and management. Thus, Asian Americans are not discussed in detail in this review.

Topics of interest include attitudes on fuel reduction and vegetation-management techniques such as prescribed burning and mechanical thinning. Perceptions concerning wildfire risk and risk-mitigation measures are included. This review presents information on both contemporary and historic fire-use patterns, traditions, and perceptions. For enhanced understanding, contemporary attitudes toward fire use and management should be set within the framework of the historical background of fire use among the groups of concern. In many cases, historical uses include the recent past and form an important body of ongoing traditions that potentially shape the way people view the role of fire and its management. For example, Native Americans such as the Methow of Washington and the Dene Tha of Alberta, who have active traditions of annual burning to clear vegetation (Boyd 1999; Lewis 1982), tend to be supportive of burning as a management tool. Groups with less-active burning programs and/or more experience with wildfire damage, such as some of the Southwestern Puebloan groups, may express greater concerns about the possible escape of prescribed fire and the potential damage to both resources and sacred sites caused by wildfires. This type of information is important for the management of public lands with their increasingly wide diversity of user groups and growing recommendations for greater stakeholder involvement and/or co-management.

Traditional Knowledge and Worldview

Although it is hazardous to uncritically accept generalizations about any culture or society, some researchers have noted that the ways in which many indigenous and relatively non-technological, land-dependent societies (Berkes 1993) view and interact with the natural world differ fundamentally from those of western industrialized society. Callicott (1982) argues that Native American attitudes toward nature are not explicitly ecological or conservative in the modern scientific sense so much as they are moral and ethical—considering animals, plants, and minerals as living entities equal with humans in the social order (see also Jostad et al. 1996). "This perspective places humans within the realm of an ecosystem, rather than as managers of its commodities or observers of its grandeur" (McAvoy et al. 2003:88). Such views are considered to underlie and affect the ways in which these groups view and use natural resources (Callicott 1982), supporting local bodies of traditional ecological knowledge used in interactions with the physical environment.

Traditional ecological knowledge is discussed by Berkes (1993) as knowledge of relationships among humans, non-humans, and the physical environment that is based on observations, interactions, and systematic feedback from the natural world (Capp and Jorgensen 1997). It is constantly updated in both the temporal and spatial dimensions. Traditional ecological knowledge is usually expressed in spiritual and cultural terms with rules that provide an ethical system for human behavior to sustain ecosystems for the generations that will follow (Capp and Jorgensen 1997).

A pertinent example of this worldview is discussed by Anderson (1993:7): the Native American cultures of the Sierra Nevada hold the "belief that in the absence of human harvesting, tending, and use the native plants are offended and consequently disappear." The validity of this belief is documented in oral traditions, scientific literature, and harvesting practices that ensure a sustained yield (Anderson 1996; Anderson and Rowney 1999; Richards and Creasy 1996). The view that plants will decrease or disappear without human use and intervention is common among indigenous communities throughout the world (Anderson 1993, 1996; Anderson and Rowney 1999) and sets the stage for active management,[1] often incorporating the intentional use of fire.

It is important to note that "traditional ecological knowledge is not unique to Native American culture. It is born of long intimacy and attentiveness to a homeland and can arise wherever people are materially and spiritually integrated with their landscape" (Kimmerer 2000: 9). Land-dependent peoples such as the Hispanic farmers and ranchers of the Southwest and the rural farmers and herders of the South also developed and used traditional ecological knowledge in their interactions with the biophysical world (García 1996; Peña and Gallegos 1993; Pyne 1982: 143-60; Rothman 1989).

The following section reviews research on historic Native American burning practices, which have considerable relevance for the current discussion on perceptions concerning fire use and management. The body of traditional ecological knowledge evident in past burning practices has the potential to affect present-day views and attitudes toward fire. The active, hands-on environmental management discussed by Anderson (1993, 1996) and Anderson and Rowney (1999) is apparent in tribal lore and memory.

Boyd (1999: 1) describes an incident related to him concerning a visit to the Methow Valley in north-central Washington by a group of Methow elders, some of whom had not been there for fifty years. When the group was halfway through the valley, one woman began to cry and stated "When my people lived here, we took good care of all this land. We burned it over every fall to make it like a park. Now it is a jungle." Other Methow tribal elders confirmed the regular burning program. The Dene Tha from northern Alberta also comment on the negative changes brought about by brush and tree encroachment and remember their tradition of annual spring burning (Lewis 1982). Despite the fact that many peoples no longer engage in traditional burning practices, their effects are remembered and valued by certain segments of the society (Anderson 1993, 1996; Bonnicksen et al. 1999; Boyd 1999; Johnson 1994; Turner 1999).

Historic Native American Fire Use and Management

There is a large and growing body of information on historic Native American burning practices and attitudes toward fire, many of which are reviewed and discussed by Williams (2002a, b).   For purposes of this discussion, the historic period encompasses pre-European contact times through encroachment by colonists and ultimate removal to reservations.

The literature indicates that the role of anthropogenic fire varied both regionally and locally. Variations stemmed from differences in biophysical environment, climate, and sociodemographic and economic conditions, such as population level and subsistence practices, which affected the utility of fire as a management tool (Pyne et al. 1996). As examples, coastal peoples of the Pacific Northwest burned rarely because their primary subsistence was derived from marine resources, while inland groups in the same area burned regularly to maintain grassy prairies to attract game (Boyd 1999; Norton et al. 1999; Williams 2000a). Information for the Northeast indicates that most indigenous fires were local and were related to subsistence practices such as slash-and-burn agriculture and maintenance of berry patches. There is not strong evidence for intentional burning on a large scale in the Northeast. The region lacks a pronounced dry season, precipitation is generally uniform from month to month, and the wind patterns to carry large fires do not occur regularly (Pyne et al. 1996; Russell 1983; Williams 2000a). Grassland areas of the Southwest, such as those of southeastern Arizona, were maintained by regular indigenous burning (Bahre 1995), while there is debate in the literature concerning the role of natural (lightning) versus human causation for fires in the ponderosa pine uplands of the Southwest (Allen 1984, 2002; Baisan and Swetnam 1990, 1997; Fish 1996; Savage and Swetnam 1990; Swetnam and Baisan 1996; Touchan et al. 1995).

In general, however, researchers agree that Native American burning had considerable environmental effect, both at the landscape and local levels (Pyne et al. 1996). There are both primary and secondary accounts that describe purposeful burning by Native American groups in various parts of North America to promote diversity of habitats and resources, environmental stability, predictability, and maintenance of ecotones (Lewis

1985; Williams 2002a, b). Many of the grassland areas found by European settlers were created or maintained by Native American burning. Many forested areas were kept free from underbrush by indigenous fire regimes (Bahre 1995; Pyne 1982, 1983). However, overgeneralizations that all indigenous peoples used fire as a management tool in all regions and at similar levels of intensity disregard important distinctions and demonstrate one of the problems in the literature that must be taken into consideration. Other problems include misinterpretation of historical documents, reliance on secondary sources, and reliance on studies that are vague or based on hearsay (Williams 2002a).

Despite these difficulties, research on past Native American fire use provides an alternate body of traditional ecological knowledge on one important land management tool for contemporary managers seeking ecosystem restoration (Kimmerer 2000). Of special importance is the fact that indigenous fires were not replications of natural fires but involved important differences in terms of seasonality, intensity, control, and purposeful site selection (Bonnicksen et al. 1999; Williams 2000a). "For the most part, tribes set fires that did not destroy entire forests or ecosystems, were relatively easy to control, and stimulated new plant growth" (Williams 2000a: 10). Equally important for this discussion is the potential effect that the body of traditional ecological knowledge represented by past burning practices may have on the fire perceptions of contemporary Native American peoples.

Contemporary Native American Fire Use, Management Practices, and Perceptions

Contemporary Native American views on resource management, encompassing fire use, are included in ethnographic examinations of various indigenous groups, as well as in attitudinal studies on the resource-management practices of differing cultural/ethnic and racial groups (Boyd 1999; Floyd 2004; Johnson 1994; Winter and Cvetkovich 2003). Most studies collect data by means of anthropological methods, such as participant observation, or by means of personal interviews, telephone surveys, or mailed surveys. Researchers gather data from tribal resource professionals, reservation residents, and Native Americans living off reservations. There is, however, less information regarding contemporary Native American views, attitudes, and practices on fire than there is for historic burning practices. The information is also more scattered and often found included with other information-collection efforts as a category on culture/ethnicity and race. Information is retrievable from these types of studies but may suffer from small sample sizes. In addition, these data may not be the first priority of the researchers undertaking the project, leading to less emphasis in analysis and reporting.

Forest-resource management and fire-management programs are increasing at the tribal level as a result of legislation providing for the transfer of authority and funding from the Bureau of Indian Affairs (BIA) to tribal governments (the 1975 Indian Self-Determination and Education Act). However, many of these programs are still in the early stages of development (Austin and Wolf 2001). Under tribal fire-management programs and plans, groups can undertake mechanical thinning, prescribed burning, and wildfire-protection programs (Austin and Wolf 2001). Many tribal foresters and ecologists view prescribed burning very positively and are using it as a means of reducing fuel accumulations, changing species composition, and managing vegetation structure and density, much as their ancestors did before them (Williams 2000b). It should be noted, however, that some programs have an active commercial-logging component and/or Anglo foresters and directors. The influence of these factors on program activities and goals has not been examined in any systematic manner.

During the 1990s, prescribed burning occurred annually on 55,000 acres (22,000 ha) of tribally managed forest, which amounts to about 20% of those lands estimated to benefit from burning (Haglund 1998; Williams 2000b). The literature reports the views of tribal resource managers concerning the positive role of forest treatments such as thinning and burning, as well as the positive view of many non-Native Americans concerning the condition of tribally managed forest lands in the Southwest (Austin and Wolf 2001; Carroll et al. 2005; Integrated Resource Solutions 2004; Raish and González-Cabán 2003). Reservation residents in Montana have also reported favorable attitudes to forest management, including mechanical thinning and prescribed burning, although there is not an extensive body of published information or wide geographic coverage on the topic (González-Cabán et al. 2003). Available forest resources and tribal capacity to develop funding and manage forestry programs affect the presence and success of these endeavors. Many groups do not have the infrastructure to support tribal programs and must rely on the BIA for both fire management and protection (Austin and Wolf 2001).

At a smaller scale, information shows continuing interest in and use of traditional knowledge of burning practices to improve subsistence and technological resources. These include berry patches, croplands and gardens, grasslands, and specific plants used in basketry and other craft production. Burning primarily occurs on reservation lands, although groups express interest in seeing cooperatively developed burning programs that could include publicly managed forests and grasslands (Austin and Wolf 2001; Johnson 1994; Thakali and Lesko 1998).

There is less specific information concerning individual perceptions of wildfire risk and risk-mitigation measures taken by reservation residents than there is on the managed-fire programs. Work in progress with the Colville Tribe of Washington on their preparedness for wildfire is an example of needed research in this direction, as is ongoing work in the Southwest exploring wildfire risk perceptions and mitigation measures among Native American groups.

A regional survey examining Southwesterners' opinions on wildland and wilderness fire management included Native Americans, as well as other cultural/ethnic and racial groups, from California, Colorado, Arizona, and New Mexico (Winter and Cvetkovich 2003). In general, Native Americans were similar in their responses to the larger population. However, the study showed that Native Americans were among the groups more likely to feel greater concern about wildland and wilderness fires in their state and were among the groups, including Whites, with highest average perceived knowledge (self-rated) about wildland and wilderness fires in their state (Winter and Cvetkovich 2003). Continuing analyses on these data will examine differences among cultural/ethnic and racial groups in greater detail.

At a larger geographic level, the National Survey on Recreation and the Environment (NSRE), conducted by the USDA Forest Service, gathers information on cultural/ethnic and racial groups, in addition to gathering information on outdoor recreation, the natural environment, and the management of public lands. The survey effort for the eighth national survey began in 1999 and continued through 2004. The survey was administered in different versions, which included varying modules of interest in addition to the basic information on recreation. Two versions of the survey included a module of questions concerning knowledge, attitudes, and preferences toward fire and fire management in wildland and wildland-urban interface areas. There were a total of 6,979 completed responses to the versions with the fire module. Analysis and reporting are in the draft phase for the fire information. Data were recorded on varying cultural/ethnic and racial groups including the following: Spanish, Hispanic or Latino; White; Black or African American; American Indian or Alaska Native; Asian; Native Hawaiian or Other Pacific Islander. For analytic purposes, the categories of Blacks, Hispanics, and Whites were used because the sample sizes of the other groups were considered too small (under 2%) (Bowker et al. 2005). The data are available on all groups for future use, however.

Recommendations for Future Research on Native American Fire Use, Management Practices, and Perceptions

There is evidence from several studies that the body of traditional ecological knowledge apparent in past resource-management practices may affect contemporary Native American attitudes, producing positive views toward active forest management using both mechanical thinning and prescribed burning. The available information shows generally favorable attitudes among tribal resource managers and among a limited sample of reservation residents in Montana toward these forest-management practices (Austin and Wolf 2001; González-Cabán et al. 2003; Integrated Resource Solutions 2004; Raish & González-Cabán 2003). Ethnographic work has demonstrated approval for and continued use of small-scale burning to improve plant and crop production on reservations ranging from British Columbia to California to Arizona (Austin & Wolf 2001; Johnson 1994; Thakali and Lesko 1998).

However, positive views toward active vegetation management and fire use, and their basis in historical practice, should be explored in greater depth among tribal groups with and without forestry programs and among Native Americans who are not trained resource-management professionals (in the western scientific tradition of natural resource management). The role of natural resource training, the possible influence of non-Native American program managers, and the commercial direction of some tribal forestry programs in producing positive attitudes toward active forest management require further study.

In general, developing a body of information on Native American opinions concerning both managed fire and wildfire requires more group-specific studies over a larger geographic area, studies specifically designed to gather data from Native Americans, and expanded sample sizes in research efforts that examine views across various cultural/ethnic and racial groups. Expanding the sample sizes and coverage in such studies will provide the opportunity for statistically significant comparisons of the diverse cultural subgroups within the larger culture. Understanding the similarities and differences will provide important input for more effective management prescriptions. Native American views on wildfire risk and risk-mitigation measures remain an area with considerable research potential.

Historic Euro-and African American Fire Use and Management

Early European colonists often adopted the burning practices of the local indigenous populations, along with many of their subsistence strategies, which were already adapted to local environmental conditions and resources. They also brought fire-use knowledge from their homelands and added that knowledge to observed local practices (Brose et al. 2001; Pyne et al. 1996). An example comes from the Southeast, where colonists adopted long-standing Native American fire-use strategies for hunting, foraging, clearing farm fields, and protecting communities. They used fire to maintain a hunting, herding, and farming economy and to control the growth of understory vegetation (Fowler 2005; Pyne et al. 1996).

Throughout the United States fire practices shifted with changing sociodemographic and economic conditions. These included increases in population density, changes from slash-and-burn cultivation to sedentary cultivation of row crops, and changes from hunting and small-scale herding to large-scale production of domesticated livestock (Brose et al. 2001; Fowler 2005; Pyne et al. 1996). Industrialization after the Civil War brought broad-scale industrial logging and railroad transport of commercial products. These developments led not only to suppression of much burning by small farmers but also to fuel build-ups that resulted in increased wildfire frequency and intensity. Ultimately, wildland fire suppression emerged with the USDA Forest Service assuming responsibility for a large portion of the fire-control activities (Brose et al. 2001; Fowler 2005; Pyne et al. 1996).

One of the groups most strongly affected by the sociodemographic, economic, and political changes that led to widespread industrial logging and fire suppression were the small farmers and herders of the rural South, both African American and Euro-American. These groups continued their hunting, herding, farming, and burning economy well into the twentieth century (Fowler 2005; Pyne 1982). They maintained a body of traditional ecological knowledge concerning management of the southern rough (understory of tall grass, saplings, and vines) that included regular burning of the woods for clearing land and maintaining range and forest habitat. This burning pattern persisted and came into often violent conflict with industrial forestry and fire-suppression policies (Pyne 1982). Fire suppression was strongly resisted in the rural South and the tradition of illicit woodsburning persisted. There is a considerable literature that treats southern woodsburning and its intentional use as a means of protest against industrial forests, enclosure of once-open hunting and rangelands, and displacement of the traditional herding and hunting economy (Bertrand and Baird 1975; Cole and Kaufman 1966; Dunkelberger and Altobellis 1975; Pyne 1982; Shea 1940). Today, 88% of the fires on federal land in the southern Appalachian Mountains are human caused due either to carelessness or arson (Wear and Greis 2002).

Contemporary Fire Use, Management Practices, and Perceptions of Diverse Cultural/Ethnic and Racial Groups

The importance of prescribed burning in maintaining southern forest habitat, already well known by the woodsburners, was accepted by the Forest Service earlier than in other regions, and therefore, prescribed burning was allowed in southern national forests by 1943 (Chapman 1912; Eldredge 1911; Pyne 1982; Schiff 1962; Stoddard 1969). Prescribed burning remains an important component of southern forest management, but it encounters increasing difficulties with air-quality management (smoke), liability risks, and residential development in close proximity to forested lands. These problems occur across national forest, state, and private lands (Haines et al. 2001). In addition to timber owners, contemporary rural forest and grassland users continue to use burning to perpetuate desired resources.

Although there is little research on the attitudes of culturally diverse user groups toward fire, ongoing work on river cane (*Arundinaria gigantea*) with the Cherokee and on sweetgrass (*Muhlenbergia filipes*) present examples of Native American and African American concern for the maintenance of traditionally used resources (Hart et al. 2004). African-American basketmakers of the Gullah people, located in the lowcountry of South Carolina, parts of Florida, and coastal Georgia, use sweetgrass to produce coiled baskets that are a major source of income. Landowners traditionally burned the coastal plains to prevent encroachment of thick shrubs and trees. This practice is now regulated and the coarser shrubs are crowding out the sweetgrass, resulting in fears of a decline in the industry. Residential development along the coast is also blocking access to sweetgrass stands and further restricting burning (Hart et al. 2004).

Examination of both locally specific case studies, such as the one on sweetgrass, and larger-scale attitudinal studies yields a growing body of information on differences in worldview, natural resource use, and conservation strategies among varying cultural/ethnic and racial groups and within groups (Anderson et al. 2000; Caro and Ewert 1995; Floyd 2004; Mountjoy 1996; Richards and Creasy 1996; Schelhas 2002). There is, however, little specific information on fire.

Those studies that are gathering, or have gathered, information on fire and fire-related topics include the previously mentioned National Survey on Recreation and the Environment (NSRE), which includes a module of questions on fire and fire management in wildland and wildland/urban interface areas. Survey information showed that fire experience, attitudes, and opinions are different across races (Bowker et al. 2005), which reiterates a cautionary note concerning the importance of avoiding lumped categories prior to determining the potential range of variability within and between groups (also discussed in Floyd 2004). Data from survey responses indicate that Blacks and Hispanics seem to have less forest-fire knowledge compared to Whites, which may be related to exposure to the news or to their recreation and travel plans. Hispanics seem more concerned about forest fire damaging their homes, while Blacks are less likely to have property insurance that would cover damages incurred from a wildfire. Other information from the survey indicated that both Blacks and Hispanics tend to be more concerned about the side effects of prescribed fire and forest-fire management programs (than Whites), with less confidence in public-land managers and the government concerning forest-fire issues (Bowker et al. 2005).

The regional survey on Southwesterners' opinions on wildland and wilderness fire included information broken out by cultural/ethnic and racial categories, as well as by language (Spanish) and years of residence in the United States (Winter and Cvetkovich 2003). This survey showed that Hispanics/Latinos and Native Americans were among the groups most likely to feel greater concern about wildland and wilderness fire in their state. These groups also were among those that showed the highest shared values and views with the Forest Service and trusted the Forest Service concerning fire management (Winter and Cvetkovich 2003). This finding is different from those of the NSRE, which showed Hispanics and Blacks having less confidence in public-land managers and the government concerning forest fire issues. Regional differences in views may be apparent in these results. In addition, the studies may suffer from the problem of aggregating all Hispanics into one cultural group during analysis.

The southwestern survey responses also showed that language (Spanish) and years of residence in the United States were important influences in viewing differences in true/false statements concerning prescribed fire, wildfire, and forest health (Winter and Cvetkovich 2003). Other non-fire research among Hispanic and other ethnic groups has shown that length of residence in the United States, arrival age, age in general, and acculturation, among other variables such as income and education level, are related to views on environmental concerns, resource use, and recreation participation and preferences (Caro and Ewert 1995; Carr and Williams 1993; Chavez 1992; Floyd 2004; Gómez 2003; Guillen et al. 2000; Johnson et al. 1997; Li et al. 2003; Tierney et al. 1998; Winter and Chavez 1999, to name a few).

On the other hand, a survey from Florida concerning alternative fuels-reduction techniques reported that support for wildfire mitigation policies is not significantly influenced by ethnicity or language, with similar responses and response rates between English and Spanish speakers (Loomis et al. 2001, 2002). As discussed for recreation and natural-resource management in general, and shown by the more limited body of information specific to fire, there is considerable variation both between and within groups. Ethnic labels can mask considerable variation of interest within ethnic groups themselves that requires further, in-depth examination (Carr and Chavez 1993; Carr and Williams 1993; Chavez 1992, 1993, 2000; Floyd 2004; Gómez 2003; Guillen et al. 2000; Johnson et al. 1997; Li et al. 2003; Schelhas 2002; Tierney et al. 1998; Winter and Chavez 1999, as examples).

Future Research and Implications for Public-land Management

The lessons for both land managers and researchers, then, concern the importance of recognizing and understanding variation both within and between groups. Public-land managers interacting with Native American groups on fire and vegetation-management issues must understand that variation exists both between and within tribal groups. Experiences working with tribes in the Great Lakes may not transfer to working with tribes in the Southwest. Tribal religious leaders and resource professionals from the same group may not view prescribed burning in the same way at the same time. Working with Native American groups can thus be specific to group, subgroup, context, and situation. Thus, management training programs that stress locally specific information and incorporate the knowledge and participation of local group members will be more successful than those that focus on broad generalizations.

The importance of recognizing inter- and intra-group variation and locally specific information also applies to the full range of cultural/ethnic and racial groups involved in land- and resource-management decisions. In particular, the role of language/acculturation, residence location, years of residence in the United States, age, and gender in influencing views on fire and fuels management issues needs further exploration. Differences within groups residing in urban versus rural settings can provide insight into the effect of residence location on views, attitudes, and experiences with fire.

As mentioned previously, studies designed to gather information specifically from diverse groups and expanded sample sizes in research efforts that examine views across various cultural/ethnic and racial groups are also needed. Such studies will be useful to understanding both common and different preferences. Understanding how each subgroup is unique will provide potentially valuable information for land managers. Although research on diversity in resource use, and especially on views and attitudes concerning fire, has not progressed as rapidly as diversity research in other areas, it is likely to grow in importance as immigration increases from Latin America and Asia (Floyd 2004). Populations from these areas tend to use forest resources and can come into conflict with traditional users, such as Native American groups, who may have legally guaranteed subsistence rights to resources in question (Floyd 2004; Richards and Creasy 1996). Understanding the role of fire in these resource equations will continue to be a research and management challenge as sociocultural, economic, and demographic changes affect both public and private lands into the twenty-first century.

Acknowledgements

We wish to thank Toddi A. Steelman, Department of Forestry, North Carolina State University, and Patricia L.Winter, Research Social Scientist, USDA Forest Service, Pacific Southwest Research Station, for their well-thought-out and insightful comments. Their efforts have improved this discussion considerably.

Notes

1. The terms "land" and "resource management" are used throughout this discussion to refer to activities and practices of the various cultural groups under discussion. It should be noted, however, that many Native American groups consider that "there is a clear, reciprocal and interdependent relationship with all of creation and that humans are inseparable from nature" (McAvoy et al. 2003: 89). Thus, they do not view themselves as managing natural resources or as natural-resource managers.

References

Allen, C. D. 1984. Montane grassland in the landscape of the Jemez Mountains, New Mexico. MS Thesis. Madison: University of Wisconsin.
———. 2002. "Lots of lightning and plenty of people: an ecological history of fire in the upland Southwest." In: T. R. Vale (ed.), *Western Wilderness: Fire, Native Peoples, and the Natural Landscape*, 143-93. Covelo, California: Island Press.
Anderson, J. A., D. J. Blahna, and D. J. Chavez. 2000. "Fern gathering on the San Bernardino National Forest: Cultural versus commercial values among Korean and Japanese participants." *Society and Natural Resources* 13: 747-62.

Anderson, M. K. 1993. Indian fire-based management in the sequoia-mixed conifer forests of the central and southern Sierra Nevada. Yosemite Research Center, Yosemite National Park. Cooperative Agreement Order Number 8027-2-002. Manuscript on file, Yosemite Research Center.

———. 1996. "Tending the wilderness." *Restoration and Management Notes* 14(2): 154-66.

———, and D. L. Rowney. 1999. "The edible plant *Dichelostemma capitatum*: Its vegetative reproduction in response to different indigenous harvesting regimes in California." *Restoration Ecology* 7(3): 231-40.

Austin, D., and B. Wolf. 2001. Fire in Indian Country: Two case studies in the southwestern United States. CLIMAS Report Series CL1-01. Tucson: University of Arizona, Institute for the Study of Planet Earth.

Bahre, C. J. 1995. "Human impacts on the grasslands of southeastern Arizona." In: M. P. McClaran, and T. R.Van Devender (eds.), *The Desert Grassland*, 230-64. Tucson: University of Arizona Press.

Baisan, C. H., and T. W. Swetnam. 1990. "Fire history on a desert mountain range: Rincon Mountain Wilderness, Arizona, U. S.A." *Canadian Journal Forest Research* 20: 1559-69.

———, and T. W. Swetnam. 1997. Interactions of fire regimes and land use in the Central Rio Grande Valley. Research Paper RM-RP-330. Fort Collins, Colorado: USDA Forest Service, Rocky Mountain Forest and Range Experiment Station.

Berkes, F. 1993. "Traditional ecological knowledge in perspective." In: J. T. Inglis (ed.), *Traditional Ecological Knowledge Concepts and Cases*. Ottawa, Canada: Canadian Museum of Nature and International Development Research Centre.

Bertrand, A. L., and A. W. Baird. 1975. Incendiarism in southern forests: A decade of sociological research. Bulletin 838. Starkville: Mississippi State University, Social Science Research Center.

Bonnicksen, T. M., M. K. Anderson, H. T. Lewis, C. E. Kay, and R. Knudson. 1999. "Native American influences on the development of forest ecosystems." In: R. Szaro, N. C. Johnson, W. T. Sexton, and A. J. Malk (eds.), *Ecological Stewardship: A Common Reference for Ecosystem Management* Vol. II, 439-70. Oxford, England: Elsevier Science.

Bowker, J. M., S.-H. Lim, H. K. Cordell, G. T. Green, S. Rideout-Hanzak, C. Y. Johnson, and C. J. Betz. 2005. A social assessment of public knowledge, attitudes, and values related to wildland fire, fire risk, and fire recovery (draft). Project Report Submitted to: Joint Fire Science Program (JFSP Grant #01-1-3-30). Athens, Georgia: USDA Forest Service, Southern Research Station. http://www.srs.fs.usda.gov/recreation/socfire.html.

Boyd, R. 1999. "Introduction." In: R. Boyd (ed.), *Indians, Fire, and the Land in the Pacific Northwest*,1-30. Corvallis: Oregon State University Press. 313 p.

Brose, P., T. Schuler, D. Van Lear, and J. Berst. 2001. "Bringing fire back: The changing regimes of the Appalachian mixed-oak forests." *Journal of Forestry* 99(11): 30-35.

Callicott, J. B. 1982. "Traditional American Indian and Western European attitudes toward nature: An overview." *Environmental Ethics* 4(4): 293-318.

Capp, J. C., and C. Jorgensen. 1997. "Traditional knowledge: Don't leave the future without it." In: K.G. Wadsworth (ed.), Transactions of the 62nd North American Wildlands and Natural Resources Conference, 199-209. Washington, D.C.: Wildlife Management Institute.

Caro, V., and A. Ewert. 1995. "The influence of acculturation on environmental concerns: An exploratory study." *Journal of Environmental Education* 26: 13-21.

Carr, D. S., and D. J. Chavez. 1993. "A qualitative approach to understanding recreation experiences: Central American recreation on the national forests of southern California." In: A. W. Ewert, D. J. Chavez, and A. W. Magill (eds.), *Culture, Conflict, and Communication in the Wildland-urban Interface*, 181-94. Boulder, Colorado: Westview Press.

———, and D. R. Williams. 1993. "Understanding the role of ethnicity in outdoor recreation experiences." *Journal of Leisure Research* 25(1): 22-38.

Carroll, M. S., D. N. Seesholtz, and L. L. Higgins. 2005. "Fire as a galvanizing and fragmenting influence on communities: the case of the Rodeo-Chediski Fire." *Society and Natural Resources* 18(4): 301-20.

Chapman, H. H. 1912. "Forest fires and forestry in the United States." *American Forests* 18: 516.

Chavez, D. J. 1992. "Hispanic recreationists in the wildland-urban interface." *Trends* 29(4): 23-25.

———. 1993. Visitor perceptions of crowding and discrimination at two national forests in southern California. Research Paper PSW-RP-216. Riverside, California: USDA Forest Service, Pacific Southwest Research Station.

———. 2000. "Invite, include, and involve! Racial groups, ethnic groups, and leisure." In: M. T. Allison, and I. E. Schneider (eds.), *Diversity and the Recreation Profession: Organizational Perspectives*, 179-94. State College, Pennsylvania: Venture Publishing.

Cole, L. W., and H. F. Kaufman. 1966. Socio-economic factors and forest fires in Mississippi counties. Preliminary Report no. 14. Starkville: Mississippi State University, Social Science Research Center.

Dunkelberger, J. E., and A. T. Altobellis. 1975. Profiling the woods-burner: an analysis of fire trespass violations in the South's national forests. Auburn University Agricultural Experiment Station Bulletin 469. Montgomery, Alabama: Auburn University Agricultural Experiment Station.

Eldredge, I. 1911. "Fire problems on the Florida National Forest." *Society of American Foresters Proceedings* 6: 166-68.

Fish, S. K. 1996. "Modeling human impacts to the Borderlands environment from a fire ecology perspective." In: P. F. Ffolliott et al. (tech. coords.), Effects of fire on Madrean Province ecosystems: A symposium proceedings, 125-134. General Technical Report RM-GTR-289. Fort Collins, Colorado: USDA Forest Service, Rocky Mountain Forest and Range Experiment Station.

Floyd, M. F. 2004. "Cultural diversity and natural resource management." In: M. J. Manfredo, J. J. Vaske, B. L. Bruyere, D. R. Field, and P. J. Brown (eds.), *Society and Natural Resources: A Summary of Knowledge*, 71-82. Jefferson, Missouri: Modern Litho.

Fowler, C. 2005. "A history of people and fire in the South." Encyclopedia of southern fire science. Athens, Georgia: USDA Forest Service, Southern Region Extension Forestry. http://www.forestryencyclopedia.net/Encyclopedia/Fire%20Science/4_fire_people/Encyclopedia_Page.2003-12-22.1208.

García, M. T. 1996. "Hispanic perspectives and values." In: B. L. Driver, D. Dustin, T. Baltic, G. Elsner, and G. Peterson (eds.), *Nature and the Human Spirit: Toward an Expanded Land Management Ethic*, 145-51. State College, Pennsylvania: Venture Publishing.

Gómez, E. 2003. Ethnicity and recreation: an abridged annotated bibliography. FS Agreement No. 02-CA-11272137-047. Manuscript on file at: USDA Forest Service, Pacific Southwest Research Station, Riverside, California.

González-Cabán, A., J. B. Loomis, and H. Hesseln. 2003. "Do cultural differences affect support for alternative wildland fire mitigation strategies: Native Americans in Montana, USA." In: Proceedings, 3rd International Wildland Fire Conference and Exhibition; 3-6 October, Sydney, Australia.

Guillen, B. F., A. Marcus-Newhall, P. L.Winter, and A. Meyer. 2000. Recreational preferences, environmental concern, intergroup conflict, and ethnic identity measures: An annotated bibliography. Manuscript on file at: USDA Forest Service, Pacific Southwest Research Station, Riverside, California.

Haglund, S. 1998. "Indian country on the forefront in new approaches to wildland fire." *Evergreen* 9(19): 44.

Haines, T. K., R. L. Busby, and D. A. Cleaves. 2001. "Prescribed burning in the South: Trends, purpose, and barriers." *Southern Journal of Applied Forestry* 25(4): 149-53.

Hart, Z. H., A. C. Halfacre, and M. K. Burke. 2004. "Community participation in preservation of lowcountry South Carolina sweetgrass (Muhlenbergia filipes) basketry." Economic Botany 58(2): 161-83.

Indian Forest Management Assessment Team (IFMAT). 1993. An assessment of Indian forests and forest management in the United States. Portland, Oregon: Intertribal Timber Council.

Integrated Resource Solutions. 2004. Interim report on phase one of public input concerning fire and fuels management in the Southwestern Region: Results from the Lincoln National Forest. Research Joint Venture Agreement Number 02-JV-11221601-218. Manuscript on file at: USDA Forest Service, Rocky Mountain Research Station, Albuquerque Laboratory, Albuquerque, New Mexico.

Johnson, C. Y., P. M. Horan, and W. Pepper. 1997. "Race, rural residence, and wildland visitation: Examining the influence of sociocultural meaning." *Rural Sociology* 62(1): 89-110.

Johnson, L. M. 1994. "Aboriginal burning for vegetation management in northwest British Columbia." *Human Ecology* 22(2): 171-88.

Jostad, P. M., L. H. McAvoy, and D. McDonald. 1996. "Native American land ethics: Implications for natural resource management." *Society and Natural Resources* 9: 565-81.

Kimmerer, R. W. 2000. "Native knowledge for native ecosystems." *Journal of Forestry* 98(8): 4-9.

Lewis, H. T. 1982. "Fire technology and resource management in aboriginal North America and Australia." In: E. Hunn, and N. Williams (eds.), *The Regulation of Environmental Resources in Food Collecting Societies*, 45-67. American Association for the Advancement of Science Selected Symposium Series No. 67. Boulder, Colorado: Westview Press.

———. 1985. "Why Indians burned: Specific versus general reasons." In: James E. Lotan, et al (tech. coords.) Proceedings—symposium and workshop on wilderness fire; 1983 November 15-18; Missoula, MT, 75-80. General Technical Report INT-GTR-182. Ogden, Utah: USDA Forest Service, Intermountain Forest and Range Experiment Station.

Li, C., H. R. Zinn, A. R. Graefe, and J. D. Absher. 2003. A multi-ethnic comparison of service quality and satisfaction in national forest recreation. RWU 4902 Technical Report. Riverside, California: USDA Forest Service, Pacific Southwest Research Station.

Loomis, J. B., L. S. Bair, and A. González-Cabán. 2001. "Prescribed fire and public support: Knowledge gained, attitudes changed in Florida." *Journal of Forestry* 99(11):18-22.

———, L. S. Bair, and A. González-Cabán. 2002. "Language related differences in a contingent valuation study: English versus Spanish." *American Journal of Agricultural Economics* 84(4): 1091-1102.

McAvoy, L., D. McDonald, and M. Carlson. 2001. American Indians: Sense of place and contested terrain. Final Report: PSW-98-0010CA. Riverside, California: USDA Forest Service, Pacific Southwest Research Station.

————., D. McDonald, and M. Carlson. 2003. "American Indian/First Nation place attachment to park lands: The case of the Nuu-chah-nulth of British Columbia." *Journal of Park and Recreation Administration* 21(2): 84-104.

Morishima, G. S. 1997. "Indian forestry: From paternalism to self-determination." *Journal of Forestry* 95(11): 4-9.

Mountjoy, D. C. 1996. "Ethnic diversity and the patterned adoption of soil conservation in the Strawberry Hills of Monterrey, California." *Society and Natural Resources* 9: 339-57.

Norton, H. H., R. Boyd, and E. Hunn. 1999. "The Klikitat trail of south-central Washington: A reconstruction of seasonally used resource sites." In: R. Boyd (ed.), *Indians, Fire and the Land in the Pacific Northwest*, 65-93. Corvallis: Oregon State University Press.

Peña, D., and J. Gallegos. 1993. "Nature and Chicanos in southern Colorado." In: R. D. Bullard, and B. F. Chavis, Jr. (eds.), *Confronting Environmental Racism: Voices from the Grassroots,* 141-160. Boston, Massachusetts: South End Press.

Pyne, S. J. 1982. *Fire in America: A Cultural History of Wildland and Rural Fire.* Princeton, New Jersey: Princeton University Press. Reprinted in paperback 1997. Seattle: University of Washington Press.

————. 1983. "Indian fires: the fire practices of North American Indians transformed large areas from forest to grassland." *Natural History* 92: 6-11.

————, P. L. Andrews, and R. D. Laven. 1996. *Introduction to Wildland Fire.* 2nd ed. New York: John Wiley & Sons. 769 p.

Raish, C., and A. González-Cabán. 2003. "Culture/ethnicity and fire: The challenge of harmonizing cultural/ethnic variations and traditional practices concerning fire use and management with current practices." In: H. J. Cortner, D. R. Field, P. Jakes, and J. D. Buthman (eds.), Humans, fires, and forests: Social science applied to fire management, 39-49. ERI Papers in Restoration Policy. Flagstaff: Northern Arizona University, Ecological Restoration Institute.

Richards, R. T., and M. Creasy. 1996. "Ethnic diversity, resource values, and ecosystem management: Matsutake mushroom harvesting in the Klamath Bioregion." *Society and Natural Resources* 9: 359-74.

Rothman, H. 1989. "Cultural and environmental change on the Pajarito Plateau, New Mexico." *Historical Review* 64(2): 185-211.

Russell, E. W. B. 1983. "Indian-set fires in the forests of the Northeastern United States." *Ecology* 64(1): 78-88.

Savage, M., and T. W. Swetnam. 1990. "Early 19th century fire decline following sheep pasturing in a Navajo ponderosa pine forest." *Ecology* 70(6): 2374-78.

Schelhas, J. 2002. "Race, ethnicity, and natural resources in the United States: A review." *Natural Resources Journal* 42(4): 723-63.

Schiff, A. 1962. *Fire and Water: Scientific Heresy in the Forest Service.* Cambridge, Massachusetts: Harvard University Press.

Shea, J. 1940. "Our pappies burned the woods." *American Forests* 46: 159-74.

Stoddard, H. L. 1969. *Memoirs of a Naturalist.* Norman: University of Oklahoma Press.

Swetnam, T. W., and C. H. Baisan. 1996. "Historical fire regime patterns in the Southwestern United States since AD 1700." In: C. D. Allen (ed.), Proceedings of the 2nd La Mesa Fire Symposium; 1994 March 29-30; Los Alamos, 11-32. General Technical Report RM-GTR-286. Fort Collins, Colorado: USDA Forest Service, Rocky Mountain Forest and Range Experiment Station.

Thakali, R., and L. Lesko. 1998. Wisdom of the ages: Traditional knowledge and forest ecosystems. Manuscript on file at: USDA Forest Service, Kaibab National Forest, Williams, Arizona.

Tierney, P. T., R. F. Dahl, and D. J. Chavez. 1998. Cultural diversity of Los Angeles County residents using undeveloped natural areas. Research Paper PSW-RP-236. Riverside, California: USDA Forest Service, Pacific Southwest Research Station.

Touchan, R. T., T. W. Swetnam, and H. D. Grissino-Mayer. 1995. "Effects of livestock grazing on pre-settlement fire regimes in New Mexico." In: J. Brown (tech. coord.), Proceedings of the Symposium on fire in wilderness and park management: past lessons and future opportunities; 1993 March 30-April 1; Missoula, MT, 268-72. General Technical Report Int-GTR-320. Ogden, Utah: USDA Forest Service, Intermountain Forest and Range Experiment Station.

Turner, N. J. 1999. "Time to Burn: Traditional use of fire to enhance resource production by aboriginal peoples in British Columbia." In: R. Boyd (ed.), *Indians, Fire, and the Land in the Pacific Northwest*, 185-218. Corvallis: Oregon State University Press.

U. S. Bureau of the Census. 2000. Statistical abstract of the United States: 2000 (120th ed.). Washington, DC: U. S. Government Printing Office.

Wear, D. N., and J. G. Greis. 2002. The southern forest resource assessment summary report. General Technical Report SRS-53. Asheville, North Carolina: USDA Forest Service, Southern Research Station. 103 p.

Williams, G. W. 2000a. "Introduction to aboriginal fire use in North America." *Fire Management Today* 60(3): 8-12.

———. 2000b. "Reintroducing Indian-type fire: implications for land managers." *Fire Management Today* 60(3): 40-48.

———. 2002a. Aboriginal use of fire: Are there any "natural" communities? Washington, D.C.: USDA Forest Service.

———. 2002b. References on the American Indian use of fire in ecosystems. Washington, DC: USDA Forest Service.

Winter, P. L., and D. J. Chavez. 1999. "Recreation in urban proximate natural areas." In: H. K. Cordell, C. J. Betz, J. M. Bowker, D. B. K. English, S. H. Mou, J. C. Bergstrom, R. J. Teasley, M. A. Tarrant, and J. Loomis (eds.), *Outdoor Recreation in American Life: A National Assessment of Demand and Supply Trends*, 268-71. Champaign, Illinois: Sagamore Publishing.

———, and G. T. Cvetkovich. 2003. A study of Southwesterners' opinions on the management of wildland and wilderness fires: Fire management version. Riverside, California: USDA Forest Service, Pacific Southwest Research Station.

Section II
Community Perspectives

Matthew S. Carroll

Tip O'Neill famously said that all politics is local. He, of course, didn't literally mean that there is no need for a president, a national Congress, state governments, etc. What he did mean was that all political decision making was ultimately "felt" and therefore reacted to, in terms of its local manifestations. One can make the case that the late House Speaker would well understand that all wildland-urban interface (WUI) wildfires are, at some level, ultimately local events. To be sure it can be argued that the size and intensity of present-day WUI fires may be at least partially the result of one hundred years of federal land-management policies and national migration patterns. Federal and state resources are often employed to deal with such fires and their aftermath. The largest of such events receive national media coverage and national attention. Ultimately, however, WUI fires affect someone's community and local ecosystem whatever ownership parcels and legal jurisdictions they may cross.

The chapters in this section of People, Fire, and Forests look at wildfire from the point of view of how communities cope with it both as a risk and (in more and more instances in recent years) as a reality. In so doing, we locate our discussion within the broad framework of understanding human/fire interactions as a function of the biophysical environment, the demographics of a given local area, and the sociocultural dynamics that background people's responses to fire events. Within this broad framework and more specifically for understanding fire at the local community level, we adopt the structure of the event-driven model of McCool et al. (2006). This model suggests that communities and land managers face different kinds of decisions before, during, and after WUI fire events. The three chapters here each examine one of these time periods and attempt to synthesize what is known about dynamics, decisions, and dilemmas faced at each of these three stages in the community/fire cycle.

The chapter by Jakes and Nelson addresses community preparedness (or lack thereof) before the fire event. In so doing the authors tackle the thorny and very topical question of why and how communities prepare for the

Matthew S. Carroll, Dept. of Natural Resource Sciences, Washington State University (carroll@wsu.edu)

eventuality of a wildfire event, and perhaps more importantly, why they often do not.

The chapter by Carroll and Cohn deals with the dynamics of the fire event itself, including such events and processes as evacuation, firefighting, and media coverage among others. It also talks about the short- and long-term impacts of these during-fire events and processes on such things as citizen trust of the government, intergovernmental relations, and local fiscal circumstances. The authors conclude that although such fire events pose significant challenges for communities, they also "provide ... a valuable opportunity for community and agency leaders to adopt more strategic and systematic approaches to organizing people for a common goal of accommodating fire events with minimal losses and disruption."

The chapter by Burchfield treats the subject of "what now?" for communities after the smoke has cleared and the immediate threat is gone. Taking inspiration from Tom Beckley's well-known (1998) paper on community forest dependence, the author talks about the "nested layers of complexity affecting community responses to fire." He describes the positive and negative aspects of outside intervention and help for community recovery and the importance of pre-existing and emergent community capacity as local entities attempt to return local life to some semblance of normal and to grapple with the need for preparing for the next fire. He concludes "Sustainable long-term mitigation will be enhanced if community/agency cooperation considers elements of residential quality of life, local economic vitality, social and intergenerational equity, improvements to environmental quality, and open and fair processes for community-level preparations for future disaster events."

Taken together, these chapters present a reasonably comprehensive but also nuanced picture of what is known in a research sense about human communities and fire. We argue that this is important because communities in many ways represent "ground zero" when one talks about human impacts of wildfire. The chapters also help provide grounding for the topics that follow, which focus on the broader institutions and policies that have evolved and continue to evolve in response to the wildfire issue.

REFERENCES

Beckley, T. M. 1998. "The nestedness of forest dependence: A conceptual framework and empirical exploration." *Society and Natural Resources* 11(2): 101-20.

McCool, S. F., D. R. Williams, J. A. Burchfield, and M. S. Carroll. 2006. "An event driven model of the effects of wildland fire on communities: A potential framework for research, management, and understanding." *Environmental Management* 37(4): 437-50.

Community Interaction with Large Wildland Fire Events: Critical Initiatives Prior to the Fire

Pamela J. Jakes and Kristen Nelson

Introduction

Communities are more than places where people live, work, and raise their children. They are the relationships, partnerships, attitudes and values that bind people, businesses, organizations and agencies together and motivate them to achieve common goals. (Firewise Communities 2001, 4)

Over the past decade, with the adoption of the National Fire Plan and development of other wildland fire initiatives such as the Western Governor's Association Ten-Year Comprehensive Strategy, there has been a major shift in philosophy regarding wildland fire, from a philosophy bent on suppression to one that seeks prevention (USDA Forest Service 2000, 2004; Western Governors' Association 2001). While federal, state, and county managers will undertake activities to prevent wildland fire on public land, the focus of many prevention efforts will be at the local or community level (Society of American Foresters 2004; USDA Forest Service 2004). Certain wildland fire preparedness actions—such as insuring adequate water systems, sufficiently wide streets, and clear and consistent street signage, and maintenance of perimeter green belts—can only be done at the community level (David 1990), yet it is the local community that may be least prepared to undertake many of the steps necessary to achieve preparedness (Cigler 1988).

Questions related to wildland fire management and communities are significant because the risks associated with the fire event are large; our knowledge of the potential or actual impacts of wildland fire on a community, before, during, and after the event is incomplete; and the capacity of communities to deal with these impacts is limited. In this paper we focus on what the literature tells us about wildland fire preparedness—community-level actions implemented before a wildland fire to minimize the potential impacts of the event. Our goal is to help communities act more effectively prior to the fire to reduce their wildland fire risk. Later chapters in this

Pamela J. Jakes, USDA Forest Service, North Central Research Station (pjakes@fs.fed.us); Kristen Nelson, Dept. of Forest Resources and Dept. of Fisheries, Wildlife, and Conservation Biology, University of Minnesota section look at the consequences of actions taken during (Carroll and Cohn) and after (Burchfield) the fire.

Community Wildland-fire Preparedness in the Human Dimensions of Fire Framework

Luloff et al. (this volume) provide a broad framework for understanding the interactions between wildland fire and communities, one that focuses on both the physical and social systems through three main constructs: the biophysical environment, sociodemographic characteristics/dynamics, and sociocultural characteristics/dynamics. Much of the literature synthesized in this chapter focuses on ecosystems characterized by high fire risk— communities surrounded by or containing dense forests of high-fire-risk species, many stressed by drought or in poor health, which makes them more susceptible to catastrophic wildland fire. Physical aspects of the environment may exacerbate the risk faced by a community.

Although sociodemographic characteristics vary, because we're dealing with communities, the research is conducted at the wildland-urban interface. The wildland-urban interface is where we find homes and other structures built adjacent to or within tracts of flammable vegetation (Winter and Fried 2000).

Finally, in terms of sociocultural characteristics, much of the literature related to communities and fire preparedness describes the actions communities have taken to minimize the risks from wildland fires, the processes that are most effective in reaching decisions about which actions to take, and the social characteristics of the community that impact its ability to support these actions.

Lessons from Natural-hazard Preparedness

Research on community wildland-fire preparedness is conducted within a larger body of research on natural-hazard preparedness. Natural hazards are defined as "threats to life, well-being, material goods, and environment from extremes of natural processes" (Cigler 1988, p 40). However, it has been pointed out that "natural disaster" may be a misnomer, since people are often guilty of making their environment more prone to natural disasters or themselves more vulnerable to hazards (Cigler 1988). Wildland fire is a case in point, as attempts to suppress wildland fire have created conditions that make large-scale wildland fires more probable, and the movement of people into wild areas has made them more vulnerable to the hazards of wildland fire.

When discussing natural-hazards management, researchers often find it useful to talk about different periods surrounding the event (Drabek 1986; Gillespie et al. 1993). In general, the literature recognizes four phases for coping with disaster: mitigation, preparedness, response, and recovery (Gillespie et al. 1993). The chapter by McCaffrey and Kumagai in this volume provides more detail about these phases and in this chapter we focus on the first two, and particularly on preparedness. Preparedness and mitigation activities are addressed in an event-driven model of decisions for managing wildland fire (McCool et al. 2006). This model recognizes three stages of wildfire events: prior to, during, and following the fire event The model also highlights the linkages between the three phases, supporting the observation that preparedness is an important predictive indicator of hazard response and recovery (Gillespie et al. 1993). In addition, partnerships and networks formed during preparedness activities can be vital during response and recovery (Boura 1999). From a community perspective, the differences between mitigation and preparedness are indistinct, as the same set of people may well be doing preparedness and mitigation work—communities often don't have the luxury of being able to delegate specific tasks to specific individuals. In this chapter, we adopt the event-driven model and use the term preparedness to refer to all activities that occur prior to the fire event. There is support for this combination in that the line between mitigation and preparedness "is somewhat blurry" (Drabek 1986, p 21).

Partners in Community Wildland-fire Preparedness

A model for community preparedness developed from fifteen case studies helps explain the roles played by individual/homeowner decisions, organizational decisions, and collective decisions in the implementation of community actions that support community wildland-fire preparedness (Jakeset al. 2003b; Krugeret al. 2003). The model builds on the idea that communities will take action in response to risk (Tilly 1973); the assumption underlying it is that individuals can come together to make collective decisions to take action as a community to maintain or improve wildland-fire preparedness. In addition, organizations, including various federal land management agencies, state resource management agencies, city councils, nongovernmental organizations, and neighborhood associations, can make decisions to take community-level actions to improve wildland-fire preparedness.

As policy maker, funder, and land manager, the federal government plays several roles in wildland-fire preparedness. The policies developed under the National Fire Plan have shifted the wildland fire approach from one that might be characterized as reactive to one that is proactive (Western Governors' Association 2001). The plan specifies that this proactive approach is to be planned and implemented using a collaborative, community-based process that relies on local knowledge and develops objectives for long-term management activities in communities and the environment.

Several federal agencies provide funding for wildland-fire preparedness. The Federal Emergency Management Agency (FEMA) has supported community wildland-fire preparedness through Project Impact. In Bend, Oregon, Project Impact funds supported community clean-up days and the creation of an emergency egress over a railroad track for a subdivision (Sturtevant and Jakes 2002). In Ruidoso, New Mexico, a Project Impact grant was used for wildland fire education and emergency management (Steelman 2004b). Funding for Project Impact was terminated in 2002, and there is some concern that FEMA will return to its historic focus on the immediate and urgent aspects of disaster response rather than the effective pre-disaster preparedness measures (Cigler 1988; Teie and Weatherford 2000), or disappear within the Department of Homeland Security.

The National Fire Plan provides additional financial and technical support for fire suppression and prevention, rehabilitation and restoration of fire-damaged wildland and high-risk ecosystems, hazardous-fuel reduction projects, and community projects to reduce risk (Rains and Hubbard 2002). However, there is concern that, although hundreds of millions of dollars have been allocated to the states to fund local wildland-fire management activities, only a small portion is actually reaching communities (Steelman et al. 2004, p 10).

As land managers, federal agencies can model fire-preparedness behavior. Agencies such as the Forest Service, Bureau of Land Management, National Park Service, Fish and Wildlife Service, and Bureau of Indian Affairs play an important role as "good neighbor" in the effort to model community preparedness for wildland fire. In the northern Black Hills south of Spearfish, South Dakota, the Fish and Wildlife Service conducted a fuels-reduction project at the D. C. Booth Fish Hatchery (Hudson et al. 2003). New Firewise landscaping was installed, and signs were posted throughout the hatchery grounds explaining the project and the role of wildland fire in local ecosystems. Hiking trails, which will serve as fuel breaks, are being planned for the area. Near Red Lodge, Montana, the Custer National Forest is home to a large number of special-use cabins—privately owned cabins constructed in dense lodgepole pine on National Forest land (Sturtevant & Kruger 2004). The Forest Service has designed a hazardous-fuel reduction project for these cabins. The focus is on creating several cabins that will serve as models for other homeowners in the area.

States play a role in community wildland-fire preparedness through organizational arrangements, programmatic decisions, and access to funding (Steelman et al. 2004). State agency staff can be uniquely placed to serve as a conduit between federal agencies and local communities. They can play a critical role as initiator in community wildland preparedness, especially in communities with low social or human capacity. For example, in northwestern Wisconsin, the Department of Natural Resources took responsibility for educating the public and coordinating preparedness activities between agencies and local industry (Jakes et al. 2003a).

Local communities control many aspects of wildfire preparedness. One of the major findings following the 1998 wildland fires in Florida was the need for improved local-level planning to mitigate wildland fire danger (Long and Monroe 1999). Communities and local government often play a lead role in the development of comprehensive or land-use plans that specify the locations of future growth and development (Britton and Lindsay 1995a, 1995b; Godschalk 1991).

The enactment of local codes, standards, and zoning that restrict development or mandate fuels reductions are seen as important tools for cities and local governments to increase community wildland preparedness (Bailey 1991). A report for the Council of Western State Foresters observed that codes, regulations, and building standards exist that would increase community wildland-fire preparedness, but few states or communities have the public or political will to implement them (Teie and Weatherford 2000). Magill (1992) has suggested that the unwillingness of communities to implement laws, codes, and standards is really a reluctance of elected officials to be associated with actions that may be viewed unfavorably by their constituents. Other studies indicate that these actions can be perceived by property owners as an unwelcome intrusion on personal freedom (Winter and Fried 2000). Some communities, however, have stepped forward. In Palm Coast, Florida, the city notifies a property owner when they need to reduce fuels (Monroe et al. 2003a). Upon notification the owner has two options: they can remove the vegetation themselves or have the city perform the service and reimburse the city for the costs. If the owner does neither, the city will clear the underbrush and charge the owner the cost plus a fine. If no payment is made, the city will place a lien on the property that must be paid before the lot can be sold or developed.

Local government can also help financially with wildland-fire preparedness. In Red River, New Mexico, the city absorbs the 30% cost share required by the state's Twenty Communities Cost-Share Program (Steelman 2004a). In addition to providing funding, local governments can facilitate wildland-fire preparedness activities. A Neighborhood Fire Smart program was initiated by the city of Ruidoso, New Mexico (Steelman 2004b); modeled after the national Neighborhood Watch crime-prevention program, it identifies block captains and other interested residents to coordinate fuel-management activities within neighborhoods and to perform one-on-one outreach.

Businesses and local organizations are also important partners in community wildland-fire preparedness. In Bend, Oregon, the SAFECO Insurance Company provided funding to initiate a public education campaign, FireFree (Sturtevant and Jakes 2002). State Farm Insurance agencies in Prescott, Arizona, purchased chippers for the city to assist in hazardous fuel reduction around private homes and purchased signs to encourage the creation of defensible space throughout the city (Steelman and Kunkel 2004a).

When existing partnerships or groups become involved in wildland-fire preparedness, entrance is gained to local networks that can spread the preparedness message. The Fire Council of Carbon County, Montana, has worked with the county commissioners to create subdivision regulations that increase fire safety in the wildland-urban interface (Sturtevant and Kruger 2004). The Forest Health Coalition, a local citizens' group, played an important role in eliminating a 1980s ordinance in Ruidoso, New Mexico, that required residents to pay a fee and obtain a permit to cut trees larger than five inches in diameter (Steelman 2004b). In Minnesota, the Gunflint Trail Association used their network of local business owners to promote fuel treatments and educate community members about wildfire (Jakes and Nelson 2002).

Physical and Social Wildfire Preparedness within a Community

The natural-hazards literature generally differentiates between actions to improve physical preparedness and those that improve social preparedness (Gillespie et al. 1993). Physical preparedness emphasizes the safety of physical facilities to minimize loss of life, injury, and property damage. For wildland fire this could include vegetation management, communication systems, water access systems, and public education programs. Social preparedness focuses on activities such as planning, training, and steps to improve financial security. Over the past few years there has been a remarkable growth in the number of qualitative case studies illustrating the implementation of physical and social preparedness actions for community wildfire initiatives (Boura 1999; Community Safety Directorate n.d.; Hudson et al. 2004; Jakes and Nelson 2002; Jakes et al. 2003a, 2003b; Kruger et al. 2003; Lang et al. 2003; McGee and Russell 2003; Monroe et al. 2003a, 2004; Nelsonet al. 2003; Steelman 2004a, 2004b; Steelman and Bell 2004; Steelman and Kunkel 2004a, 2004b, 2004c; Sturtevant and Jakes 2002, 2003; Sturtevant and Kruger 2004; Teie and Weatherford 2000). Findings from several of these studies are highlighted below.

Physical preparedness
Communities can be found throughout the country that have engaged in vegetative management programs to improve wildland-fire preparedness. In Roslyn, Washington, the Washington Department of Natural Resources, Kittitas County Fire Marshal, USDA Forest Service Cle Elum Ranger District, and local fire departments and fire districts created a 150- to 200-feet-wide shaded fuel break around Roslyn, the adjacent town of Ronald, and along the highway corridor connecting the two (Kruger and Sturtevant 2004). The object of the shaded fuel break is not to stop a wildland fire, but to keep it on the ground and of low intensity so crews will have a better chance of controlling it.

In developing vegetation-management projects, differences can arise over the acceptability of different fuels treatments. As observed by Brunson in regards to ecosystem management, "Practices and conditions that are acceptable in one setting will not be acceptable in another ... Acceptability is judged within a social context" (Brunson 1993, p 118). Citizen support is essential for the successful implementation of fuels-management programs (Shindler 2002).

Of course there are also challenges in conducting vegetation-management projects, during the removal and utilization stages. There can be a shortage of qualified workers or prohibitive transport costs (Steelman and Bell 2004). The National Fire Plan acknowledges this issue by supporting Economic Action Programs. Funds from this program are used to develop and expand markets for material removed during fuels-reduction and vegetation-management projects (Rains and Hubbard 2002). Some communities have been successful in helping develop businesses that utilize material from fuels-mitigation projects (Monroe et al. 2004; Steelman 2004a, 2004b; Steelman and Bell 2004); however the utilization challenge continues to loom large over any fuels-reduction initiative (Becker and Viers, this volume).

Research has shown that communication systems during a wildland fire can be critical in reducing risks for community residents. Several communities, including Ruidoso, New Mexico, and Palm Coast, Florida, have installed reverse-911 telephone systems that allow emergency management personnel to notify residents of an impending emergency or disaster (Steelman 2004b; Monroe et al. 2003a).

In another case, Boreal Access, a local business-association Web site, and the Cook County Firewise Committee created a highly interactive Web site for public education and notification about wildfire issues. This site educates homeowners, but also serves as a link to local groups organizing wildland-fire preparedness activities (Jakes and Nelson 2002).

Social preparedness

Physical preparedness is the outcome of the social processes and institutions that are essential for community action. A few that have emerged in the wildland-fire studies are partnerships and laws/ordinances, discussed earlier, as well as planning institutions and decision-making networks. Planning institutions and decision-making networks require tools to facilitate the organization of information for decision makers. The Bureau of Land Management and USDA Forest Service operating in La Plata County, Colorado, have approached the National Environmental Policy Act process creatively, with a programmatic document for prescribed burning and an umbrella environmental assessment for mechanical thinning (Steelman and Bell 2004). This creative approach to planning has allowed the agencies to move forward to reduce hazardous fuels by reducing duplicate paperwork.

Education is a social measure that can target specific groups within the community, groups that may serve as successful conduits of information and message importance. In many communities, children can be important communication partners. In Roslyn, Washington, the creation of defensible space around the school grounds piqued the curiosity of students (Kruger and Sturtevant 2004). As a result, teachers, the county fire marshal, and Department of Natural Resources and USDA Forest Service fire-management officers developed a Junior FireWise program, which has been added to the middle school curriculum.

Collaboration is often cited as a critical social measure for increasing or improving community wildland-fire preparedness (Kruger et al. 2003; Sturtevant et al. 2005; Teie and Weatherford 2000). Collaboration around specific wildland-fire preparedness initiatives can begin with existing networks or it may be necessary to start from scratch. Neighborhood and landowner associations can serve as strong foundations (Jakes and Nelson 2002; Nelson et al. 2003; Steelman 2004b). The Healthy Forests Restoration Act of 2003 emphasizes the need for federal agencies to work collaboratively with communities in planning and implementing hazardous fuel reduction projects (Society of American Foresters 2004). However, collaboration will not occur without public knowledge and understanding of ecological and social conditions: "Only when the public truly understands the nature of the wildland/urban interface fire problem will the community-based coalitions needed to effectively mitigate the problem be successful." (Teie and Weatherford 2000, p 29)

The Applegate Fire Plan represents a highly collaborative community-driven process to plan fuels-reduction projects on public and private land (Sturtevant and Jakes 2003). For the federal and state agencies involved, the plan solidifies a process that has been ongoing for decades—gathering information, balancing priorities, planning strategies, and cooperating across property lines—but this time the process occurs in dialogue and partnership with one another and community members.

Despite examples like the Applegate Partnership, many collaborative forestry groups in the West, including some focused on wildland fire preparedness, are floundering: "Collaborative forestry groups are not achieving their land management goals at the rate and scale they had anticipated, with the result that both agency and non-agency collaboration are experiencing frustration and burnout" (Moote and Becker 2003).

In a major effort to synthesize the literature related to wildland fire and collaboration, Sturtevant et al. (2005) discuss many of the challenges and benefits of collaboration. Much of the literature supports the belief that collaboration produces better outcomes for everyone.

A Social Foundation for Community Wildland-fire Preparedness

Successful implementation of physical and social wildland-fire preparedness depends on the presence of appropriate conditions within the community (Jakes et al. 2003b; Kruger et al. 2003). Pretty (2000) has discussed how the success of communities and other social systems in natural-resource management relies on the accumulation of capital—natural capital, social capital, human capital, physical capital, and financial capital. One study of fifteen communities across the U.S. found support for similar ideas in the area of wildfire preparedness. In this study, the key foundational elements for success were identified as landscape, government involvement, human capacity, and social capacity (Jakes at al. 2003b). In Australia, agency involvement, human capacity, and social capacity were also found to be important to the success of wildland-fire preparedness activities (McGee and Russell 2003). These studies suggest that wildland-fire preparedness activities not only build on, but can help build can build, human and social capacities.

Conclusions

The community wildland-fire preparedness literature is a rich collection of case studies highlighting what individual communities are doing to increase preparedness. These data have been organized around themes such as steps in the decision-making process (Steelman and Kunkel 2004b) and key elements for success (Jakes et al. 2003b, 2004; Kruger et al. 2003). As final thoughts, we offer several questions evolving from this synthesis:

· Do we have enough case studies to begin synthesizing what we have learned?

· If the fire event model is really a circular process, how do a community's activities related to rehabilitation and restoration feed preparedness?

· What is the "political will" that results in one community enacting ordinances, codes, and regulations that facilitate community wildland-fire preparedness, while another cannot or will not?

· How can we help public land-management agencies be good neighbors and model effective wildland-fire preparedness on their land adjacent to communities?

· What has been the diffusion of community preparedness programs such as FireFree, FireSafe, and FireWise, and what has been the effectiveness of these programs?

· How are the social mechanisms of community preparedness any different from or the same as other community natural-resources management initiatives or natural-hazard preparedness in general?

· How can we, as scientists, give back to the communities we study, perhaps work with them to continue learning?

REFERENCES

Bailey, D. W. 1991. "The wildland-urban interface: Social and political implications in the 1990's." *Fire Management Notes* 52 (1):11-18.

Boura, J. 1999. *Community fireguard: Creating partnerships with the community.* County Fire Authority Occasional Paper No. 2. Mt. Waverley, Victoria, Australia: County Fire Authority.

Britton, N. R., and J. Lindsay. 1995a. "Integrating city planning and emergency preparedness: Some of the reasons why." *International Journal of Mass Emergencies and Disasters* 13 (1):93-106.

———, and J. Lindsay. 1995b. "Demonstrating the need to integrate city planning and emergency preparedness: Two case studies." *International Journal of Mass Emergencies and Disasters* 13 (2):161-78.

Brunson, M. W. 1993. " 'Socially acceptable' forestry: What does it imply for ecosystem management?" *Western Journal of Applied Forestry* 8 (4):116-19.

Cigler, B. A. 1988. "Current policy issues in mitigation." In: L. K. Comfort (ed.), *Managing Disaster: Strategies and Policy Perspectives.* Durham, North Carolina: Duke Press Policy Studies, 39-52.

Community Safety Directorate. n.d. *Bushfire blitz 2000/2001: An evaluation of program implementation and outcomes.* State of Victoria, Australia: County Fire Authority.

David, J. B. 1990. "The wildland-urban interface: Paradise or battleground?" *Journal of Forestry* 88 (1): 26-31.

Drabek, T. E. 1986. *Human System Responses to Disaster: An Inventory of Sociological Findings.* New York: Springer-Verlag.

FireWise Communities. 2001. *FireWise communities workshop: Participant workbook.* Quincy, Massachusetts: FireWise Communities.

Gillespie, D. F., R. A. Colignon, B. M. Mahasweta, S. A. Murty, and M. Rogge. 1993. Partnerships for community preparedness. Boulder: University of Colorado.

Godschalk, D. R. 1991. "Disaster mitigation and hazard management." In T. E. Drabek and G. J. Hoetmer (eds.), *Emergency Management: Principles and Practices for Local Government.* Washington, D.C.: International City Management Association, 131-60.

Hudson, R., E. Lang, and K. Nelson. 2003. *Spearfish, South Dakota, and the Northern Black Hills: Steps to improve community preparedness for wildfire.* Community Preparedness Case Study #5. St. Paul, Minnesota: USDA North Central Research Station.

———, S. Agrawal, and M. Monroe. 2004. *Communities near the Sandhill Crane National Wildlife Refuge: Steps to improve community preparedness for wildfire.* Community Preparedness Case Study #10. St. Paul, Minnesota: USDA Forest Service, North Central Research Station.

Jakes, P. J., and K. Nelson. 2002. *Gunflint Trail Community: Steps to improve community preparedness for wildfire.* Community Preparedness Case Study #1. St. Paul, Minnesota: USDA Forest Service, North Central Research Station.

———, K. Nelson, and E. Lang. 2003a. *Barnes-Drummond and Northwestern Wisconsin: Steps to improve community preparedness for wildfire.* Community Preparedness Case Study #7. St. Paul, Minnesota: USDA Forest Service, North Central Research Station.

———, K. Nelson, E. Lang, M. Monroe, S. Agrawal, L. Kruger, and V. Sturtevant. 2003b. "A model for improving community preparedness for wildfire." In P. J. Jakes (compiler), *Homeowners, communities, and wildfire; Science findings from the National Fire Plan.* St. Paul, Minnesota, USDA Forest Service. General Technical Report NC-231:4-9.

———, L. Kruger, M. Monroe, K. Nelson, and V. Sturtevant. 2004. "Partners in wildland fire preparedness: Lessons from communities in the U.S." In *Human behavior in fire: Public fire safety—professionals in partnership.* Proceedings of the 3rd International Symposium on Human Behavior in Fire. September 1-3; Belfast. London, UK: Interscience Communications Limited, 139-50.

Kruger, L. E., S. Agrawal, M. Monroe, E. Lang, K. Nelson, P. Jakes, V. Sturtevant, S. McCaffrey, and Y. Everett. 2003. "Keys to community preparedness for wildfire." In P. J. Jakes (compiler), *Homeowners, communities, and wildfire; Science findings from the National Fire Plan.* St. Paul, Minnesota, USDA Forest Service. General Technical Report NC-231:10-17.

———, and V. Sturtevant. 2004. *Roslyn, Washington: Steps to improve community preparedness for wildfire.* Community Preparedness Case Study #9. St. Paul, Minnesota: USDA Forest Service, North Central Research Station.

Lang, E., R. Hudson, P. Jakes, and K. C. Nelson. 2003. *Spearfish, South Dakota and the Northern Black Hills: Steps to improve community preparedness for wildfire.* Community Preparedness Case Study #5. St. Paul, Minnesota: USDA Forest Service, North Central Research Station.

Long, A. J., and M. C. Monroe.1999. "New interface strategies in Florida." In *Proceedings of the Society of American Foresters 1999 National Convention.* September 11-15; Portland, Oregon. Bethesda, Maryland: Society of American Foresters, 397-402.

Magill, A. 1992. "People—fire managers must talk with them." *Fire Management Notes* 53-54 (2):3-7.

McCool, S., D. Williams, M. Carroll, and T. Ubben. 2006. *Social science to improve fuels management: Impacts of wildland fires on communities.* General Technical Report NC-269. St. Paul, Minnesota: USDA Forest Service, North Central Research Station.

McGee, T. K., and S. Russell. 2003. " 'It's just a natural way of life …' An investigation of wildfire preparedness in rural Australia." *Global Environmental Change Part B: Environmental Hazards* 5 (1-2): 1-12.

Monroe, M., S. Agrawal, and P. J. Jakes. 2003a. *The Palm Coast community: Steps to improve community preparedness for wildfire.* Community Preparedness Case Study #4. St. Paul, Minnesota: USDA Forest Service, North Central Research Station.

———, S. Agrawal, and P. J. Jakes. 2003b. *Waldo, Florida: Steps to improve community preparedness for wildfire.* Community Preparedness Case Study #6. St. Paul, Minnesota: USDA Forest Service, North Central Research Station.

———, S. Agrawal, S., and R. Hudson. 2004. *Bastrop, Texas: Steps to improve community preparedness for wildfire.* Community Preparedness Case Study #12. St. Paul, Minnesota: USDA Forest Service, North Central Research Station.

Moote, A., and D. Becker. 2003. *Exploring barriers to collaborative forestry.* Report of the Barriers to Collaborative Forestry Workshop; September 17-19; Flagstaff, Arizona. Flagstaff: Ecological Restoration Institute.

Nelson, K., E. Lang, P. J. Jakes, and R. Hudson. 2003. *Berkeley Township, New Jersey: Steps to improve community preparedness for wildfire.* Community Preparedness Case Study #8. St. Paul, Minnesota: USDA Forest Service, North Central Research Station.

Pretty, J. 2000. "Towards sustainable food and farming systems in industrialized countries." *International Journal of Agricultural Resources, Governance and Ecology* 1 (1): 77-94.

Rains, M. T., and J. Hubbard. 2002. "Protecting communities through the National Fire Plan." *Fire Management Today* 62 (2):4-12.

Shindler, B. 2002. "Citizens in the fuel-reduction equation: problems and prospects for public forest managers." In: S. A. Fitzgerald (ed.), *Fire in Oregon's Forests: Risks, Effects, and Treatment Options.* Portland, Oregon: Oregon Forest Resources Institute, 139-47.

Society of American Foresters. 2004. *Preparing a Community Wildfire Protection Plan: A Handbook for Wildland-urban Interface Communities.* Washington, D.C.: Society of American Foresters.

Steelman, T. A. 2004a. "Community responses to wildland fire threats in New Mexico: Red River." Available at www.ncsu.edu/project/wildfire/red_river.html.

———. 2004b. "Community responses to wildland fire threats in New Mexico: Ruidoso." Available at www.ncsu.edu/project/wildfire/ruidoso.html.

———, and D. Bell. 2004. "Community responses to wildland fire threats in Colorado: La Plata County." Available at www.ncsu.edu/project/wildfire/Colorado/la_plata.html.

———, and G. F. Kunkel. 2004a. "Community responses to wildland fire threats in Arizona: Prescott." Available at www.ncsu.edu/project/wildfire/Arizona/prescott/p_improve.html.

————, and G. F. Kunkel. 2004b. "Community responses to wildland fire threats in New Mexico: Santa Fe." Available at www.ncsu.edu/project/wildfire/santa_fe.html.

————, and G. F. Kunkel. 2004c. "Effective community responses to wildfire threats: Lessons from New Mexico." *Society and Natural Resources* 17 (8):679-700.

————, G. Kunkel, and D. Bell. 2004. "Federal and state influence on community responses to wildfire in AZ, CO and NM." *Journal of Forestry* 102(6):21-27.

Sturtevant, V., and P. J. Jakes. 2002. *The Bend Community and FireFree: Steps to improve community preparedness for wildfire.* Community Preparedness Case Study #2. St. Paul, Minnesota: USDA Forest Service, North Central Research Station.

————, and P. J. Jakes. 2003. *The Applegate Fire Plan: Steps to improve community preparedness for wildfire.* Community Preparedness Case Study #3. St. Paul, Minnesota: USDA Forest Service, North Central Research Station.

————, and L. Kruger. 2004. *Red Lodge, Montana: Steps to improve community preparedness for wildfire.* Community Preparedness Case Study #13. St. Paul, Minnesota: USDA Forest Service, North Central Research Station.

————, M. A. Moote, A. Cheng, A., and P. J. Jakes. 2005. Social science to improve fuels management: A synthesis of research on collaboration. St. Paul, Minnesota, USDA Forest Service, North Central Research Station. General Technical Report NC-257.

Teie, W. C., and B. F. Weatherford. 2000. *A Report to the Council of Western State Foresters: Fire in the West, the Wildland/urban Interface Fire Problem.* Rescue, California: Deer Valley Press.

Tilly, C. 1973. "Do communities act?" *Sociological Inquiry* 43 (3-4): 209-40.

USDA Forest Service. 2000. *Protecting people and sustaining resources in fire-adapted ecosystems: A cohesive strategy.* Washington, D.C.: USDA Forest Service.

————. 2004. "The Healthy Forests Initiative and Healthy Forests Restoration Act: An interim field guide." FS-799. Washington, D.C.: USDA Forest Service, U.S. Department of the Interior, Bureau of Land Management. FS-799. Available at http://www.fs.fed.us/projects/hfi/field-guide/web/.

Western Governors' Association. 2001. "A collaborative approach for reducing wildland fire risks to communities and the environment: 10-year comprehensive strategy". Available at http://www.westgov.org/wga/initiatives/fire/final_fire_rept.pdf.

Winter, G., and J. Fried. 2000. "Homeowner perspectives on fire hazard, responsibility, and management strategies at the wildland-urban interface." *Society and Natural Resources* 13 (1): 33-40.

Community Impacts of Large Wildland Fire Events: Consequences of Actions during the Fire

Matthew S. Carroll and Patricia J. Cohn

This paper portrays one segment of an event-driven model about the local community impacts of large residential-interface wildfire events. Beginning with the assumption that such events occur within a context framed by the biophysical setting, sociodemographic conditions, and the psychological-cultural context, this work reviews the scant published literature on the human-community impacts of wildfire and the more abundant hazards and disaster literature to distill key events and processes that occur within communities during wildfire events in light of the aforementioned contextual elements. Specifically, the paper examines: 1) events and processes during fires; 2) issues related to such events and processes; and 3) long-term impacts of events, decisions, and processes occurring during fires. We conclude by suggesting that although particular events and processes are inherent in community wildfire events, particular outcomes are not inevitable. By identifying key decision points, community and agency leaders can affect the outcome of fire events on communities in important ways.

Introduction

Through research in fire ecology over the course of several decades, we have come to understand fire as an endemic disturbance element in many forest and brushland ecosystems (Agee 1994; Arno and Allison-Bunnell 2002; Arno and Feidler 2005; Hessburg and Agee 2003). More recently social scientists, historians, and an increasing number of those who live in the wildland-urban interface (WUI) on much of the North American continent have come to understand that increasingly severe wildland fires that burn into or around residential areas are a source of social disturbance that have short- and in some cases long-term effects on human communities (Rodriguez-Mendez et al. 2003). Much as ecologists see fire as both a cause and an effect of

Matthew S. Carroll, Dept. of Natural Resource Sciences, Washington State University (carroll@wsu.edu; Patricia J. Cohn, Research Associate, Washington State University ecological dynamics, social scientists are increasingly viewing interface fire as both a cause and an effect of social dynamics, particularly in the case of fire-affected human communities. This said, it seems fair to say that our sociological understanding of fire lags far behind our understanding of its biophysical aspects, with our grasp of the dynamic interaction of fire and society perhaps the least developed of all (Bonnickson and Lee 1979; Hessburg and Agee 2003).

Luloff et al. (this volume) provide a broad framework for understanding human-forest fire interactions that takes as its three main constructs the biophysical environment, sociodemographic characteristics/dynamics, and sociocultural characteristics/dynamics. McCool et al. (2006) look more narrowly at the question of the impacts of fire on the human community and propose an event-driven model consisting of a temporal framework that examines community-fire dynamics before, during, and after a given fire event. This chapter seeks to summarize what is currently known about human-community dynamics during a major fire event. We draw primarily from the relatively small literature specifically focused on the community impacts of wildfire and secondarily (and by necessity far more selectively) on the broader and more extensive literature on the human-community impacts of disaster events such as floods, earthquakes, urban-structure fires, and hurricanes.

Given that this paper is focused on social dynamics during fires, it follows that our emphasis is on the impacts that fires have on human settlements and not the inverse (which also is a subject worthy of thought and analysis, see Bonnickson and Lee 1979; Hessburg and Agee 2003; Jakes and Nelson 2007).

We begin by describing the major events and processes that typically occur in and around fire-affected communities that are relevant to social impacts. This information is derived largely from a handful of recently conducted case studies on fire events. We then summarize what is known from the published literature about the specific social impacts of fire events as they play out in affected communities. These impacts are described across ascending levels of social organization from the individual level up to and including the community level. We conclude with a brief discussion of the consequences from decisions and actions made during fire events.

Fire Event Processes

The literature on the community impacts from fire events suggests that a number of processes play out in virtually every major fire event. Many of these same or similar processes are also documented in the literature on natural disasters. In this section, we present what is known from both fields on the following processes: evacuation, firefighting, law enforcement, media coverage, communication, purchases and hiring, and the arrival of assistance organizations.

Evacuation

As more people live in or near public forests, evacuation of these communities during wildfires is becoming common. The main concerns associated with wildfire evacuation situations are the same as those for other types of natural disasters: notification, timing, evacuation of pets and livestock, ingress and egress, and people who refuse to leave or delay leaving (Drabek 1994; Halvorson 2002; Heath 2001). The presence of tourist attractions and vacation residences in or near the WUI adds another complication (Drabek 1994).

Perhaps the major concern of emergency services personnel is persuading people to leave. Perry (1994) and Drabek (1994) proposed evacuation behavior and compliance models that predict willingness or likelihood to evacuate. Among the variables affecting evacuation decisions are: confirmation of the warning, credibility of the source, content of the warning message, perceived risk, location of family members, and level of preparedness (Drabek 1994; Perry 1994), gender, pre-existing personal arrangements for accommodations/shelter, and level of belief in the occurrence of the event (Drabek 1994). And finally, sociodemographic or sociocultural characteristics, situational constraints, and personal resources affect one's ability to leave (Tierney et al. 2001). Other findings indicate that people who have had previous experience with disasters are less likely to leave. However, the consistency of notice and the specificity of the warning do not appear to have an effect on willingness to stay or leave. Decisions on whether or not to leave are also affected by increased perceptions of risk, security, vulnerability, and loss (Drabek 1994; Halvorson 2002; Riad et al. 1999).

Wildfire evacuees have their concerns about evacuation, chief among them being the status of their homes, as well as pets and livestock (evacuation, care), and accessing their homes while the evacuation order is in force (Benight et al. 2004; Carroll et al. 2000; Cohn et al. 2006; Graham 2003; Taylor et al. 2005). That more evacuees stay with friends and relatives than stay in shelters (Graham 2003; Halvorson 2002) makes it difficult to inform them about the status of their homes and neighborhood and firefighting progress, and provide access to recovery resources. As was found in the general disaster literature, some fire evacuees from the Hayman (Colorado) and Rodeo-Chediski (Arizona) fires reported that they would be far more reluctant to evacuate should another fire event occur. Part of this reluctance stemmed from a desire to stay and fight the fire around their home and property and part from the inability to return until authorities allowed it (Carroll and Cohn 2003; Graham 2003).

Law enforcement

During a wildfire event, law enforcement personnel usually have the responsibility for evacuation procedures, traffic control, public safety, access restrictions, and crime prevention. Their actions may conflict with the mission of fire-suppression teams: structure and resource protection (Bender 2003). For example, escorted trips for evacuated homeowners to retrieve medication and other necessities and post-fire van tours of burned areas were seen by the sheriff's office as necessary, reassuring, and helpful in reducing tension during the Missionary Ridge Fire (Colorado). The federal fire-management team saw these exceptions to the evacuation order as interfering with fire-suppression activities and as public safety and liability risks. The presence of law enforcement officers behind the fire lines and without red cards and firefighting clothing was also bothersome to incident command team members (Bender 2003).

Law enforcement agencies and services are stretched during wildfires. Agencies juggle additional staffing and volunteers, extended patrols, evacuations, the news media, and hot lines in addition to handling routine crimes and public safety concerns. Another issue is the impact of emergency operations on county budgets, reimbursement from state and federal agencies, and the seemingly torturous and lengthy Federal Emergency Management Agency (FEMA) reimbursement process for emergency expenditures (Graham 2003; State of California 2004).

Public safety officials involved with the 2002 wildfires in Arizona and Colorado expressed the need for better communications between suppression and law enforcement entities and for improved communications systems (Bender 2003; Carroll et al. 2000; Graham 2003). Communications between fire teams and deputies were hindered by incompatible radios and dispatch operators were deluged with calls from the public wanting information on the fire. Similar problems were experienced during the California wildfires of 2003 (State of California 2004).

Residents and members of the public also have public safety concerns. Chief among them are entry restrictions, or access to homes and property during and immediately after the fire. Residents want access to their homes during the evacuation period, primarily to retrieve additional belongings, and are also concerned over the possibility of looting and theft during and after the fire (Graham 2003; Halvorson 2002). While widespread crime and looting are not common after natural disasters Drabek (1994), the above studies did report isolated incidents of theft and post-fire scavenging.

Media coverage

Flames and burned foundations make great images for the nightly news (Beebe and Omi 1993), more so than images of growing forests. Smith's (1992, 1995) analysis of media coverage of wildfires and other natural disasters found that media coverage of wildfires tended to be sensationalistic, at times inaccurate, and focused on the drama of the event, the responsible agent, and the impacts of the fire on humans and communities. Today, wildfires are still described in apocalyptic terms—devastating, devouring, consuming, and blackening—as they were during the Yellowstone fires in 1988 (Smith 1995).

The character of media coverage of wildfire is attributed to several factors, including the information sources and their ability to gain and hold the attention of reporters; the extent to which the story resonates with cultural values; and the salience of the event (Quarantelli 1996; Smith 1992, 1995). During disasters, reporters tend to turn to their usual sources of information and the perspective of those sources dominates the coverage. Media personnel confined to command posts impart that perspective. As a result, the viewpoints of citizens and emergent groups may not be presented and reporting may be biased towards an official perspective. Also, time and travel constraints, editorial decisions, the reporter's values, and the entertainment angle shape the news coverage (Quarantelli 1996; Smith 1995).

Different news media respond and report differently during disaster situations (Quarantelli 1996). Television and radio reports have more immediacy, while newspaper coverage is better during the post-disaster phase. Local radio stations are not only used for general coverage, but are also an important way to relay personal messages among local residents, an occurrence noted during several recent wildfires (Carroll et al. 2005; Graham 2003; Taylor et al. 2005). The different media also use citizen sources differently. Radio stations use citizens for information, while newspapers and television use them as subjects of human interest stories.

During the 2002 wildfires in Colorado and the 2003 fire events in southern California, research revealed that local residents obtained information about the fire from many sources, with the Internet, television, and personal networks (friends, relatives, neighbors, and those who were working on the fire or did not evacuate) among the more frequently listed (Benight et al. 2004; Graham 2003; Taylor et al. 2005). Interviewees stated that the information they received from personal networks was more current and accurate than Forest Service or television reports, with reports from the latter source seen as misleading and inaccurate (Graham 2003; Taylor et al. 2005). During the Hayman fire, a local coffee shop became an information center for residents to exchange information (Benight et al. 2004; Graham 2003).

Another aspect of communication is the type of information the affected residents want and need and when they get it. Studies during wildfires in Colorado, Arizona, California, and Montana, reported that affected residents wanted current information on where the fire was and what it was doing, and especially where the fire was in relation to their residence (Benight et al. 2004; Graham 2003; Halvorson 2002; Kumagai et al. 2004a, 2004b; Taylor et al. 2005). Evacuated residents wanted to know the status of their home—had it burned or not? The inability to get the most current information at any time about their homes and about when they could return was a source of stress and tension; providing this type of information was not a priority for fire managers who tended to be focused on the technical aspects of the fire and suppression efforts (Carroll et al. 2000; Graham 2003; Kumagai et al. 2004a, 2004b).

The news media and fire managers have taken advantage of the array of communication and information-gathering/processing devices such as computers, cell phones, satellite photos, and GIS, but these technologies have a number of problematic aspects related to disaster planning and management (Quarantelli 1997). Among the more obvious are information overload, the spreading of inappropriate, inaccurate, or misleading information, and technology failure. Less-obvious problems are an increasing difficulty with intra/interlevel information flow; lack of or an inadequate social/cultural structure to use the technology, e.g., presence/absence of a safety culture; and technology failures that amplify existing disasters.

As noted in the law enforcement section, a chronic communications problem is the incompatibility of radio equipment used by the federal and local/county agencies and the often inadequate radio equipment at the local and county levels (Graham 2003; National Association of State Foresters 2003; State of California 2004; U.S. General Accounting Office 1999).

Suppression tactics and strategy

The first priority in federal firefighting is firefighter and public safety (National Interagency Fire Center 2001). The emphasis on safety has shaped decision making and tactics, as have amount and type of firefighting resources, public opinion, and reliability of information (Taylor et al. 1988). Risk aversion has also played a role, leading fire managers to want to suppress all fires quickly in order to prevent the loss of life and resources. This, however, has had the unintended effect of contributing to fuel loading and thus increasing the risk of catastrophic fire and the loss of life (Saveland 1985).

Wildfire suppression falls under the management of designated suppression teams based on established, interagency protocols. These teams make decisions on basic strategies of fire suppression (e.g., containment versus property protection) and a host of tactical questions such as the use of backfires, the types of equipment used (aerial/ground), and type and source of personnel (agency versus local). The many strategic and tactical decisions involved in managing a large wildland fire open the door for communities to second-guess the decisions of the fire-suppression team, particularly when life and property are affected. Thus, while firefighters are often praised for their valiant efforts to protect local property, considerable controversy can also develop over how the fire was managed and policy factors that contributed to the catastrophe in the first place (Carroll et al. 2005; Kumagai et al. 2004a, 2004b).

Horlick-Jones (1995) suggests that disasters often contain elements of a release of anxiety set off by the perception of a betrayal of trust by contemporary institutions. Kumagai (2004a, 2004b) studied blaming behavior in wildland-fire settings, suggesting that under some circumstances, people tend to make oversimplified causal attributions about what caused the damage to their homes and communities from wildland fires. As a result of this causal attribution, people blame the responsible fire officials for events that are beyond those officials' power to control or for things that they simply did not do. It is important to note that the specific triggers of faulty causal attributions have yet to be fully identified and that it can be difficult to make a distinction between irrational or unfair blaming and legitimate differences of opinion about causes of fire damage and appropriate firefighting in some situations.

There is evidence for general public support for flexible fire-suppression policies (e.g., contain and control, allow to burn), yet there is a general expectation for firefighters to put out any fire quickly regardless of training, equipment, or policy (Burnset al. 2003; Cortneret al. 1990). The expectation that a firefighter is a firefighter is a firefighter (as opposed to distinguishing between structural firefighters and wildland firefighters) appears to contribute to frustration when federal firefighters are not stationed in residential areas or are perceived as "standing around doing nothing" while houses burn (Carroll et al. 2005; Graham 2003; Kumagai et al.2004b). That these firefighters lack the training and mandate to fight structure fires does not mean much to homeowners during a wildfire. Local residents and firefighters in particular may become frustrated by what they perceive as the lack of effective use of local knowledge and local resources in fighting fires, particularly in the critical early phases (Burns et al. 2003; Carroll et al. 2005; Carroll et al. 2000; Graham 2003; Kumagai et al. 2004a; Rodriguez-Mendez et al. 2003; Taylor et al. 2005).[1]

Hiring, buying, and leasing

Public facilities such as schools and community centers are often utilized for evacuation shelters and other facilities, such as playing fields, fair grounds, parks, pastures, or range land, are used for fire camps and staging areas. Equipment, supply, and lodging purchases, vehicle and land leases, and off-duty spending by firefighters all have an impact on the local economy of a community near a fire. Project fires require the mobilization and equipping of fire crews, including National Guard and Army troops, as well as finding places to feed and house them.

Research addressing economic impacts from wildfire focuses on short-term disruptions to a community or region and long-term impacts on the timber market, health, tourism, and property values, as well as suppression costs, relief expenditures, and property damage (Butry et al. 2001; Prestemon et al. 2001). It is difficult to obtain data to measure economic impacts from wildfire such as lost wages, quality of life, and landscape restoration and rehabilitation (Butry et al. 2001) and there is even less information about specific practices, such as local hiring and contracting, how such decisions are made, and whether there are ways to do this that are minimally disruptive and lessen the often negative differential economic impacts in affected communities.

While overall the positive impacts from government purchasing and leasing may equal or exceed losses from other sectors, these are differential impacts and some sectors or individuals end up as winners and others as losers. For example, the fires of 2000 virtually shut down the tourism and outfitting and guiding businesses in Montana (Laverty and Hartzell 2001). Recreation, tourism, and travel businesses suffered in the communities affected by the Missionary Ridge and Hayman fires in Colorado and there were concerns that some types of recreation, such as fishing and camping, would take many years to recover due to the resource impacts from the fire (Burns et al. 2003; Graham 2003). Tourism in northeast Florida dropped after extensive fires in 1998 (Butry et al. 2001). Hesseln et al. (2003, 2004) found that the extent and size of wildfires and prescribed burns affected recreational use demand on national forests in New Mexico and Montana, respectively.

Non-governmental assistance organizations

The best known of the governmental and quasi-governmental organizations that arrive while the fire is burning to help with community recovery are FEMA, Red Cross, and the Salvation Army. However, nongovernmental organizations also play a role in assistance and recovery and are often perceived more favorably (Carroll et al. 2005; Paul 1999). Some of these groups are associated with churches, and others are initiated under FEMA auspices, while still others are truly grassroots organizations that spring up to handle the influx of donations sent in response to the disaster. Although the amount of assistance and how fast it arrives is important to the recovery process (Paul 1999), local assistance groups and volunteer efforts are a key component in community coping and recovery, and reach high-risk or underserved populations that the national organizations may not (Rosse 1993).

Wilson and Oyola-Yemaiel (1998) described two types of post-disaster assistance groups. Locally formed assistance groups or emergent coordinative groups connect neglected or underserved groups with recovery resources. So-called interstitial groups coordinate services and pool resources among existing organizations (see Bates and Harvey 1978; Peacock 1991). These groups are most likely to form after large-magnitude disasters in which social and institutional structures are severely disrupted.

After the Oakland Hills (California) firestorm in 1991, Hoffman (1999) documented the arrival of assistance organizations as well as the emergence of self-help community groups. The emergence of locally created and staffed recovery organizations was also documented after the Hayman (Graham 2003), Rodeo-Chediski (Carroll et al. 2005), the Bitterroot Valley (Idaho: Halvorson 2002), and the 2003 southern California (California Fires Coordination Group 2004) fires. Both emergent and outside-assistance groups were considered to be an important part of the post-fire recovery process after the Hayman andRodeo-Chediski fires, and the California wildfires of 2003 (Carroll et al. 2005; California Fires Coordination Group 2004; Graham 2003; Taylor et al. 2005). The Hayman Forest Fire Victims Task Force and the Heber-Overgaard (Arizona) Community Recovery Team served as collectors for outside donations and focused their distribution of these funds to underserved groups, i.e., those with no or inadequate insurance who did not qualify for other assistance programs (Carroll et al. 2005; Graham 2003).

Existing organizations and networks (e.g., social services) may also adapt their mission and services to post-disaster needs (Wilson and Oyola-Yemaiel 1998). During and after the East Bay Hill (California) fire, nonprofit social service organizations provided health and social services to victims, and public health agencies provided counseling and assistance to emergency personnel, hospitals, and schools, and also provided community organization help and education programs (Gordon and Maida 1992).

Despite the ability of outside assistance groups to enhance community recovery, they can also complicate community recovery (Hoffman 1999). This is most likely to happen when the ideas and actions of outside groups conflict with those of emergent self-help groups, which rely on existing social and cultural institutions and networks to build local recovery organizations. Other obstacles that may affect both local and outside groups include lack of coordination between agencies, informing the public about the services and service centers, staffing problems, (including too many volunteers in some places and not enough in others), and difficulty reaching underserved populations (Gordon and Maida 1992).

Impacts and Consequences of Fire Events

Agencies make many decisions during a fire event that hold possible consequences, both positive and negative, for communities. These consequences occur at a variety of scales, but again, little research has been conducted to assess these consequences. The evaluation of decisions during the cycle of a fire event is a fundamental component of a constructive, adaptive, learning environment. Investments in loss-prevention or mitigation measures for community protection can be considerable, and comprehensive auditing of the costs and benefits of common management tools will determine the extent of their long-term application.

Social science has tended to focus on understanding the consequences of fire in the human domain; these consequences occur at the household, neighborhood, community, and institutional scales (McCool et al. 2006) . While many consequences are immediate, others are displaced temporally. Still other consequences occur at different organizational levels.

There are obvious biophysical factors influencing the scale of wildland-fire consequences, such as the intensity and size of a fire, the location of the fire with reference to human communities, weather conditions, and fuel availability. There are also sociodemographic factors, or the social composition of a particular community, that may well influence impacts. For example a community inhabited by longtime rural residents might have more collective experience with fire and how to deal with it than one consisting of more recent arrivals. While we do not wish to minimize the importance of biophysical and sociodemographic influences, our attention here is on the sociocultural dynamics inherent in interactions between fire and human communities. Specifically, we focus on the impacts fire events have on the day-to-day lives of people who live in fire-affected communities. Our focus extends beyond the physical event of the fire itself and extends to the impacts of and reactions to decisions made by fire-suppression teams, law enforcement officers, emergency management officials, and even other residents in the midst of the event.

Individual level impacts

Mortality is the ultimate individual impact of a fire event. In this category we focus on deaths of community members, rather than those of firefighters (which is a separate, albeit very important, topic). The Oakland Hills fire (1991) and the California wildfires of 2003 claimed twenty-five and twenty-four lives, respectively, and over two hundred people (firefighters and residents) were injured in the latter fires (California Fires Coordination Group 2004). A post-burn flash flood from the Aspen (Arizona) fire killed one person and damaged three homes (Schaffner 2003) and sixteen people died in post-fire flooding and mudslides resulting from the southern California wildfires of 2003 (California Fires Coordination Group 2004).

Suppression tactics and the availability of fire-suppression resources in any fire situation may affect the extent of loss or damage to home and property or increased smoke production. These, combined with the stress associated with the evacuation process, may affect mortality, and physical and mental health. For example, Carroll and Cohn (2003) and Graham (2003) cited the opinions of local health officials and community leaders in Arizona and Colorado that a small number (not specified) of elderly people had died prematurely in the wake of large fire events, presumably as the result of stress and disorder in their lives during and after the fires. Beyond morbidity, Graham (2003) cited interview evidence that elderly people appeared to suffer disproportionately more stress, anxiety, and depression from the fire event than other age groups in the study area of the Hayman fire. Halvorson (2002) noted similar findings in the wake of the Bitterroot Valley fires of 2000. Residents with preexisting cardiopulmonary and respiratory conditions suffered greater effects from smoke (Mott et al. 2002) and health officials noted widespread respiratory irritation and discomfort as a result of wildfire smoke (Graham 2003; Halvorson 2002; Sorensen et al. 1999).

Interviews with social service providers and mental health professionals revealed a dramatically increased need for short-term mental health services in communities affected by fires (Carroll et al. 2005; Graham 2003). In a smaller number of cases, the fire events appeared to trigger or exacerbate more serious longer-term emotional problems (Graham 2003). In recent catastrophic fires, virtually all residents who experienced the fire events in question experienced some level of psychological stress (Burns et al. 2003; Carroll et al. 2000; Graham 2003; Halvorson 2002). Various mental health problems including "jumpiness," sleep disturbance, trouble concentrating, general lethargy, and loss of appetite were reported by Maida et al. (1989) after the Baldwin Hills (California) fire.

Family-level impacts
Short of the death or severe disabling of a family member, the loss of a home is perhaps the most dramatic impact a fire can have on the life of a family. Some of the more notable losses include over fifty homes in the Bitterroot Valley fires (Halvorson 2002), 340 in the 1998 Florida fires (Butry et al. 2001), 280 in the Cerro Grande (New Mexico) fire (U.S. General Aaccounting Office 2003), 333 in the Aspen fire (USDA Forest Service 2003a), and several hundred buildings each in the Hayman and Rodeo-Chediski fires (Carroll et al. 2005; Graham 2003). California wildfires have produced the heaviest losses: one thousand homes in the 1993 Laguna/Malibu fires; over thirty-two hundred homes in the 1991 Oakland Hills fire; and 3,361 homes (fifteen thousand structures in all) in the California wildfires of 2003 (California Fires Coordination Group 2004).

Residents who lost homes in wildfires reported that documenting their losses for insurance purposes was a significant burden both from an emotional and time perspective. They also reported a wide range of experiences with their insurance companies in terms of recovering lost equity. Some reported "coming out pretty well" financially while others reported significant losses of equity due to underinsurance (Burns et al. 2003; Graham 2003; Hoffman 1999). Anecdotal reports indicate that similar problems are occurring in southern California in the wake of 2003 wildfires (California Department of Insurance 2004). The federal government assumed responsibility for damages from the Cerro Grande fire (2000), and was still processing claims as of 2003 (U.S. General Accounting Office 2003).

Neighborhood-level impacts
In the case of the Wenatchee (Washington) fires, Carroll et al. (2000) also found that emotional impacts of fire events tended to be distributed at the neighborhood level because the fires affected some neighborhoods and spared others. A similar dynamic was described by Hoffman (1999, p144) for victims of the 1991 Oakland Hills fire: "... survivors develop a divergence from those unharmed around them, and vice versa. We in Oakland soon found that our sentiments and actions were so foreign to those 'unsinged' surrounding us ..."

Social group-level impacts

Wildfires have provided the basis for extending and, in some cases, amplifying preexisting disagreements and conflict over federal forest management between those advocating active forest management and those arguing for environmental protection (Burns et al. 2003; Carroll et al. 2005; Carroll et al. 2000; Graham 2003; Halvorson 2002). The rhetoric on both sides tends to oversimplify the real cause of the fire events, with each side emphasizing those aspects of the causation of such fires that are consonant with their worldviews (Burns et al. 2003; Kumagai et al. 2004a, 2004b).

Carroll et al. (2005) and Graham (2003) noted that some of those who had lost property, wages, or business income due to wildfires were in a better position than others to absorb or replace the loss. For example, many homeowners have replacement insurance, fewer renters do. Homeowners can choose to rebuild homes or not, whereas renters interviewed stated they had fewer options, particularly in areas where rental property is scarce. Those with seasonal jobs tended to suffer more income loss than those with year-round jobs as did those with tourism/recreation-dependent jobs.

Community-level impacts

The disaster literature documents the presence of a therapeutic community or "pulling together" in the wake of a natural disaster as residents reach out to help each other and those in need, especially during and immediately after the event. This is also evident after fires (Carroll et al. 2005, Carroll et al. 2000; Graham 2003; Hoffman 1999). The disaster literature also documents cases in which natural or human-caused disasters result in conflicts within communities, which may go on for years after the event (see Erikson 1976; Kroll-Smith and Couch 1990). Thus far, the literature on the impact of fire has yet to document this level of internal community conflict. Neighborhood-to-neighborhood tension was documented by Carroll et al. (2000) on the Wenatchee fires of 1994 and on the Oakland Hills fire by Hoffman (1999). Cultural tension arose between some non-tribal local residents and the White Mountain Apache tribe and the local office of Bureau of Indian Affairs over the ignition and early suppression efforts on the Rodeo fire (Carroll et al. 2005). Some internal community tension and conflict, such as that between residents who wished to continue to focus blame on the individual who allegedly started the Chediski fire and those who wanted to "move on" (Carroll et al. 2005) and that internal to local volunteer fire departments over how to respond to decisions and actions of the federal Type One incident-command team (Carroll et al. 2005; Graham 2003; Kumagai et al. 2004b; Rodriguez-Mendez et al. 2003) has also been documented. With the notable exception of extreme cases (Erikson 1976), post-disaster conflict does not drastically change the community in the long term (Quarantelli and Dynes 1976).

Specific business sectors appear to suffer disproportional impacts from fire events (Burns et al. 2003; Carroll et al.2005; Carroll et al. 2000; California Fires Coordination Group 2004; Graham 2003; Halvorson 2002). Among these were seasonal businesses, businesses with perishable stock such as local nurseries, agricultural businesses, and businesses that relied on seasonal tourist dollars. County officials in Colorado, following the Hayman fire, were concerned over the loss of property tax revenues that would be felt most acutely by the local fire districts (Graham 2003). Carroll et al. (2005) also reported the loss of community-owned physical infrastructure in the form of a local fire station in the Rodeo-Chediski fires. There was also widespread concern over damage to municipal watersheds and local infrastructure (Burns et al. 2003; Graham 2003) and local flooding in areas affected by the Hayman (Graham 2003), Rodeo-Chediski (Carroll et al. 2005), Buffalo Creek (Colorado: Benight & Harper 1997), the Bitterroot Valley (Halvorson 2002), and the 2003 southern California fires (California Fires Coordination Group 2004). Pima County (Arizona) issued flood warnings after the Aspen fire (Pima County 2003).

Local public-safety infrastructure is pushed beyond existing limits by large fire events, especially two-way radio, phone, and cell phone capacity (Bender 2003; Carroll et al. 2005; Graham 2003). Other needs include training in wildfire suppression for firefighters trained primarily in structure protection (Graham 2003; National Association of State Foresters 2003; State of California 2004) and a faster pre-fire federal-inspection and certification process for locally available firefighting equipment and operators such as bulldozers and water trucks (Carroll et al. 2000; Graham 2003).

Another community issue is the overlap/underlap and lack of coordination of helping resources in fire-affected communities. In several cases the underlap problem for fire victims with short-term needs was partially addressed by the emergence of local groups to help underserved local residents (Carroll et al. 2005; California Fires Coordination Group 2004; Graham 2003; Halvorson 2002).

Cross-cutting impacts
Some community impacts of fire cut across the levels of organization noted above. One of these is the loss or transformation of place as the result of a fire event (Burns et al. 2003; Halvorson 2002). For example, interviewees reported that at first they could not recognize the exact site where their houses had been when they were brought back into their burned neighborhoods (Carroll and Cohn 2003). A similar impact is that on locally

based recreation. Wildfires have damaged or destroyed the favorite hunting, hiking, or camping spots of local residents (Burns et al. 2003; Graham 2003; USDA Forest Service 2003b). Interviewees talked about losing these favorite areas and the fact that such spots would "never be the same again" (Burns et al. 2003; Graham 2003). Another type of impact was mentioned by WUI residents: although homes, infrastructure, and other physical items can be rebuilt after a fire, the social infrastructure is not so easily reconstructed (Burns et al. 2003). Such losses can be felt at the level of the individual, the family, the neighborhood, and the community, depending on the scale of the particular fire in a given location.

Conclusion

This review clearly demonstrates that the community/social impacts of fire events are complex and are often expressed differently at different levels of social organization. Now that we are coming to understand that fire events are inevitable in many inhabited North American landscapes, preparations to reduce the potential for disruptive or even lethal consequences will require attention at multiple levels. Throughout the life cycle of fire events, both agency and community-level decisions can influence the extent and intensity of the impacts of wildfire. The current salience of the fire issue in the public eye provides a valuable opportunity for community and agency leaders to adopt more strategic and systematic approaches to organizing people for a common goal of accommodating fire events with minimal losses and disruption.

The focus of this discussion has been on the impacts from events and processes that occur during fires. It goes without saying that a systematic understanding of fire/community impacts requires an integrated understanding of community dynamics before, during, and after fire events. Nonetheless, there is value in dissecting each stage in the fire-event life cycle as a route to a more integrated understanding of the entire event. Our review has identified what we believe to be a number of inherent or more or less inevitable processes and events that emerge in and around communities during major wildfire events. However, it does not follow that because events and processes are inevitable that particular outcomes are pre-ordained. A logical step in this area of research is to identify key decision points and key actors or occupants of key roles whose specific decisions can substantively affect outcomes of such events for communities (McCool et al. 2006).

Space does not permit a full exploration of this topic, but a couple of examples may be illustrative. One common theme from the literature on large fire events is the difficulty in federal/local radio communications because of a lack of adequate and cross-jurisdictionally compatible radio equipment. Although a strain on radio equipment is likely inevitable in any major fire event, investing across governmental levels in compatible radio equipment would seem to be a logical step for communities and counties planning for emergency preparedness. Solving this problem would require both federal and local actors working in advance of any given fire event.

Another example is the frequently cited disconnect in fire information provision/needs during fire emergencies. Public information officers on large fires tend to focus on the technical aspects of the fire and firefighting progress (fire intensity, number of miles of fireline, numbers of personnel and equipment, acreage burned). Residents want accurate, timely, and place-based information (where is the fire in relation to my neighborhood and my house? has my house burned? and when can I return?). Internet-based geospatial technology resources (e.g., real-time GIS, satellite imagery) provide the neighborhood and street level of detail residents want.

Much has been written about the new reality of a need for security preparedness in a post-September 11 and post-Hurricane Katrina world. We would propose that fire presents an analogous situation for interface communities. The better question is often no longer if a fire event occurs, but when. Given this premise, we argue that an understanding of the processes and events inherent during fires is critical. Further, we suggest that within such an understanding, planners and decision makers should focus on the decision points where they can affect the outcomes important to communities. The few days during a fire event can have an effect on community/agency relationships for years, making advance planning for and thoughtful decision making during fire events an important undertaking.

NOTES

1. This is a particularly complicated issue worthy of a publication unto itself. Considerations include the advanced certification of local equipment and firefighters, the safety of federal and local firefighters, and the federal firefighting mandate that delegates structure protection to other agencies.

REFERENCES

Agee, J. K. 1994. *Fire and weather disturbances in terrestrial ecosystems of the eastern Cascades.* Portland, Oregon, USDA Forest Service. Pacific Northwest Research Station, General Technical Report PNW -320.

———, and S. Allison-Bunnell. 2002. *Flames in Our Forest: Disaster or Renewal?* Washington, D.C.: Island Press.

———, and C. E. Fiedler. 2005. *Mimicking Nature's Fire: Restoring Fire-prone Forests in the West.* Washington, D.C.: Island Press.

Bates, F., and C. Harvey. 1978. *Structure of Social Systems.* New York: John Wiley & Sons.

Beebe, G. S., and P. N. Omi. 1993. "Wildland burning: The perception of risk." *Journal of Forestry* 91(9): 19-24.

Bender, D. 2003. *The impacts of a major wildfire on the sheriff's office: What to expect when the circus comes to town.* Unpublished report. Durango, Colorado: La Plata County Sheriff's Office.

Benight, C. C., E. Gruntfest, and K. Sparks. 2004. "Colorado wildfires 2002." Available at http://www.colorado.edu/hazards/qr/qr167/qr167.pdf.

———, and M. L. Harper. 1997. "Buffalo Creek fire and flood report." Available at http://www.colorado.edu/hazards/qr/qr96.html.

Bonnickson, T. M., and R. G. Lee 1979. "Persistence of a fire exclusion policy in southern California: A biosocial interpretation." *Journal of Environmental Management* 8(3): 277-93.

Burns, S., M. Porter-Norton, M. Mosher, and T. Richard. 2003. "People and fire in Western Colorado: Focus group attitudes, beliefs, opinions, and desires regarding wildfire in the wildland-urban interface of Colorado's Westslope." Available at http://ocs.fortlewis.edu/peopleandfire_final.pdf.

Butry, D. T., E. D. Mercer, J. P. Prestemon, J. M. Pye, and T. P. Holmes. 2001. "What is the price of catastrophic wildfire?" *Journal of Forestry* 99(11): 9-17.

California Department of Insurance. 2004. "Insurance commissioner John Garamendi calls on legislature to protect homeowners in aftermath of devastating southern California wildfires." Available at http://www.fema.gov/pdf/library/draft_cfcg_report_0204.pdf.

California Fires Coordination Group. 2004. "The California Fires Coordination Group Report to the Secretary of Homeland Security." Available at http://www.fema.gov/pdf/library/draft_cfcg_report_0204.pdf.

Carroll, M. S., and P. J. Cohn 2003. *Inductive case study for Rodeo-Chediski Fire, Apache-Sitgreaves National Forests.* Report prepared for the USDA Forest Service, Apache-Sitgreaves National Forests, Report No. RFQ R3-01-02-60. Pullman, Washington: Washington State University.

———, P .J. Cohn, D. N. Seesholtz, and L. L. Higgins. 2005. "Fire as a galvanizing and fragmenting influence on communities: The case of the Rodeo-Chediski fire." *Society and Natural Resources* 18(4): 301-20.

———, A. J. Findley, K. A. Blatner, S. Rodriguez-Mendez, S. E. Daniels, and G. B. Walker. 2000. *Social assessment for the Wenatchee National Forest wildfires of 1994 targeted analysis for the Leavenworth, Entiat, and Chelan Ranger Districts.* Portland, Oregon, USDA Forest Service. General Technical Report PNW-479.

Cohn, P. J., M. S. Carroll, and Y. Kumagai. 2006. "Evacuation behavior during wildfires: Results of three case studies." *Western Journal of Applied Forestry* 21(1): 39-48.

Cortner, H. J., P. D. Gardner, and J. G. Taylor. 1990. "Fire hazards at the urban-wildland interface: What the public expects." *Environmental Management* 14(1): 57-62.

Drabek, T. E. 1994. *Disaster evacuation and the tourist industry.* Program on Environment and Behavior Monograph No. 57. Boulder, Colorado: University of Colorado Institute of Behavioral Science.

Erikson, K. T. 1976. "Loss of communality at Buffalo Creek." *American Journal of Psychiatry* 133(3): 302-5.

Gordon, N. S., and C. A. Maida. 1992. *The immediate community response to disaster: The East Bay Hills fire.* Quick Response Research Report No. 51. Boulder, Colorado: University of Colorado Natural Hazards Research and Applications Information Center.

Graham, R. (ed). 2003. *Hayman Fire case study.* Ogden, Utah, USDA Forest Service Rocky Mountain Research Station. General Technical Report RMRS-114.

Halvorson, S. J. 2002. "The fires of 2000: Community response and recovery in the Bitterroot Valley, Western Montana." Available at http://www.colorado. edu/hazards/qr/qr151/qr151.html.

Heath, S. 2001. "Human and pet-related risk factors for household evacuation failure during a natural disaster." *American Journal of Epidemiology* 153(7): 659-65.

Hessburg, P. F., and J. K. Agee. 2003. "An environmental narrative of Inland Northwest United States forests, 1800-2000." *Forest Ecology and Management* 178(1-2): 23-59.

Hesseln, H., J. B. Loomis, A. González-Cabán, and S. Alexander. 2003. "Wildfire effects on hiking and biking demand in New Mexico: A travel cost study." *Journal of Environmental Management* 69(4): 359-68.

———, J. B. Loomis, and A. González-Cabán. 2004. "The effects of fire on recreation demand in Montana." *Western Journal of Applied Forestry* 19(1): 47-53.

Hoffman, S. M. 1999. "The worst of times, the best of times: Toward a model of cultural response to disaster." In: A. Oliver-Smith and S. M. Hoffman (eds.), *The Angry Earth: Disaster in Anthropological Perspective.* New York: Routledge, 134-55.

Horlick-Jones, T. 1995. "Modern disasters as outrage and betrayal." *International Journal of Mass Emergencies and Disasters* 13(3): 305-15.

Kroll-Smith, J. S., and S. R. Couch. 1990. *The Real Disaster is Above Ground: A Mine Fire and Social Conflict.* Lexington, Kentucky: University of Kentucky Press.

Kumagai, Y., J. C. Bliss, S. E. Daniels, and M. S. Carroll. 2004a. "Real-time research on causal attribution of wildfire: An exploratory multiple methods approach." *Society and Natural Resources* 17(2): 113-27.

———, S. E. Daniels, M. S. Carroll, J. C. Bliss, and J. E. Edwards. 2004b. "Causal reasoning processes of people affected by wildfire: Implications for agency-community Interactions and communication strategies." *Western Journal of Applied Forestry* 19(3):184-94.

Laverty, L., and T. Hartzell. 2001. "A report to the President in response to the wildfires of 2000: Managing the impact of wildfires on communities and the environment." September 8, 2000. Available at http://www.fireplan.gov/reports/8-20-en.pdf.

Maida, C. A., N. S. Gordon, A. Steinberg, and G. Gordon. 1989. "Psychosocial impacts of disasters: Victims of the Baldwin Hills fire." *Journal of Traumatic Stress* 2(1): 37-48.

McCool, S. F., D. R. Williams, J. A. Burchfield, and M. S. Carroll. 2006. "An event driven model of the effects of wildland fire on communities: A potential framework for research, management, and understanding." *Environmental Management* 37(4): 437-50.

———, D. Williams, M. Carroll, and T. Ubben. 2006. *Social science to improve fuels management: Impacts of wildland fires on communities.* General Technical Report NC-269. St. Paul, Minnesota: USDA Forest Service, North Central Research Station.

Mott, J. A., P. Meyer., D. Mannino, and S. C. Redd. 2002. "Wildland forest fire smoke: Health effects and intervention evaluation, Hoopa, California, 1999." *Western Journal of Medicine* 176(3): 157-62.

National Association of State Foresters. 2003. *The changing role and needs of local, rural and volunteer fire departments in the wildland-urban interface. Recommended actions for implementing the 10-year comprehensive strategy. An assessment and report to Congress.* June 30, 2003. Available at http://www.stateforesters.org/pubs/Final%20Rural%20Fire%20Report.pdf.

National Interagency Fire Center. 2001. "Review and update of the 1995 Federal Wildland Fire Management Policy." Available at http://www.nifc.gov/fire_policy/index.htm.

Paul, B. K. 1999. "Flash flooding in Kansas: A study of emergency response and victims' perceptions." Available at http://www.colorado.edu/hazards/qr/qr118.html.

Peacock, W. G. 1991. "In search of social structure." *Sociological Inquiry* 61(3): 281-98.

Perry, R. W. 1994. "A model of evacuation compliance behavior." In: R. R. Dynes and K. J. Tierney (eds.), *Disasters, Collective Behavior and Social Organization.* Newark: University of Delaware Press, 85-98.

Pima County. 2003. "Pima County Aspen Fire recovery, Pima County Public Works flood warning information, July 15, 2003." Available at http://www.aspenfirerecovery.org/Flood.htm.

Prestemon, J. P., J. M. Pye, and T. P. Holmes. 2001. "Timber economics of natural catastrophes." Available at http://www.srs.fs.usda.gov/econ/pubs/misc/jpp011.pdf.

Quarantelli, E. L. 1996. "Local mass media operations in disasters in the USA." *Disaster Prevention and Management* 5(5): 5-10.

———. 1997. "Problematical aspects of the information/communication revolution for disaster planning and research: Ten non-technical issues and questions." *Disaster Prevention and Management* 6(2):94-106.

———, and R. R. Dynes. 1976. "Community conflict: Its absence and its presence in natural disasters." *Mass Emergencies* 1:139-52.

Riad, J. K., F. H. Norrris, and R. B. Ruback. 1999. "Predicting evacuation in two major disasters: Risk perception, social influence, and access to resources." *Journal of Applied Social Psychology* 29(5): 918-34.

Rodriguez-Mendez, S., M. S. Carroll, K. A. Blatner, A. J. Findley, G. B. Walker, and S. E. Daniels. 2003. "Smoke on the hill: A comparative study of wildfire and two communities." *Western Journal of Applied Forestry* 18(1): 60-70.

Rosse, W. L. 1993. "Volunteers and post-disaster recovery: A call for community self-sufficiency." *Social Behavior and Personality* 8(5): 261-66.

Saveland, J. M. 1985. "Risk in fire management." In: J. N. Long (ed.), *Fire management: The challenge of protection and use.* Proceedings of a symposium. Logan, Utah: Department of Forest Resources, Utah State University, 85-97.

Schaffner, M. 2003. "The Campo Bonito Wash flash flood of August 14, 2003: A heavy rain event on a recent burn." Available at http://www.wrh.noaa.gov/wrhq/03TAs/0310/.

Smith, C. 1992. *Media and Apocalypse: News Coverage of the Yellowstone Forest Fires, Exxon Valdez Oil Spill, and Loma Prieta Earthquake.* Westport, Connecticut: Greenwood Publishing Group.

———. 1995. "Fire issues and communication by the media." In: J. K. Brown, R. W. Mutch, C. W. Spoon, and R. H. Wakimoto (eds.), *Proceedings of a symposium on fire in wilderness and park management.* Ogden, Utah, USDA Forest Service Intermountain Research Station, General Technical Report INT-320: 65-69.

Sorensen, B., M. Fuss, Z. Mulla, W. Bigler, S. Wiersma, and R. Hopkins. 1999. "Surveillance of morbidity during wildfires-Central Florida, 1998." *Morbidity and Mortality Weekly Report* 48(4): 78-79.

State of California. 2004. "Governor's Blue Ribbon Fire Commission: Report to the Governor." Available at http://www.oes.ca.gov/Operational/OESHome. nsf/PDF/BlueRibbonReporttoGov/$file/BlueRibbonRept.pdf.

Taylor, J. G., E. H. Carpenter, H. J. Cortner, and D. A Cleaves. 1988. "Risk perception and behavioral context: U.S. Forest Service fire management professionals." *Society and Natural Resources* 1(3): 253-68.

———, S. C. Gillette, R. W. Hodgson and J. K. Downing. 2005. *Communicating with wildland interface communities during wildfire.* Open File report 2005-1061. Fort Collins, Colorado: U.S. Geological Survey, Fort Collins Science Center.

Tierney, K.J., M.K. Lindell, and R.W. Perry. 2001. *Facing the Unexpected: Disaster Preparedness and Response in the United States.* Washington, D.C: Joseph Henry Press.

USDA Forest Service. 2003a. "Aspen Fire archival site." Available at http://www. fs.fed.us/r3/coronado/aspen/index.html.

———. 2003b. "Biscuit Fire final assessment." Available at http://www.biscuitfire. com/final_exe_summ.htm.

U.S. General Accounting Office. 1999. *Federal wildfire activities: Issues needing attention.* GAO/RCED-99-282. Washington, D.C.: U.S. Government Printing Office.

———. 2003. "FEMA Cerro Grande claims: Payments properly processed, but reporting could be improved." Available at http://www.gao.gov/index.html.

Wilson, J., and A. Oyola-Yemaiel. 1998. "Emergent coordinative groups and women's response roles in the central Florida tornado disaster." Available at http://www.colorado.edu/hazards/qr/qr110/qr110.html

Community Impacts of Large Wildfire Events: Consequences of Actions After the Fire

James Burchfield

Introduction

Although wildfire has historically provided the vehicle for forest formation and transformation in the western United States (Agee 1996; DeBano et al. 1998; Pyne 1982), the frequency of very large, forest-based wildfires has increased over the past two decades (Arno and Allison-Bunnell 2002). Lingering drought and increased fuel accumulations have been major contributors to this shift, along with other factors such as prior land use practices and insect infestations (USDA Forest Service 2003). In recent years, residents of rural, suburban, and exurban communities embedded in these fire-adapted ecosystems are being forced to respond to the multiple consequences of wildfires, even though people and agencies have not been well equipped to address these disturbance events in the wildland interface in the past (Cortner and Gale 1990). Current trends point to an unabated rise in human populations moving into these western ecosystems (Bradshaw 1987; Johnson and Fuguitt 2000), elevating the profile of wildfire risks and fomenting a political urgency for remedial actions.

This paper reviews the current literature on the consequences to human communities of a recent wildfire event, and it utilizes a three-dimensional framework of biophysical, social-demographic, and social-cultural impacts to describe the complexities of the wildfire phenomenon. Evident in this review is the paucity of research on the impacts of fire on human communities, arguing for a much more energized research agenda to understand how people may cope with this inevitable and frequently unwelcome summer visitor to their neighborhoods and communities. However, our current understanding points to a few important lessons for resource managers:

(1) Continuing population growth in the interior West will burden agencies to supply wildfire rehabilitation and recovery. The situation will become ever more complex, and attention to coordination and efficiency will be vital.

James Burchfield, College of Forestry and Conservation, University of Montana
(james.burchfield@umontana.edu)

(2) Opportunities for management innovation, land use regulation, and institutional change within the wildland interface are highest in the aftermath of wildfires, since the salience of the event diminishes quickly and people will return to business as usual.

(3) Community-level recovery from a wildfire is difficult to predict in the highly heterogeneous network of western communities. Fires affect exurban neighborhoods more directly than whole communities.

A few central concepts that have emerged from the literature on natural disasters will permeate any evaluation of post-fire responses. As Drabek (1986) observes, post-impact consequences of natural disasters fall within discernable time periods: there is an "emergency action" post-impact period; a reconstruction/restoration phase that includes rebuilding and rehabilitation; and a mitigation phase that extends until the next event. As time passes after the disaster, the conspicuousness of the event diminishes, and people's behaviors revert to patterns closer to pre-disaster levels (Drabek 1986; Passerini 2000). Quarantelli and Dynes (1976) compiled over one hundred field studies of disasters, observing changes in levels of community conflict and norms in post-disaster time periods. During the immediate post-impact, or "emergency," period, there is a relative absence of community conflict, as people pull together to address pressing needs. Latent or new conflicts may emerge, however, in the reconstruction and mitigation phases, based on a series of variables such as the cause of the disaster, the behavior of disaster-management agencies, or inequities that may result from recovery efforts. Thus, the awareness and solidarity that emerge immediately after a disaster are fragile. With respect to wildfires, this diminishing salience presents a difficult challenge to those wishing to reduce future risks, since the long-term costs to citizens to mitigate the impacts of future events is high and their incentives are low (see Daniel, this volume). However, there are cases, such as after the Oakland Hills fire in California in 1993, where a proportion of residents adopt significant changes in residential behaviors because of a fire event (Gordon and Maida 1992; Greenlee 1992).

The location, scale, and intensity of a fire event also present influential variables in human responses. A small fire in a remote wilderness may not evoke an emphatic public reaction, whereas the Yellowstone fires of 1988 and the southern California wildfires in October 2003 mobilized national attention (after all, the Monday Night Football game had to be moved from San Diego to Arizona). Repeated occurrences of disasters or inevitable future threats also precipitate action (Sims and Baumann 1983). Birkland (1996) found that dramatic, highly publicized disasters can lead to sweeping policy changes. The political shakeup in the aftermath of Hurricane Katrina in the fall of 2005 presents the most evident example of this phenomenon.

Wildfire has become a dominant issue in forest management in the western United States. With the passage of the Healthy Forest Restoration Act in late 2003 (spurred through the Senate after the southern California wildfires that same fall), agencies such as the Forest Service are actively engaging community representatives and other partners through important cooperative planning efforts such as Community Wildfire Protection Plans. A greater understanding of human responses to fire will offer valuable insights to the generation of sound public policies that provide protections for the health and safety of citizens while advancing additional public goals for sustaining healthy, productive forest ecosystems.

Biophysical Consequences

There is a vast literature on the impact of fire on the forest ecosystem and how it serves as a primary vector for forest regeneration, the establishment of forest species, the creation/recreation of forest structure, and the maintenance of forest habitat conditions for wildlife species. Examples include Agee (1996), DeBano et al. (1998), and Whelan (1995). Far less available are scholarly treatments that examine the interactions of fire with human communities, although historian Stephen Pyne has provided useful overviews of the role of fire in human cultural development (Pyne 1982, 1997; Pyne et al. 1996). That fire affects soils and watershed stability are two obvious biophysical consequences that will be addressed briefly below, yet the scope of this review does not allow treatment of the majority of biophysical issues. Suffice it to say that substantial research will continue on areas important to human interests such as the invasion of exotic species into burned areas, the effect of burn intensity on soil productivity and nutrient exchange, the maintenance of biological diversity via fire influence on vegetative patch dynamics, and the effects of fire on habitats of wildlife preferred by people, such as game or rare species. A particularly controversial aspect of the biophysical response to fire is the disposition of standing dead trees left after fires, which are frequently the target of social demands for "salvage" utilization to capture wood volume before degradation by insects and/or fungal decay agents. The impacts of timber salvage operations on biophysical characteristics are highly varied and poorly understood. Reviews of salvage harvesting after major wildfires or other disturbances (Lindenmayeret al. 2004; Robinson and Zappieri 1999) demonstrate the potential for poorly designed salvage operations to diminish structural and ecosystem complexity, as well as the potential of well-designed operations to restore important lost structural attributes in burned forest plantations via mimicry of natural fire disturbances.

The impacts of fires on forest soils and watersheds remain an important concern for managers, ecologists, and residents who strive to understand the role of fire in nutrient cycling, erosion, forest productivity, and water budgets. Literature surveys on the effects of wildfires on soils and watershed processes (Certini 2005; Ice et al. 2004) emphasize the significance of fire severity (its intensity and duration) on overall watershed impacts. For the first year after a fire, infiltration rates are reduced because of the formation of water-repellent (hydrophobic) soils, allowing very rapid surface runoff and the potential for flash floods. The vegetative recovery of the site greatly decreases this surface runoff, and within two years this hydrophobicity is typically gone. Of more serious concern to communities are mass failures and debris flows, caused by a major storm event and exacerbated by the absence of strong, living roots for the first five to ten years after a fire (Wondzell and King 2003). Major rain events or rain-on-snow events can trigger landslides and/or mudflows that move with such speed and power as to be life threatening. The degree of mass soil movement depends on a variety of factors, including burn severity, rainfall intensity, slope percentage, and parent material, with erosion greatest in granitic and sedimentary soils (Brooks et al. 1997). The most critical factor for communities downslope from a major wildfire is the occurrence of a major storm event during the first year or two after a fire, which can cause either flash flooding or debris flows (Wondzell and King 2003).

Stabilization of watersheds is the primary objective of special Burned Area Emergency Rehabilitation (BAER) teams that are assigned to fire events as the last step in wildfire-incident management. BAER teams perform the following functions: hillslope treatments, including mulching, seeding, contour felled logs, contour trenching, slash spreading, and the placement of sediment traps (frequently with straw "waddles" that slow or capture surface runoff); channel treatments that include straw-bale check dams, log check dams, and rock and gabion dams; and road treatments, including culvert upgrades, trash racks/storm panels, drain dips, and waterbars. Robichaud et al. (2000) completed a comprehensive evaluation of the effectiveness of BAER team post-fire treatments, and found the amount of protection provided by any one of these treatments to be small, though over $48 million was expended on these efforts over the past decade. Hillslope treatments appeared most effective in terms of costs/benefits, while road treatments, although highly significant in terms of watershed stabilization, are often cost prohibitive to implement.

Sociodemographic Consequences

The abrupt change in physical appearance of a forest immediately after a wildfire can affect people greatly, as the blackened ground and standing dead trees present chilling reminders of the destructive capabilities of wildfires. When looking at nearby burned landscapes, residents described the loss of the forest in terms of emotional suffering (Halvorson 2000), and the transformation of the pleasing colors and textures of forests to undifferentiated expanses of bare hillsides reduced the aesthetic qualities of the landscape (Kaplan et al. 1998). Although flushes of grasses and forbs after fires are evident quite soon after rains in burned areas, long-term vegetative recovery can last decades, depending on site conditions and fire intensity (Miller et al. 2000). In terms of aesthetic appreciation, Taylor and Daniel (1984) found less acceptability for more severely burned areas than lightly burned areas, yet there is limited research on the thresholds of scenic recovery from revegetation that make post-fire areas as acceptable as unburned areas. Anecdotal evidence from contact with realtors in the Bitterroot Valley (Idaho) indicate that recently blackened acres are undesirable to newcomers purchasing land ("If the land is burned, it just won't sell," Erickson 2004, personal communication). Yet in general, housing prices in the intermountain western region most affected by fires over the last decade are not diminishing (Office of Federal Housing Enterprise Oversight 2004). In counties experiencing relatively rapid growth, such as Missoula County, Montana, even the repeated fires in this county in 2000, 2002, and 2003 have not slowed the growth of home prices in the exurban environment (Missoula Association of Realtors 2004).

Typically, only a small proportion of a county will burn in a given year and relatively few residents will be evacuated or directly affected by the footprint of fires. However, the potential for fire to return to the county is very high, and fires cause, at a minimum, widespread indirect impacts from smoke and suppression operations. Even though the frequency of large wildfires in the West has been widely reported in national media and the risk of fire in the wildland interface has been noted in numerous public outlets, wildfires are not a sufficient deterrent to overcome the forces of western development that Riebsame (2000) and other demographers (Johnson and Fuguitt 2000; Masnick 2001) have identified as significant attractants to a mobile population. This behavior mirrors the findings of Wright (1979) in his study of the demographic consequences of natural disasters in the decade of 1960-1970, and he concludes "there are no discernable effects of the natural disaster events occurring in that period which materially altered population and housing growth trends" (p 27).

Table 1 identifies five of the largest fires since 1987 (National Interagency Fire Center 2004), the acres burned, and the change in county populations from 1980; in all cases, whether in Montana, California, or Idaho, inmigration to fire-adapted ecosystems continues unabated. Unfortunately, these data on population do not capture second-home developments, which create even more extensive pressure on western landscapes; nor is it known whether fire damage to areas adjacent to second homes drives seasonal visitors to other locations or affects decisions to rebuild a second home after a wildfire.

One other sociodemographic consequence of fire deserves attention—wildfire's effect on economic values. Burtry et al. (2001) calculated the costs of the 1998 Florida fires as close to $700 million, mainly from losses of timber and infrastructure on property (personal health-care costs from these fires were low). The traditional rationale for fire suppression in many parts of the United States has been as investment protection, and in some cases (as in the Florida example) these suppression costs may be justified. However, fire suppression in areas where there are limited private infrastructure or timber values raises legitimate questions on the rationale for significant suppression expenditures. The costs for firefighting continue to rise as fires become more extensive, suppression technologies become more sophisticated, and fire-suppression leaders increase priority actions for firefighter safety. Hesseln (2001) argues for a fundamental restructuring of federal fire-management programs to address both inefficiencies and the cost and benefits of suppression.

Table 1. Population Change Before and After Large Fires

County and State	Fire name	Acres burned	Year burned	Population 1980	1990	2000	2002 (est.)
Toulumne, CA	Siege of '87	640,000	1987	33,928	48,456	54,501	55,850
Fremont, ID	Yellowstone	1,585,000	1988	10,813	10,937	11,819	11,859
Lewis & Clark, MT	Canyon Creek	250,000	1988	43,039	47,495	55,716	56,554
Elmore, ID	Foothills	257,000	1992	21,565	21,205	29,130	29,481
Ravalli, MT	Bitterroot	510,000	2000	22,493	25,010	36,070	37,868

Source: US Census Bureau 2004

Sociocultural Consequences

After the smoke clears people are affected both psychologically and socially by fire events, and throughout the stages of recovery, different types of responses occur at individual, community, and agency levels.

The trauma of overcoming a fire event affects individual community members along multiple gradients, including those relating to previous experience with fire, the types of impacts the fires had on their lives and properties, and the degree of control perceived by residents during the event (Kumagai et al. 2004). After a fire experience people exhibit new levels of awareness about the risks and seriousness of fire threats (Abt et al. 1991). However, these levels of awareness are not necessarily associated with an individual's actual risk exposure, but can also depend on other value-affecting variables such as length of residency, age cohort, and experience with community-based risk amelioration (Baxter et al. 1992). Not surprisingly, psychological recovery from fires is also tied to an individual's capacity to handle stress, and coping self-efficacy measures can help predict individuals' ability to recovery from this type of trauma (Benight and Harper 1997). Post-fire stresses can also last years after the event, as studies from the 1983 Australian brushfires (McFarlane 1990; McFarlane and Papay 1992) and the East Bay Hills fire in Oakland, California (Koopman et al. 1997) demonstrate.

Dealing with the stress of wildfires can also change people's impressions of the cause of fire damages. In a study of two fires in California, Kumagai et al. (2004) demonstrate that those without information or contact with fire-suppression staff tend to blame human agents for fire damages (for example, when backfires are utilized in fire suppression), whereas others with more contact with firefighters and knowledge of the fire perceive greater control, and thus attribute damages to natural causes instead of human failings. Control over one's decisions during a fire may also affect the interpretation and recovery from the event. Crouse (2002) observes higher occurrence of Post Traumatic Stress Disorder among those residents who remain in place during a fire, uncertain about their potential evacuation, while those who are evacuated possess an assurance of their immediate safety and the predictability of their near-term situation.

Halvorson's (2002) study of the consequences of the 2000 fires in Montana's Bitterroot Valley indicates an immediate period of grieving among returning residents. The author reinforces findings from other disaster research (for example, the work of Beggs et al. (1996) following the consequences of Hurricane Andrew) of the importance of strong, extensive community-level networks to speed and facilitate the recovery process.

Community responses to fire are not uniform across all individuals or households (Carroll et al. 2000; Rodriguez-Mendez et al. 2003). Factors such as attitudes toward forest management, pre-existing social conflicts, and residents' worldviews may affect their interpretation and responses to fires. Rubin (1985) emphasizes the role of leadership and governance in mollifying the differential impacts of a disaster, since effective administration can defend and respect other social values such as equity and timeliness. Community responses are also affected by established attitudes toward those agencies responsible for both land management and fire suppression. If dominant land management agencies like the Forest Service are viewed as irresponsible land stewards, then post-fire actions require more than fire-damage mitigation, and should include actions to re-establish trust and public confidence in general land management practices, such as vegetation management, that affect fire behaviors. The strengthening of public trust in agencies is as much a function of process as results (Dryzek 2000; Forester 1999; Shindler et al. 1999), and implies a far more participatory approach to land use decision making (including fire and fuel management) than has been practiced in the past.

The recent work of Carroll et al. (2005) on community-level recovery from large wildfires supports other findings in the disaster literature on the cohering effect of the event during emergency recovery operations and the potentially centripetal effects of the reconstruction/restoration phases (Drabek 1986; Quarantelli and Dynes 1976). During Arizona's Rodeo-Chediksi fire of 2002 and in the immediate post-fire stage, the authors observed that these major fires had a "galvanizing" impact on the affected communities, drawing diverse groups together to protect community infrastructure and activating cooperative behavior to provide necessary services. After the emergency stages of recovery passed, however, other conflicts that had been embedded within the community emerged over inequities in the delivery of community resources allocated to recovery. Old cultural tensions between affected groups (here, the White Mountain Apaches and Anglo-American Arizonans) were sharpened by the experience of the fire. As mitigation efforts progressed in these Arizona communities, some new partnerships developed to generate long-term improvements in forest conditions and residential preparedness. Yet old-standing rancor remained between elements of timber-harvesting interests and the environmental community. Conflict and cohesion within communities affected by fires can emerge at different times and for different purposes, but they tend to coexist throughout all post-fire phases.

Agency roles during both the emergency and longer-term reconstruction/ restoration recovery periods can be highly influential in guiding the healing process for communities (Daniels et al. 1996; Duncan 1997).

Clarity of communication and transparency of agency decision processes, especially those decisions regarding the allocation of scarce resources, can advance recovery and reduce the potential for misinformation that could lead to frustration and fragmentation. The prior establishment of trusted relationships between local leaders and land management staff reduces the potential for friction in these communications, and the pre-fire "social foundation" described earlier by Jakes and Nelson (this volume) establishes the necessary links to address conflict openly. An established agency capacity to work across institutional boundaries also helps mobilize critical community-level volunteer services after a fire, since many of these volunteer services, such as transportation, may require agency conduits for efficient delivery. Community-level organizations provide a vital legitimacy and awareness of local needs for both restoration recovery and longer-term mitigation actions (Burns et al. 2003; Cortner and Gale 1990; Halvorson 2002). The combination of agency and volunteer networks can help avoid misdirected interventions.

Coordination and integration among different organizational actors involved in recovery speed the process and lead to more sustained progress in the mitigation and subsequent preparations for additional events (Monday 2002). Recent major wildfires in the west and financial incentives emerging from the federal government's National Fire Plan are stimulating widespread efforts to improve local coordination before, during, and after fires, especially through the development and circulation of Community Wildfire Protection Plans. After a series of fires in Montana's Bitterroot Valley during the years 2000-2003, the local Resource Conservation and Development Area produced a widely circulated guidebook for citizens that identified federal, state, and local agency programs and services to assist residents after a fire event. Community recovery requires multiple inputs, such as the restoration of utilities, financial and technical assistance to businesses and homeowners, and infrastructure repair. Sustainable long-term mitigation will be enhanced if community/agency cooperation considers elements of residential quality of life, local economic vitality, social and intergenerational equity, improvements to environmental quality, and open and fair processes for community-level preparations for future disaster events (Monday 2002).

The capacity for community-level institutions to manage the post-fire crisis and to address inevitable conflicts effectively may well rest on latent abilities for a community to respond to change. This "community capacity" has been the subject of an intense sociological discourse over the past decade, and numerous observers have identified the contributions of social and human capital as foundational to smooth community transitions to new circumstances (Beckley 1995; Harris et al. 2000; Kusel 1996). Post-disaster recovery is a process affected by both institutional capabilities and the quality of administration (Rubin 1985), so organizational abilities and predispositions to work cooperatively may foster a more broadly acceptable restoration/reconstruction period. Elevated levels of community capacity may also help stimulate a collaborative learning strategy for fire recovery, an approach employed by Daniels et al. (1996) after the 1994 fires near Wenatchee, Washington. Their work focused on clear, tangible steps to improve the post fire situation and define feasible levels of change. Participants in this process expressed an increased sensitivity to views other than their own regarding recovery and a willingness to cooperate for mutual progress.

Opportunities for institutional changes or land use planning modification are highest in the aftermath of a large fire, since the event elevates pubic awareness of risk and the potential for regulatory remediation (Abt et al. 1991; Burby et al. 2000). Since advance planning can reduce fire hazard (Rice 1991), the reconstruction phase provides new public incentives to adopt more stringent codes for housing developments, redraw protective zone boundaries, or consider zoning opportunities. Because homeowner actions can be critical in affecting structural loss (Cohen 2000), county- or community-level guidelines may also be promulgated to encourage building materials and landscape designs to improve structural survivability. The track record on the ability of communities to make these changes is mixed. Although the conditions for progress in land use planning may be ripe because of heightened awareness, significant barriers to land use change, such as private property interests, may supercede reform even after a disaster (Irwin 1987). Further, although it seems logical for local governments to encourage land use restrictions or other active measures to mitigate the potential risks of wildfires, they have few political incentives to advance the highly charged decisions for development restraint (Davis 2001).

Other sociocultural factors, such as the type and intensity of human uses of public forests, can create other post-fire tensions at the community level. For example, the release of nutrients and the change in water availability on the forest floor after a fire generate highly favorable conditions for the growth of desirable mushroom species, and the first warm days of spring attract legions of mushroom pickers to burned areas (Rinella 2002). These mushroom pickers compete for harvest territories, and local residents may feel they have been excluded from opportunities to gather mushrooms for their own use. Similarly, road or area closures that occur after fires can exclude community members from traditional uses and amplify existing controversies over access opportunities to public lands. Area closures also have a negative effect on the business opportunities for outfitting and guide services whose clients have expectations for unfettered access to their favorite sites.

The change in landscape characteristics after a fire, such as forest structure and appearance, influences the desirability of many forest uses. The emotional attachments of forest users to places within the forests are based in past memories and events (Williams et al. 1992), and a change in aesthetic or instrumental qualities may alter this attachment. The speed of natural post-fire recovery also affects recreation demands on public lands. Taylor (1990) discusses both short- and long-term impacts of wildfire on recreational use and observes that highly severe fires discourage the acceptability of several common recreational activities, such as camping and hiking. Englin et al. (2001) monitored post-fire use by recreationists in three western states and discovered an immediate pulse of use by non-motorized users immediately after a fire, attracted by the openness and novelty of the immediate post-fire landscape. Recreation use then dropped off for the subsequent seventeen years, only to gradually recover as vegetation returned. Hesseln et al. (2003) and Loomis et al. (2001) recognized somewhat similar findings of a temporal drop-off in recreation use, although there were enough contradictions between the results to suggest that recreation values after fires might vary across different states and regions. Hesseln (2003) and colleagues concluded that predictions about changes in recreational demand from fires should not be broadly applied.

Conclusion

Research to date indicates that wildfire recovery parallels other natural disasters in terms of a staged process: emergency recovery, reconstruction/ restoration, and mitigation. Fires have the potential to serve as catalysts for social change, although lessons from other disasters are sufficiently mixed to be inconclusive. Sometimes "therapeutic communities" emerge in recurrent disaster types, such as floods and tornadoes (Perry and Lindell 1978). However, Passerini (2000) argues that social contextual variables are more significant in driving community mobilization, regardless of disaster type or periodicity, and McCaffrey and Kumagai (this volume) highlight the importance of variables such as salience, knowledge, risk perception, and experience as influential in community responses. Levels of economic opportunity and social or human capital also might play crucial roles in community responses. The ability of a community to respond smoothly to near pre-fire status is not guaranteed. Other disaster research even reminds us of unusual cases, like the Buffalo Creek flood in West Virginia in 1972, in which a disaster can tear apart the tenuous working associations, or "axes of variation," along which rural culture is constructed (Erickson 1976).

It is difficult to draw firm conclusions on the community-level impact of fires, since modern western communities are highly variable and difficult to categorize (Brick 2000; Riebsame 2000). Fires affect exurban "neighborhoods" more directly than whole communities, since much western development emerges as amalgams of housing clusters associated with topographically driven road systems. Fires may also have highly variable consequences for individuals, depending on the situation and the psychological disposition of the affected party. For some residents of the wildland-urban interface, a fire that destroys their "dream" house or the view from their retirement home can be devastating, or the trauma surrounding the recurrent smoke and uncertainty can cause lingering psychological problems. For others, fire may be a transformative event creating new opportunities. For example, a resident who lost his house in San Diego in 2003 received generous insurance payments and now finds himself financially "free and clear" (Franklin 2004). The specific context of an individual's predisposition to stress and the relative level of impact of a fire (the "singed" versus "unsinged" as described in Carroll and Cohn, this volume) can be decisive in terms of an individual's recovery.

The interactions among biophysical, sociodemographic, and sociocultural variables make the assessment of community-level impacts after a fire dependent on specific circumstances. The level of preparedness of a community toward fire events, as well as the amount of social cohesion and social capital can be highly influential in the manner in which a community may recover. These variables are in turn affected by the rate of community change in sociodemographic characteristics, including considerations such as the speed of in-migration and emerging economic opportunities. Variation in traditional use patterns of forests across different communities cause predictions about fire impact on forest use to be more regionally specific than generalizable. The integration and coordination among volunteer organizations and the general relationship between community-level institutions and the agencies responsible for fire suppression will also affect community recovery and the ability to move beyond the immediate losses into a more sophisticated, comprehensive mitigation phase.

This review has identified the nested layers of complexity affecting community responses to fire, and it recognizes the importance of an active and multidisciplinary research agenda to address the many gaps in our understanding. Since wildfires are here to stay and the human population will continue to expand into these fire-prone areas, there is a need for focused, longitudinal studies that examine pre-, during-, and post-fire conditions across an array of affected communities. Armed with the knowledge of the range of community responses to fire and the relative significance of factors affecting these responses, public sector agencies can better design community-based fire-management programs to help residents adapt to this dynamic environment.

REFERENCES

Abt, R. C., M. K. Kuypers, and J. B. Whitson. 1991. "Perception of fire danger and wildland/urban policies after wildfire." In: S. C. Nodvin, T. A. Waldrop (eds.), *Fire and the environment: Ecological and cultural perspectives; proceeding of an international symposium;* 1990 March 20-24, Knoxville, Tennessee. Asheville, North Carolina, USDA Forest Service. General Technical Report SE-69: 257-262.

Agee, J. K. 1996. *Fire Ecology of Pacific Northwest Forests.* Washington, D.C.: Island Press.

Arno, S. F., and S. Allison-Bunnel. 2002. *Flames in Our Forest: Disaster or Renewal?* Washington, D.C.: Island Press.

Baxter, J., J. Eyles, and D. Willms. 1992. "The Hagersville tire fire: Interpreting risk through a qualitative research design." *Qualitative Health Research* 2(2): 208-37.

Beckley, T. M. 1995. "Community stability and the relationship between economic and social well-being in forest dependent communities." *Society and Natural Resources* 8(3): 261-66.

Beggs, J. J., V. A. Haines, and J. S. Hurlbert. 1996. "The effects of personal network and local community contexts on the receipt of formal aid during disaster recovery." *International Journal of Mass Emergencies and Disasters* 14(1): 57-78.

Benight, C. C. and M. L. Harper. 1997. *Buffalo Creek fire and flood report.* Quick response report QR96. Boulder, Colorado: Natural Hazards Research and Applications Information Center, University of Colorado.

Birkland, T. 1996. "Natural disasters as focusing events: Policy communities and political response." *International Journal of Mass Emergencies and Disasters* 14(2): 221-43.

Bradshaw, T. D. 1987. "The intrusion of human population into forest and range lands of California." *Proceedings of the Symposium on Wildland Fire 2000,* April 27-30, 1987, South Lake Tahoe, California. Berkeley, California, USDA Forest Service General Technical Report PSW-101: 15-21.

Brick, P. 2000. "Of imposters, optimists, and kings: Finding a political niche for collaborative conservation." In: P. Brick, D. Snow, and S. Van De Wetering (eds.), *Across the Great Divide: Exploration in Collaborative Conservation and the American West.* Washington, D.C.: Island Press, 172-79.

Brooks, K. N., P. F. Ffolliott, H. M. Gregersen, and L. F. DeBano. 1997. *Hydrology and the Management of Watersheds* (2nd ed.). Ames: Iowa State University Press.

Burby, R., R. Deyle, D. Godschalk, and R. Olshanksy. 2000. "Creating hazard resilient communities through land-use planning." *National Hazards Review* 1(2): 99-106.

Burns, S., M. Portner-Norton, M. Mosher, and T. Richard. 2003. *People and fire in Western Colorado: Focus group attitudes, beliefs, opinions, and desires regarding wildfire in the wildland-urban interface of Colorados' west slope: A working report.* Durango, Colorado: Office of Community Services, Fort Lewis College.

Burtry, D. T., E. D. Mercer, J. P. Prestemon, J. M. Pye, and T. P. Holmes. 2001. "What is the price of catastrophic wildfire?" *Journal of Forestry* 99(11): 9-17.

Carroll, M. S., A. J. Findley, K. A. Blatner, S. Rodriguez-Mendez, S. E. Daniels, and G. B. Walker. 2000. *Social assessment for the Wenatchee National forest wildfires of 1994: Targeted analysis for the Leavenworth, Entiat, and Chelan Ranger Districts*. Portland, Oregon: USDA Forest Service. General Technical Report PNW-479.

———, P. Cohn, D. Seesholtz, and L. Higgins. 2005. "Fire as a galvanizing influence on communities: The case of the Rodeo-Chediski fire." *Society and Natural Resources* 18(4): 301-20.

Certini, G. 2005. "Effects of fire on properties of forest soils: A review." *Oecologia* 143 (1): 1-10.

Cohen, J. D. 2000. "Preventing disaster: Home ignitability in the wildland-urban interface." *Journal of Forestry* 98(3): 15-21.

Cortner, H. J. and R. D. Gale. 1990. "People, fire, and wildland environments." *Population and Environment: A Journal of Interdisciplinary Studies* 11(4): 245-57.

Crouse, E. M. 2002. *Prolonged disaster and the effects of uncertainty: The Montana wildfires*. Masters Thesis, University of Montana, Missoula.

Daniels, S. E., G. B. Walker, M. S. Carroll, and K. A. Blatner. 1996. "Using collaborative learning in fire recovery planning." *Journal of Forestry* 94(8): 4-9.

Davis, C. 2001. "The West in flames: The intergovernmental politics of wildfire suppression and prevention." *Publius: The Journal of Federalism* 31(3): 97-110.

DeBano, L. F., D. G. Nealy, and P. F. Ffolliott. 1998. *Fire Effects on Ecosystems*. New York: John Wiley.

Drabek, T. E. 1986. *Human System Responses to Disaster: An Inventory of Sociological Findings*. New York: Springer-Verlag.

Dryzek, J. 2000. *Deliberative Democracy and Beyond: Liberals, Critics, and Conversations*. New York: Oxford University Press.

Duncan, F. 1997. "How a community heals: lessons learned from Buffalo Creek." *Fire Management Notes* 57(3): 11-14.

Englin, J., J. Loomis, and A. González-Cabán. 2001. "The dynamic path of recreational values following a forest fire: A comparative analysis of states in the intermountain west." *Canadian Journal of Forest Research* 31(10): 1837-44.

Erickson, D. 2004. Donna Erickson, Realtor, Montana Westgate Realty, Hamilton, Montana. Personal communication, May 26.

Erickson, K. 1976. *Everything in its Path: Destruction of Community in the Buffalo Creek Flood*. New York: Simon and Shuster.

Forester, J. 1999. *The Deliberative Practitioner: Encouraging Participatory Planning Processes*. Cambridge, Massachusetts: MIT Press.

Franklin, M. B. 2004. "After the fire, I'm starting over free and clear." *Kiplinger's Personal Finance* 58(4): 116.

Gordon, N. S., and C. A. Maida. 1992. *The immediate community response to disaster: The East Bay Hills fire*. Quick response report, QR51. Boulder, Colorado: Natural Hazards Research and Applications Information Center, University of Colorado.

Greenlee, J. M. 1992. "Oakland, California faces the beast-again." *International Bulletin Wildland Fire* 1(1): 8-10.

Halvorson, S. 2002. *The fires of 2000: Community response and recovery in the Bitterroot Valley, Western Montana*. Quick response report, QR151. Natural Hazards Research and Applications Information center, University of Colorado. Boulder.

Harris, C., W. McLaughlin, G. Brown, and D. Becker. 2000. *Rural communities in the Inland Northwest: An assessment of small rural communities in the Interior and Upper Columbia River Basins.* Portland, Oregon: USDA Forest Service. General Technical Report PNW-477.

Hesseln, H. 2001. "Refinancing and restructuring federal fire management." *Journal of Forestry* 99(11): 4-8.

———, J. Loomis, and A. González-Cabán. 2003. "The effects of fire on hiking demand: A travel cost study of Colorado and Montana." In: P. Omi, L. Joyce (eds.), *Fire, fuel treatments, and ecological restoration: Conference proceedings;* 2002 16-18 April; Fort Collins, Colorado. Fort Collins, Colorado: USDA Forest Service. Proceedings RMRS-P-29: 177-86.

Ice, G., D. Neary, and P. Adams. 2004. "Effects of wildfire on soils and watershed processes." *Journal of Forestry* 102(6): 16-20.

Irwin, R. L. 1987. "Local planning considerations for the wildland-structural intermix in the year 2000." In: J. E. Davis and R. B. Martin (eds.), *Proceedings of the Symposium on Wildland Fire 2000,* April 27-30, 1987, South Lake Tahoe, California. Berkeley, California, USDA Forest Service General Technical Report PSW-101: 38-46.

Johnson, K. M., and G. V. Fuguitt. 2000. "Community and change in rural migration patterns 1950-1995." *Rural Sociology* 65 (1): 27-49.

Kaplan, R., S. Kaplan, and R. L. Ryan. 1998. *With People in Mind: Design and Management of Everyday Nature.* Washington, D.C.: Island Press.

Koopman, C., C. Claussen, and D. Spiegel. 1997. "Multiple stressors following a disaster and dissociated symptoms." In: C. S. Fullerton and R. J. Ursano (eds.), *Post-traumatic Stress Disorder: Acute and Long-term Responses to Trauma and Disaster.* Washington, D.C.: American Psychiatric Press, 21-35.

Kumagai, Y., J. Bliss, S. Daniels, and M. Carroll. 2004. "Research on causal attribution of wildfire: An exploratory multiple-methods approach." *Society and Natural Resources* 17(2): 113-28.

Kusel, J. 1996. "Well-being in forest dependent communities, Part I: A new approach." In: University of California; SNEP Science Team and Special Consultants (eds.), *Sierra Nevada Ecosystem Project: Final report to Congress, Volume II, Assessments and scientific basis for management options.* Davis: University of California Centers for Water and Wildland Resources, 361-73.

Lindenmayer, D. B, D. R. Foster, J. F. Franklin, M. L. Hunter, R. F. Noss, F. A. Schmeigelow, and D. Perry. 2004. "Salvage harvesting practices after natural disturbance." *Science* 303 (5662): 1303.

Loomis, J., A. González-Cabán, and J. Englin. 2001. "Testing for differential effects of forest fires on hiking and mountain biking demand and benefits." *Journal of Agricultural Resource Economics* 26(2): 508-22.

McFarlane, A. C. 1990. "An Australian disaster: The 1993 bushfires." *International Journal of Mental Health* 19(2): 36-47.

———,. and P. Papay. 1992. "Multiple diagnoses in posttraumatic stress disorder in the victims of a natural disaster." *Journal of Nervous and Mental Disease* 180(8): 498-504.

Masnick, G. 2001. "America's shifting population: Understanding migration patterns in the West." *Changing Landscape* 2(2):8-15.

Miller, C., P. Landres, and P. Alaback. 2000. "Evaluating the risks and benefits of wildland fire at the landscape level." In: L. F. Neuenschwander and K. C. Ryan (eds.), *Crossing the Millennium: Integrating Spatial Technologies and Ecological Principles for a New Age in Fire Management.* Proceedings of the Joint Fire Sciences Conference and Workshop June 15-17 1999, Boise, Idaho. Boise, Idaho: National Interagency Fire Center, 78-87.

Missoula Association of Realtors. 2004. "General market information." Available at http://www.missoularealestate.com/index.php/fuseaction/market.trends.html. Accessed May 24, 2004.

Monday, J. L. 2002. "Building back better: Creating a sustainable community after a disaster." *Natural Hazards Informer* (1): 1-11.

National Interagency Fire Center. 2004. "Wildland fire statistics." Available at http://www.nifc.gov/stats/historicalstats.html. Accessed May 26, 2004.

Office of Federal Housing Enterprise Oversight. 2004. "House price index." Available at http://www.ofheo.gov/HPIRegion.asp?Formmode=Summary. Accessed August 12, 2004.

Passerini, E. 2000. "Disasters as agent of social change in recovery and reconstruction." *National Hazards Review* 1(2): 67-72.

Perry, R. W. and M. Lindell. 1978. "The psychological consequences of natural disaster: A review of research on American communities." *Mass Emergencies* 3: 105-15.

Pyne, S. J. 1982. *Fire in America: A Cultural History of Wildland and Rural Fire.* Princeton, New Jersey: Princeton University Press. Reprinted in paperback 1997. Seattle: University of Washington Press.

———. 1997. *World Fire: The Culture of Fire on Earth.* Seattle, Washington: University of Washington Press.

———, P. L. Andrews and R. D. Laven. 1996. *Introduction to Wildland Fire: Fire Management in the United States* (2nd ed.). New York: John Wiley and Sons.

Quarantelli, E. L., and R. R. Dynes 1976. "Community conflict: Its absence and its presence in natural disasters." *Mass Emergencies* 1: 139-52.

Rice, C. L. 1991. *Land-use planning may reduce fire damage in the urban-wildland intermix.* GTR-PSW-127. Berkeley, California: USDA Forest Service General Technical Report PSW-127.

Riebsame, W. E. 2000. "Geographies of the new West." In: P. Brick, D. Snow, and S. Van de Wetering (eds.), *Across the Great Divide: Explorations in Collaborative Conservation in the American West.* Washington, D.C.: Island Press.

Rinella, S. 2002. "Fungus rising." *New Yorker* 78(21): 30-32.

Robichaud, P. R., J. L. Beyers and D. G. Neary. 2000. *Evaluating the effectiveness of postfire rehabilitation treatments.* Fort Collins, Colorado, USDA Forest Service. General Technical Report RMRS-63.

Robinson, G., and J. Zappieri. 1999. "Conservation policy in time and space: Lessons from divergent salvage logging on public lands." *Conservation Ecology* [online] 3(1):3. Available at http://www.consecol.org/vol3/iss1/art3/.

Rodriguez-Mendez, S., M. S. Carroll, K. A. Blatner, A .J. Findley, G. B. Walker, and S. D. Daniels. 2003. "Smoke on the hill: A comparative study of wildfire and two communities." *Western Journal of Applied Forestry* 18(1): 60-70.

Rubin, C. B. 1985. "The community recovery process in the United States after a major natural disaster." *International Journal of Mass Emergencies and Disasters* 35(1): 9-28.

Shindler, B., K. A. Cheek, and G. Stankey. 1999. *Monitoring and evaluation citizen-agency interactions: A framework developed for adaptive management.* Portland, Oregon, USDA Forest Service. General Technical Report PNW-452.

Sims, J. H. and D. D. Baumann. 1983. "Educational programs and human response to natural hazards." *Environment and Behavior* 15(2): 165-89.

Taylor, J. 1990. Playing with fire: Effects of fire in the management of southwestern recreation resources." In: J. S. Krammis (ed.), *Effects of fire management in southwestern natural resources: Proceedings of the symposium,* November 15-17, 1988, Tucson, Arizona. Fort Collins, Colorado: USDA Forest Service. General Technical Report RM-191: 112-121.

————, and T. C. Daniel. 1984. "Prescribed fire: Public education and perception." *Journal of Forestry* 82(6): 361-65.

U.S. Census Bureau. 2004. "State and county QuickFacts." Available at http://quickfacts.census.gov/qfd/. Accessed May 26, 2004.

USDA Forest Service. 2003. "Wildland fire statistics." Available at http://www.nifc.gov/stats/wildfirestats.html. Accessed May 6, 2004.

Whelan, R. J. 1995. *Ecology of Fire*. London: Cambridge University Press.

Williams, D. R., M. E. Patterson, J. W. Roggenbuck, and A. E. Watson. 1992. "Beyond the community metaphor: Examining emotional and symbolic attachment to place." *Leisure Sciences* 14: 29-46.

Wondzell, S., and J. King. 2003. "Postfire erosional processes in the Pacific Northwest and Rocky Mountain regions." *Forest Ecology and Management* 178(1-2): 75-87.

Wright, J. 1979. *After the Clean-up: The Long Range Effects of Natural Disasters*. Beverly Hills, California: Sage Publications.

Section III
Socioeconomic and Institutional Factors

Cassandra Moseley

The first section of the book focused primarily on wildfire and individuals—how individuals perceive wildfire and other natural hazards—and the second section on communities—how local groups of people respond to the potential and reality of wildfire. This last section of the book turns to larger-scale analysis, focusing primarily on economic and political institutions. As a group, the authors in this section reveal how fire policy developed historically and how it is currently changing in the face of new ideas about interagency collaboration and adaptive management. We also learn from them about markets of fire suppression and fire-hazard reduction, and how public policy affects and is affected by these marketplaces.

Holmes and his co-authors examine the hazard insurance market and government disaster-assistance programs. Their concern is with the role that these two institutions might be playing in reducing the tendency for individuals to protect themselves against loss and increasing the likelihood that they will take more risk than they otherwise might. Only a few decades ago, federal disaster relief was rare; people relied on insurance or had to fend for themselves. The costs of natural disasters are increasing not because the number of natural hazards is increasing, but because people have been moving to high-hazard areas such as the hurricane-prone South, flood plains, and the fire-prone wildland-urban interface. People's willingness to move to these areas may be in part because insurance and government assistance limit their risk.

Rather than seeing the market as a concern, Becker and Viers want to see it as a solution to the problem of high fire hazard. They want to identify opportunities that the marketplace might offer to use fire-hazard reduction to create community economic-development opportunities. They are skeptical that public funds will provide the resources needed for all of the thinning required to adequately reduce fire hazard and restore fire-adapted ecosystems. They hope that markets can be developed for small-diameter material so as to reduce the costs of treatments and help them to become an economic-development opportunity. But, just as there are barriers to public

Cassandra Moseley, Ecosystem Workforce Program, University of Oregon (cmoseley@uoregon.edu)

funding for fire hazard, so too are there many institutional barriers in the marketplace: lack of consistent supply of material, value of material too low to pay for removal, and inadequate processing capacity if the material were to be removed.

Both Moseley in her chapter and Wise and Yoder in theirs move us away from economic towards political institutions. In the first part of her chapter, Moseley reviews the historical development of fire policy, finding that although there have been significant changes in fire policy driven by large-fire years, suppression has remained the predominate focus for a century. This is true even in the most recent policy shifts of the National Fire Plan. Although policy discussion has been on increasing coordination, hazard reduction, and the like, federal funding continues to be primarily for suppression. After this historical account, Moseley seeks to understand the distribution of costs and benefits of these policies of long-term suppression, and now mitigation, particularly among the businesses and workers involved in these activities. Although the literature is quite limited, she finds that both fire suppression and hazard reduction create economic opportunities. Those opportunities, however, are not equally distributed across ethnicities and communities. Rural communities, for example, face tough competition for fire-hazard reduction contracts from urban-based companies. And Hispanics are more likely to work in jobs with poor job quality than whites.

Wise and Yoder, also focused on fire policy, are most interested in identifying the ways in which fire policy is changing. They see increasing interagency coordination at a federal level and between the federal government and state agencies, the creation of monitoring and evaluation systems, and other components that might indicate a shift from a hierarchical to an adaptive management system.

Although the topics of these chapters are wide ranging and adequate research on key issues is, at times, in short supply, they make clear that both markets and public policy structure our society's relationships to wildfire. These relationships are grounded in history but are currently evolving. Some of the promises of recent policy changes such as the National Fire Plan and other programs remain just that—promises—hopeful signs but incomplete progress. Wise and Yoder find some movement towards adaptive management but Becker and Viers find mostly barriers to community development based on utilization of small-diameter trees. Moseley finds economic opportunity in fire suppression and increased hazard reduction but social inequities in how that opportunity is distributed. Holmes and his collaborators see insurance and disaster relief as creating perverse incentives but also find new flood-hazard programs that suggest models to help people change the ways they assess natural disaster risk.

Efficient and Equitable Design of Wildfire Mitigation Programs

Thomas P. Holmes, Karen L. Abt,
Robert J. Huggett, Jr., and Jeffrey P. Prestemon

Introduction

Natural resource economists have addressed the economic efficiency of expenditures on wildfire mitigation for nearly a century (Gorte and Gorte 1979). Beginning with the work of Sparhawk (1925), the theory of efficient wildfire mitigation developed along conceptual lines drawn from neoclassical economics. The objective of the traditional least-cost-plus-loss model is to minimize the sum of ex ante expenditures on fire prevention (pre-suppression), the costs of fire suppression, and the ex post costs of economic damages. In the closely related benefit/cost model, the objective is to maximize the sum of damages avoided (the benefits) minus pre-suppression and suppression costs. Both models assume that an increase in pre-suppression expenditures decreases suppression costs and economic damages (Figure 1).

A major obstacle impeding the empirical application of the theoretical model is that the specific functional relationship between costs and economic losses (or damages avoided) is generally unknown. This empirical problem arises because wildfires are dangerous, complex phenomena and experimental control plots, replicating the critical variables existing on burned areas, are almost never available. Thus, it has been extremely difficult to estimate what would have happened on an actual wildfire if pre-suppression and suppression expenditures had been applied at lower or higher levels. Empirical applications of the theoretical model have relied on other approaches such as simulation (Bellinger et al. 1983). Despite this limitation, the theoretical model has been extended to other problems in forest management, such as forest insect control (Herrick 1981), and theoretical refinements continue to be advocated (Donovan and Rideout 2003).

Thomas P. Holmes, USDA Forest Service, Southern Forest Research Station (tholmes@fs.fed.us); Karen L. Abt, Robert J. Huggett, Jr., Jeffrey P. Prestemon, USDA Forest Service, Southern Forest Research Station

Figure 1. An expanded wildfire economic model for use in the wildland-urban interface.

In this chapter, we examine a second, previously overlooked limitation with traditional microeconomic models of wildfire mitigation. This problem concerns the economic behavior of forest landowners and others living within forested areas referred to as the wildland-urban interface. Because the endpoint of the traditional economic model of wildfire mitigation is the value of timber protected (or lost), and because the frame of reference for the analysis is public forestland, the behavior of private forestland owners in response to wildfire-mitigation incentives has not been adequately addressed.

The rapid escalation of wildfire-suppression costs and financial damages over the past several years led to the National Fire Plan. The major change in federal wildland fire policy reflected in the plan was a shift from a reactive to a proactive approach that emphasizes community-based actions to reduce wildland fires (National Fire Plan 2001). Given this shift in emphasis, it is critical to understand the economic incentives faced by individuals and communities when they are asked to undertake wildfire-mitigation activities. More precisely, we argue that insurance compensation, disaster relief, and wildfire suppression reduce the incentives of homeowners to undertake individual or collective actions to mitigate wildfires (the leftward pointing arrows in Figure 1), and that the issue of who should pay for restoration of capital losses (private insurance, government-subsidized insurance, government disaster relief) does not enter the traditional model. These limitations need to be addressed.

To set the context for the remainder of the chapter, we first provide a historic overview of the development of market (insurance) and social (disaster assistance) responses to natural hazards. Next, we present evidence on the trends in costs and losses from wildfire over the past several decades. This evidence provides the motivation for the ensuing discussion of macroeconomic factors that have influenced the trends in costs and losses, as well as emerging equity impacts (who pays for economic losses). We finish with a summary of the issues and policy implications.

Development of Social and Market Responses to Natural Hazards

Since antiquity, humans have responded to natural hazards by creating cooperative arrangements to buffer themselves from losses (Kates 1971, McCall 1987). Oliver-Smith (1996) describes how people living in pre-industrial society adapted their behavior to natural disturbance patterns and developed social structures that increased their probability of survival. For example, traditional pastoralists in Africa made rational adaptations to cyclical droughts by creating "protective" social groups, engaging in livestock transfers with members of their group, and migrating with their herds (McCabe 1988). The transfer of livestock from members of the group with abundant cattle to those suffering livestock losses represents a primitive form of social insurance.

Formal markets for property insurance developed after the Great Fire of London in 1666, which destroyed about 80% of the city (Kovacs 2001). Property insurance works by creating a pool of contributions, known as "premia," from members, who can be compensated for contracted losses by the funds collected. This scheme works best where risks are randomly and independently distributed across members of the pool, and where annual losses to individual members are large relative to their assets, but collective losses are small relative to the size of the pool. The law of large numbers guarantees that the annual variation in average losses will decrease as the number of members of the pool increases, thus providing the insurance company with considerable control over annual payouts. Insurers realized from the Great Fire of London that contagion posed a threat to the insurability conditions, and thus required implementation of risk-reduction measures, such as improved building codes and close proximity to a fire brigade, in order to join the pool (Pyne 2001).

Natural catastrophes such as hurricanes, floods, and earthquakes have historically caused problems for the insurance industry because these events damage many or most properties within a geographical area. If risks are spatially correlated, insurance companies need to raise market rates above those that are actuarially fair in order to cover the "social risk" (Hirshleifer and Riley 1979). Under these conditions, consumers may decide not to purchase insurance because of budget constraints or the belief that "it can't happen to me" (Palm 2003). Where coverage is less than complete, some people remain financially exposed to natural disasters.

Because insurance coverage for natural hazards in the U.S. is less than complete, the federal government has stepped in to provide disaster relief. Although Congress passed the first piece of disaster legislation in

1803, comprehensive (as distinct from disaster-specific) legislation was not forthcoming until the Disaster Relief Act of 1950. During the past half-century, public attitudes toward natural disasters have shifted from fatalistic—disasters are a part of nature that is accepted as part of life—to viewing disaster assistance as an entitlement (Barnett 1999). This change is evidenced by the fact that the federal government provided only 1% of disaster relief in 1953 but more than 70% by the mid-1970s (Clary 1985).

In a bad wildfire year, the need for federal disaster assistance can be great. The California wildfires of 2003 burned over 750,000 acres and destroyed over 3,600 homes. Insured losses from these wildfires were close to $2 billion (Insurance Information Institute 2005). Because the demand for recovery funds was not completely met by private insurance, the federal government also provided over $483 million in disaster assistance, an amount equal to roughly 25% of the insured losses (California Fires Coordination Group 2004). Most of this federal relief was in the form of low-interest loans that the Small Business Administration provided.[1]

An increased level of concern with the escalation in federal disaster assistance has caused policymakers to emphasize the linkage between ex post disaster assistance and ex ante community mitigation activities. This shift in policy is characterized by the provisions of the National Flood Insurance Act of 1968, which requires residents of special flood-hazard areas to purchase flood insurance if financing for the property comes from a federal loan or grant or if funds come from an institution that is insured by the federal government (Palm 2003). Provision of flood insurance by the federal government is contingent upon communities undertaking actions that will mitigate potential flood damages.

Rising financial costs of climate- and weather-related disasters have caused unprecedented insurance industry losses and calls for a greater federal role in financing catastrophic relief (Nutter 2002). Insurance companies protect themselves from catastrophic losses, to some degree, by purchasing insurance from re-insurance companies. The re-insurance market attempts to diversify risks from natural catastrophes by pooling risks over large geographic areas, often including international markets. But the potential losses from natural hazards are often so large that the private sector, even supported by the re-insurance industry, has not been willing to shoulder the entire burden. Hence, government-led quasi-private insurance strategies have emerged as stop-gap measures, at the state and federal levels. Some states have created re-insurance pools for hurricane damage ("wind pools") that help keep rates lower in the private market. Another strategy is for states to create residual markets for homeowners in hurricane- or earthquake-prone locations who cannot obtain coverage in voluntary markets (Nutter 2002).

Floods cause more damage than any other natural hazard in the U.S. and account for the highest levels of federal disaster assistance in most years (Palm 2003). Within the market for private insurance, most insured losses from natural disasters result from hurricanes (33% of total), tornadoes (32% of total), and earthquakes (13%) (Insurance Information Institute 2005). Wildfires have only accounted for about 3% of total insured losses from natural hazards in the United States. Although typical homeowner fire-insurance policies cover losses from wildfires, concern over the rapid rise in insured losses due to wildfires has caused the insurance industry to require wildfire-mitigation activities as a precondition for insurance policies in some regions in California and the Southwest that are at especially high risk of wildfire losses.

Trends in Costs and Losses from Wildfires

Wildfire data obtained from the National Interagency Fire Center (2004) were plotted and a polynomial trend was fitted to the data (Figure 2). The data reveal an increasing trend in total acres burned by wildfire from 1980 to 2003. This rise follows a decreasing trend in total acres burned from 1960 to roughly 1980. The pattern has been partially attributed to a warming trend in the western U.S., causing the snowpack to melt earlier in the spring, and resulting in more severe drought conditions over much of the summer. Continued drought conditions in the western U.S. are anticipated for the foreseeable future (Strategic Issues Panel on Fire Suppression Costs 2004).

The upswing in the number of acres burned by wildfires is reflected in the trend in federal wildfire-suppression cost, adjusted for inflation (SU cost, Figure 2), particularly since 19822. In 1988, wildfire-suppression costs in the U.S. exceeded $1 billion for the first time. Since the year 2000, the billion-dollar level has been exceeded each year.

Although reliable information on the total financial damages from natural hazards is difficult to obtain, data are available on insured losses (Insurance Information Institute 2005). During the 1970s and 1980s, insured losses from catastrophic wildfires rarely exceeded $100 million (Table 1). However, the 1991 wildfires in Oakland Hills, California, destroyed nearly 3,200 homes (California Fires Coordination Group 2004) and caused about $2.3 billion in insured losses. This was the twentieth-most-costly insured loss ever recorded worldwide (Swiss Re 2004).

Since the 1970s and 1980s, insured losses from wildfires have dramatically increased and most catastrophic wildfires occurred in southern California, an area experiencing rapid population growth and escalating property values. This period of escalation in insured losses coincides with the period

Figure 2. U.S. wildfire history and federal wildfire suppression costs. Sources: NIFC 2004 and Strategic Issues Panel on Fire Suppression Costs 2004.

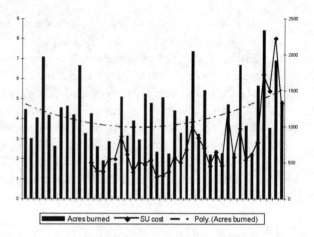

of escalation in wildfire-suppression expenditures, providing evidence that overall economic costs (the sum of costs plus losses) are also increasing.

Factors Influencing Increased Costs and Losses from Natural Disasters

We identify several micro- and macroeconomic factors that have contributed to the escalation in costs and losses resulting from natural hazards, including wildfires. Emerging trends in macroeconomic variables (migration, wealth, income, and housing prices) have been compounded by underlying microeconomic behaviors that reflect the incentives that people face when making risk-mitigation decisions. On the other hand, providing timely, believable information about natural-hazard risk helps individuals make rational economic decisions that reduce values at risk. We discuss each of these factors in turn.

Migration

The escalation in insured losses from natural events might suggest that the natural world is becoming increasingly violent. However, Changnon (2003) shows that the increasing trend of insured losses from catastrophic weather events disappears when loss data are adjusted for population levels and inflation. This leads him to conclude that "Human actions have in many ways caused the economic and environmental losses from natural disasters to become greater than years ago" (p. 287). If more people are migrating to areas that are at risk of natural disasters, such as hurricanes, earthquakes, and wildfires, and if these people are transferring and creating more wealth in these areas, then we would expect that economic losses would likewise increase, even if the rate of natural disasters is constant.

Table 1. Insured losses from catastrophic wildfires in the U.S., 1970-2003.

Year	Location	Insured losses ($millions 2003)
2003	San Diego and San Bernardino Counties, CA	2,035
2002	Rodeo-Chedeski Complex, AZ	123
2000	Cerro Grande, NM	150
1993	Los Angeles and Orange Counties, CA	923
1991	Oakland and Alameda Counties, CA	2,297
1990	Santa Barbara County, CA	373
1985	Florida	56
1982	Los Angeles, Ventura, and Orange Counties, CA	31
1980	Several Counties, Southern CA	132
1979	Hollywood Hills, CA	13
1978	Los Angeles and Ventura Counties, CA	42
1977	Santa Barbara, Montecito, CA	61
1970	Oakland-Berkley Hills, CA	118

Source: Insurance Information Institute 2005

Of particular relevance in the overall trend in losses due to natural disasters has been the migration to coastal areas, particularly in the southern and southeastern states, which are particularly prone to hurricanes. The National Oceanic and Atmospheric Administration reports that U.S. coastal areas experienced a population increase of 41% from 1960 to 1990, demonstrating a growth rate 3% higher than the nation as a whole (Ross & Lott 2003; U.S. Census Bureau 2004a)3. In total, 53% of the national population resides in coastal counties that account for 17% of the U.S. landmass (National Oceanic and Atmospheric Administration 1998).

Migration trends also appear to influence the escalation of economic costs and losses attributable to wildfires. Recent studies have shown that rural population growth in the U.S. has largely resulted from the attractiveness of natural environments, including forested areas (Deller et al. 2001; English et al. 2000). Johnson and Beale (1994) reported that, during the 1990s, the fastest-growing counties in the United States were nonmetropolitan counties that were destinations for retirement-age migrants or were outdoor-recreation centers.

Housing prices
A second factor contributing to the escalation in costs and losses attributable to natural hazards is the trend in housing prices. A rise in the general price level over time—inflation—increases the price of vulnerable human capital as the value of all goods and services rises. For example, from 1960 to 2000 the general price level rose by 482% (U.S. Department of Commerce 2002)[4].

Housing price inflation may be particularly acute in locations with favorable environmental amenities. English et al. (2000) found in a study of 1990 house values that the average house was worth nearly $13,000 more in tourism-dependent counties than in non-tourism counties. The scarcity of real property can result in higher at-risk values, as the price for land and housing is bid up in areas with desirable natural amenities. In most areas, the supply of available private land is nearly fixed, constrained by physical features and jurisdictional rules. Against a nearly fixed supply, rising demand due to increases in real wealth per capita and population create rapid property-value increases. Relatively rapid population growth in wildland-urban interface areas with attractive natural amenities combined with an increase in the real value of housing stock might reasonably explain much of the trend in increasing losses from wildfires.

Wealth and income

Wealth represents the accumulation of capital over time. Household wealth is created by savings from personal income after consumption expenditures and tax payments have been deducted. During the twentieth century, the household savings rate in the U.S. has been relatively stable at approximately 15-20% of disposable personal income, and the proportion of disposable personal income that is saved for retirement ("life-cycle saving") nearly tripled over the same period (Lee 2001). Investments in real estate are an important type of wealth accumulation and, during the period from 1945 to 1990, real-estate investments averaged about 4.4% per annum of disposable personal income (more than double the rate for the period 1897-1929) (Lee 2001). In the U.S., per capita incomes, adjusted for inflation, rose by 148% between 1960 and 2000 (U.S. Census Bureau 2004a, 2004b; U.S. Department of Commerce 2003). Thus, income growth and the accumulation of wealth through investment in real estate have placed an increasing amount of capital at risk of loss from natural hazards. This problem may be particularly acute for retirees who have migrated to the wildland-urban interface and invested life-cycle savings in real estate.

Although the overall trend in wealth has been upward in the U.S., over the past two decades income inequality has been increasing as well (Aghion et al. 1999). Chevan and Stokes (2000) argue that this trend may be due in part to the "McDonald's effect," whereby unionized, highly paid blue-collar jobs have been replaced by non-unionized lower-paying service jobs. Income inequality may be important in tourism-dependent communities within the wildland-urban interface because the tourism sector is dependent on service jobs. Although population growth has been rapid in tourism-dependent communities (Johnson and Beale 1994), income inequality in such communities may create different economic stresses for people within different economic strata.

Natural disasters may also create poverty traps. Although the linkages between poverty and natural disasters have been discussed primarily in the context of low-income countries (e.g., Morduch 1994), Fothergill and Peek (2004) have argued that even in the U.S. the poor are more vulnerable to natural catastrophes because of where they live and their poorer quality of housing. Thus, natural disasters may be among the factors that prevent people living in poverty from bettering their lives economically. Because people living below or near the poverty line, who rent or own poor-quality housing, are less able to afford investments in mitigation or insurance, they rely more heavily on governmental compensation when a disaster strikes. Thus, increasing income inequality could lead to increased recovery costs.

Moral hazard

If we wish to understand the economic rationality of actions that people take to protect themselves and their property from natural hazards, we must consider the full range of incentives and opportunities faced by property owners. The transfer of risk from the individual to the principal (i.e., insurance company) via insurance affects the incentives faced by the individual (McCall 1987). The major factor linking protective actions of individuals to private insurance is known as "moral hazard." If individuals who purchase private insurance contracts are not inclined to undertake protective measures that would reduce either the probability of loss (self-protection) or the magnitude of loss if it did occur (self-insurance), and if insurance companies cannot perfectly monitor the actions of the policyholder, a moral hazard is created for the insurance company (Kotowitz 1987). Viewed the other way around, if insurance prices do not reflect efforts at self-protection or self-insurance, then individuals will not have an incentive to adopt risk-reduction measures (Hirshleifer and Riley 1979). Ehrlich and Becker (1972) showed that market insurance is a substitute for self-insurance, and as the price of market insurance increases (decreases), people will spend more (less) on self-insurance.

Samaritan's dilemma

The expectation that the government will provide disaster assistance in the wake of a natural disaster causes people to under-invest in protective measures, a phenomenon known as "the Samaritan's dilemma." Lewis and Nickerson (1989) argued that the decision by consumers to underinsure is rational given the expectation that the government will provide compensation for losses that exceed the limits set by an insurance contract.

Kelly and Kleffner (2003) confirmed this and showed how government disaster assistance can reduce mitigation expenditures by individuals. Coate (1995) argued that the fundamental problem stems from the fact that the government cannot commit ex ante to a fixed level of support should a disaster occur. Experimental evidence has shown that a disaster-recovery program of financial aid lowers most forms of wildfire risk-mitigation expenditures (McKee et al. 2004).

These theoretical and empirical studies suggest that self-protection and self-insurance measures such as those advocated by community wildfire-mitigation programs (e.g., reducing vegetation close to the home and using fire-resistant materials in roofs and gutters) may not be adopted by homeowners for rational economic reasons. If the government were to commit ex ante to provide disaster relief only to homeowners living in communities that have implemented measures to reduce the risk of wildfire, then the incentives to take protective action would be increased.

Risk information

A basic economic tenet is that people make decisions based on the information that is available to them. If information is incomplete or is of dubious quality, then people may rationally decide not to act on that information or may make seemingly irrational decisions. Uncertainty regarding the extent to which community-based wildfire-mitigation activities reduce wildfire risk may explain why some people are reluctant to invest in these activities.

A number of economic studies have shown that, when reliable information is available regarding the risk of natural hazards, individuals use that information in making economic choices. Brookshire et al. (1985) investigated California housing markets in areas subject to earthquakes. What these researchers discovered is that people are willing to pay higher (lower) real estate prices for houses in lower (higher) earthquake risk zones. These authors concluded that a 1974 law passed by the state of California requiring earthquake risk information be available to consumers allowed individuals to self-insure by trading off risk and price. Similar results were reported by Troy and Romm (2004). They found that the average home located on floodplains across California sold for 4.2% less than comparable non-floodplain homes after passage of the California Natural Hazard Disclosure Law, but that no difference in price was found before passage of that law. The provision of timely, believable information about the risk of catastrophic events may be a critical factor in individual decisions to self-insure.

Discussion and Policy Implications

Over the past two decades, the upward trend in the number of acres burned by wildfires has been matched by growth in wildfire-suppression costs, insured economic losses, and disaster assistance. A number of macroeconomic factors have contributed to the trends in wildfire-suppression costs and losses within the wildland-urban interface, including in-migration to scenic areas, increasing wealth, and an escalation in real estate values. As greater wealth is placed at risk, more money is spent by the federal government to protect it from wildfires and provide assistance for losses. Research is clearly needed to systematically document and analyze the trends in population growth, migration, and the accumulation of capital in wildfire risk areas within the wildland-urban interface.

A fundamental issue facing policy makers is the prevalent social attitude that the federal government should and will provide assistance during a disaster (such as wildfire suppression) and that governmental relief will be forthcoming in the aftermath of a catastrophe. Although few would argue against the need for some level of federal disaster aid, federal assistance is commonly viewed as an entitlement even when those needing assistance chose not to invest in insurance or mitigation measures beforehand. Economic theory suggests that if property owners believed that disaster relief would not be forthcoming from the federal government unless effective risk-mitigation measures had been implemented beforehand, then their incentives for self-protection would be enhanced. These actions may reduce the probability of damages, may reduce future migration to, or rebuilding in, risky locations, and might begin to shift the responsibility of protection from the federal government to individuals and neighborhoods who share the risk. Research is needed to systematically evaluate the economic efficiency of mandatory and voluntary wildfire-mitigation programs.

Making disaster assistance conditional on ex ante mitigation, however, would have severe consequences for the poor. There is evidence that natural disasters are felt more acutely by the poor than the more wealthy for a variety of factors, including the likelihood that the poor live and move to risk-prone areas, have relatively low-quality housing, and possess less ability to travel the bureaucratic pathways necessary to claim disaster assistance. Because the poor are less able to purchase insurance or make investments in self-protection, they rely more heavily on federal disaster assistance to help them recover from natural disasters. Research into the impact of wildfires on people living in poverty, or close to the poverty line, is sorely needed.

Property owners use reliable information about risk in making choices regarding both purchase and provision of self-insurance. If wildfire risk factors are capitalized into property values, as has been demonstrated for earthquake and flood risks, then risk-adjusted property values may provide a degree of financial self-insurance for property owners, because they would have less wealth at risk. In addition, private insurance costs may be more affordable for risk-adjusted property owners, again because the value of the property at risk would be lower. This can only occur if wildfire risks are adequately mapped in the wildland-urban interface and the information made readily available to consumers.

Many community action programs aimed at lowering wildfire risk have been established throughout the wildland-urban interface. However, we would emphasize that the success of wildfire risk-reduction programs depends to a large degree on understanding the economic incentives that people face when making risk-reduction choices, and incorporating the proper incentives into program implementation.

NOTES

1. Most, but not all, of the loans are repaid by property owners. The net present value (NPV) of direct federal disaster relief expenditures comprises interest rate subsidies and the costs of loan defaults, and these averaged 27% of the insured losses during the mid-1990s (Barnett 1999). Applying this average to the 2003 California wildfires yields an estimated NPV of direct costs to the government of $130.4 million. It has been estimated that, during the period FY 1980-96, the NPV of direct costs to the federal government for all natural disasters averaged $535 million per year (Barnett 1999).
2. Suppression-cost data shown in Figure 2 were obtained from the report published by the Strategic Issues Panel on Fire Suppression Costs (2004). USDA Forest Service data include expenditures for initial attack and suppression, whereas those for Department of Interior agencies only include suppression expenditures. Because Department of Interior data were only reported beginning in 1985, estimates were back-cast to 1970 based on the ratio of DOI to Forest Service expenditures during the period 1985-2003.
3. The total U.S. population increased from 181 million to 249 million between 1960 and 1990 (U.S. Census Bureau 2004a); in 2000, it was estimated at 282 million (U.S. Census Bureau 2004b).
4. It should be recognized that published reports of loss-value trends sometimes do not adjust for general price inflation.

REFERENCES

Aghion, P., E. Caroli, and C. Garcia-Penalosa. 1999. "Inequality and economic growth: The perspective of the new growth theories." *Journal of Economic Literature* 37 (4):1615-60.
Barnett, B. J. 1999. "US government natural disaster assistance: Historical analysis and a proposal for the future." *Disasters* 23 (2):139-55.
Bellinger, M. D., H. F. Kaiser, and H. A. Harrison. 1983. "Economic efficiency in fire management on nonfederal forest and range lands." *Journal of Forestry* 81 (6):373-78.
Brookshire, D. S., M. A. Thayer, J. Tschirhart, and W. D. Schulze. 1985. "A test of the expected utility model: Evidence from earthquake risks." *Journal of Political Economy* 93 (2):369-89.

California Fires Coordination Group. 2004. A Report to the Secretary of Homeland Security. Washington, D.C.: Federal Emergency Management Administration.

Changnon, S. A. 2003. "Shifting economic impacts from weather extremes in the United States: A result of societal changes, not global warming." *Natural Hazards* 29 (2):273-90.

Chevan, A., and R. Stokes. 2000. "Growth in family inequality, 1970-1990: Industrial restructuring and demographic change." *Demography* 37 (3):365-80.

Clary, B. B. 1985. "The evolution and structure of natural hazard policies." *Public Administration Review* 40 (special issue):20-28.

Coate, S. 1995. "Altruism, the Samaritan's dilemma, and government transfer policy." *American Economic Review* 85 (1):46-57.

Deller, S. C., T. H. Tsai, D. W. Marcouiller, and D. B. K. English. 2001. "The role of amenities and quality of life in rural economic growth." *American Journal of Agricultural Economics* 83 (2):352-65.

Donovan, G. H., and D. B. Rideout. 2003. "A reformulation of the cost plus net value change (C+NVC) model of wildfire economics." *Forest Science* 49 (2):318-23.

Ehrlich, I., and G. S. Becker. 1972. "Market insurance, self-insurance, and self-protection." *Journal of Political Economy* 80 (4):623-48.

English, D. B. K., D. W. Marcouiller, and H. K. Cordell. 2000. "Tourism dependence in rural America: Estimates and effects." *Society and Natural Resources* 13 (3):185-202.

Fothergill, A., and L. A. Peek. 2004. "Poverty and disasters in the United States: A review of recent sociological findings." *Natural Hazards* 32 (1):89-110.

Gorte, J. K., and R. W. Gorte. 1979. Application of economic techniques to fire management—A status review and evaluation. Ogden, Utah, USDA Forest Service. General Technical Report INT-53.

Herrick, O. W. 1981. "Forest pest management economics—Application to gypsy moth." *Forest Science* 27 (1):128-38.

Hirshleifer, J., and J. G. Riley. 1979. "The analytics of uncertainty and information—An expository survey." *Journal of Economic Literature* 17 (4):1375-1421.

Insurance Information Institute. 2005. "Facts and statistics." Insurance Information Institute. http://www.iii.org/media/facts/statsbyissue/catastrophes/

Johnson, K. M., and C. L. Beale. 1994. "The recent revival of widespread population growth in non-metropolitan areas of the United States." *Rural Sociology* 59 (4):655-67.

Kates, R. W. 1971. "Natural hazard in human ecological perspective: Hypotheses and models." *Economic Geography* 47 (3):438-51.

Kelly, M., and A. E. Kleffner. 2003. "Optimal loss mitigation and contract design." *Journal of Risk and Insurance* 70 (1):53-72.

Kotowitz, Y. 1987. "Moral hazard." In J. Eatwell, M. Milgate, and P. Newman (eds.), *The New Palgrave—A Dictionary of Economics*. London, England: The Macmillan Press Ltd.

Kovacs, P. 2001. "Wildfires and insurance." Institute for Catastrophic Loss Reduction. http://www.iclr.org/research/publications_wildfires.htm

Lee, C. 2001. "Life-cycle saving in the United States, 1900-90." *Review of Income and Wealth* 47 (2):165-79.

Lewis, T., and D. Nickerson. 1989. "Self-insurance against natural disasters." *Journal of Environmental Economics and Management* 16 (3):209-23.

McCabe, J. T. 1988. "Drought and recovery: Livestock dynamics among the Ngissonyoka Turkana of Kenya." *Human Ecology* 15 (2): 371-90.

McCall, J. J. 1987. "Insurance." In J. Eatwell, M. Milgate, and P. Newman (eds.), *The New Palgrave—A Dictionary of Economics*. London, England: The Macmillan Press.

McKee, M., R. P. Berrens, M. Jones, R. Helton, and J. Talberth. 2004. "Using experimental economics to examine wildfire insurance and averting decisions in the wildland-urban interface." *Society and Natural Resources* 17 (6):491-507.

Morduch, J. 1994. "Poverty and vulnerability." *American Economic Review* 84 (2):221-25.

National Fire Plan. 2001. "A collaborative approach for reducing wildland fire risks to communities and the environment: 10-year comprehensive strategy." National Fire Plan. http://www.fireplan.gov/reports/7-19-en.pdf

National Interagency Fire Center. 2004. "Wildland fire statistics." National Interagency Fire Center. http://www.nifc.gov/stats/wildlandfirestats.html

National Oceanic and Atmospheric Administration. 1998. "Population: Distribution, density, and growth." In T .J. Culliton (ed.), State of the Coast Report. http://www.noaa.gov

Nutter, F. W. 2002. "The role of government in financing catastrophes." *The Geneva Papers on Risk and Insurance* 27 (2):283-87.

Oliver-Smith, A. 1996. "Anthropological research on hazards and disasters." *Annual Review of Anthropology* 25:303-28.

Palm, R. 2003. "Demand for disaster insurance: Residential coverage." In H. Kunreuther (ed.), *Paying the Price*. Washington D.C.: National Academy of Sciences.

Pyne, S. 2001. *Fire—A Brief History*. Seattle: University of Washington Press.

Ross, T., and N. Lott. 2003. "A climatology of 1980-2003 extreme weather and climate events." National Oceanic and Atmospheric Administration. http://www.noaa.gov

Sparhawk, W. N. 1925. "The use of liability ratings in planning forest fire protection." *Journal of Agricultural Research* 30:693-762.

Strategic Issues Panel on Fire Suppression Costs. 2004. "Large fire suppression costs—Strategies for cost management." National Fire Plan. http://www.fireplan.gov/resources/2004.html

Swiss Re. 2004. Natural catastrophes and man-made disasters in 2003: Many fatalities, comparatively moderate insured losses. Zurich, Switzerland: Swiss Reinsurance Company.

Troy, A., and J. Romm. 2004. "Assessing the price effects of flood hazard disclosure under the California natural hazard disclosure law (AB 1195)." *Journal of Environmental Planning and Management* 47 (1):137-62.

U.S. Census Bureau. 2004a. "Historical national population estimates: July 1, 1900 to July 1, 1999." United States Census Bureau. http://eire.census.gov/popest/archives/pre1980/popclockest.txt

———. 2004b. "Annual estimates of the population for the United States and States, and for Puerto Rico: April 1, 2000 to July 1, 2003." United States Census Bureau. http://eire.census.gov/popest/data/states/NST-EST2003-ann_est.php

U.S. Department of Commerce. 2002. "Consumer price indices, 1913-2002." Bureau of Labor Statistics. http://www.bls.gov/data

U.S. Department of Commerce. 2003. "Gross domestic product, current and 'real' GDP, 1946I - 02IV." http://www.bea.doc.gov/bea/dn1.htm

Matching the Utilization of the By-products of Forest Fuel Reduction with Community Development Opportunities

Dennis R. Becker and Joel Viers

Introduction

Thinning of overstocked forests is believed to improve forest health and reduce the risk of extreme fire (Pollet and Omi 2002). Accordingly, scientists, policy makers, and the public are calling for extensive thinning across the western United States. Fuel-reduction projects will generate a tremendous volume of wood material and there is an increasing interest in and focus on the community development potential of thinning. Yet development opportunities may or may not be forthcoming depending on specific local or regional circumstances affected by the interaction among biophysical dimensions of wildfire risk reduction, economic and industry factors, and sociocultural preferences. One contemporary but non-traditional area of research is the utilization of fuel reduction by-products for community development. The many physical and social aspects of this relationship are touched upon here to provide a more comprehensive and action-oriented approach to opportunities in forest thinning-based development and research.

Recent catastrophic wildfires and insect and disease epidemics in national forests led to the creation of the National Fire Plan and passage of the 2003 Healthy Forest Restoration Act. Such legislation, while emphasizing the western United States, has implications for communities across the country. Whether focused on the wildland-urban interface or remote forest areas, the scale of proposed thinning is immense. The Government Accountability Office (1999) estimates that 39 million acres in the interior west are affected by over-accumulation of fuels ; the USDA Forest Service (2000) estimates 126 million acres of public lands are at high risk of losing key ecosystem components to wildfire. Considering that wilderness, riparian zones, and other sensitive areas will limit the scope of appropriate thinning, as much as

Dennis R. Becker, Department of Forest Resources, University of Minnesota (drbecker@umn.edu); Joel Viers, Ecological Restoration Institute, Northern Arizona University

70 million acres in the western U.S. alone could be available for some form of fuels-reduction treatment (USDA Forest Service 2003).

As noted in the community-preparedness literature presented by Jakes (this volume), a key component of reducing wildfire risk is proactive forest thinning and removal of small-diameter trees and debris from the wildland-urban interface. If removed material can be used for economic benefit, fuels-reduction projects may present opportunities for community development. However, opportunities are constrained by the need to use this material sustainably, in a socially acceptable manner, and in accordance with forest ecosystem-restoration and fuel-reduction objectives. Successful forest-based community development will depend on a fuels-reduction approach that first and foremost improves forest health and, second, fulfills economic and cultural objectives. Taking advantage of small-diameter wood-utilization opportunities will require this integrated approach.

Conceptualizing an Integrated Approach to Utilization

Forest-health restoration and wildfire fuels-reduction efforts are not presumed to be dependent upon sustainable community development. There is, however, an opportunity to explicitly link sustainable development to forest restoration and fuel-reduction needs provided a number of factors are addressed. First, the physical characteristics of thinned forest material, such as variations in tree size, age, distribution, and species composition, must be matched to wood-processing technologies, because they dictate the range of wood products possible and economically feasible for a given area (Bédard 2002). The resource availability—the volume and consistency of the supply of material—is critical as it governs processing options and sustainability (Wagner et al. 1998). Viable consumer markets must also exist, for without them there is no outlet for products or financial capital to stimulate investment. Finally, utilization options must be matched with community livelihoods and capacities. Resource characteristics, availability, markets, and community capacity collectively define the range of utilization opportunities for any given area. These parameters are shown in Figure 1 to emphasize the interaction between the biophysical dimensions of wildfire risk reduction, economic and industry factors, and human communities. Important elements of this interaction are described with implications for forest products industries, contractors, capital requirements, and institutional market mechanisms.

Forest Resource Characteristics

Quality

Suppressed small-diameter trees dominate the national forests, particularly in the West where they provide fuel densities to stoke catastrophic wildfires (Covington and Moore 1994; Pollet and Omi 2002). In absolute numbers, the quantity available for harvest is immense, but not all the material is commercially desirable. As a rule, these small trees are crowded and unhealthy, with a greater incidence of disease and mortality, and are shorter and produce smaller, lower-quality logs, than trees in healthy, naturally occurring forests. So as tree size decreases, wood volume drops precipitously and harvest and processing costs increase exponentially (Barbour et al. 2003; Horsfield 1982; Wagner et al. 2000).

The physical properties of the trees also determine timber value, which, depending on species, may only be suitable for certain uses (Erickson et al. 2000; Koch 1996; Willits et al. 1997; Wolfe and Moseley 2000). One example is ponderosa pine, which grows mainly in the Southwest and inland Northwest. A high proportionof juvenile wood, which is the wood at the core of the tree, makes small-diameter ponderosa pine unsuitable for all but the least-demanding structural applications (Erickson et al. 2000; Voorhies and Blake 1981). Quantity and size of knots, warping, and other defects reduce its product grade and market value, which in turn limits utilization options (Lowell and Green 2001). On the other hand, other suppressed-

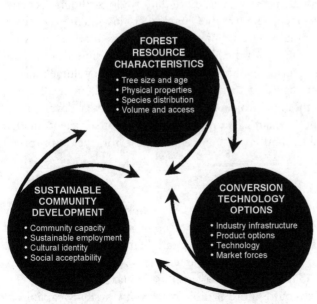

Figure 1. Interaction among forest resource characteristics, product options, and community development opportunities related to small-diameter timber utilization.

growth species like Douglas fir may possess structural characteristics superior for high-value applications like decorative molding and flooring (LeVan-Green and Livingston 2001). Localized resource characteristics and subsequent utilization constraints are basic considerations when developing an integrated strategy for fuel reduction and community development.

Issues of access and supply

Although the low value of small-diameter material is a pervasive obstacle, supply and availability also limit utilization options. The most basic supply issue is access. In some areas there may be legal designations that limit thinning: for example, wilderness, sites closed for endangered species, or areas under litigation. Land management planning inconsistencies, and appropriations can delay thinning projects because of timing, personnel, or funding. Projects may also be limited by social and political pressure, by physical terrain, or geographic proximity to recreation areas. Road access, timber distribution, aggregate volume, species mix, and distance to wood-processing facilities all affect the availability and consistency of resource supply.

Supply issues help determine the types and flow of material, affecting the range of utilization options. The production of landscaping timbers or firewood, for example, requires little in specialized equipment or stringent quality guidelines; thus there are few constraints on the type of material that can be used. Dimensional lumber and engineered wood beams, on the other hand, require higher-quality and more uniform logs. Biomass energy generation is capable of consuming large quantities of low-quality, relatively undifferentiated thinning material, but such use requires a large, consistent supply over the operating life of the plant, not to mention significant capital investment in manufacturing facilities. Therefore, adequate volume must be available at a low enough cost to amortize investments (Han et al. 2004; Morris 1999). For a thinning project to be a viable community-development opportunity there must be sufficient quantity of trees, of sufficient quality, consistently accessible, and at a competitive cost for the appropriate utilization options.

Conversion technology options

INDUSTRY INFRASTRUCTURE AND CAPACITY. Adapting existing industry infrastructure, developing products, and creating market niches all hold particular challenges and opportunities for small-diameter timber utilization. As once-prized large sawlogs become scarcer, the forest products industry is being forced to adapt to a smaller average-diameter log input. This will almost certainly require more flexible commodity systems capable of responding to changes in product mix, which can mean that investors risk reduced returns for their processing-technology investment. As witnessed by corporate farm conversions in the Midwest, textile production in the South, and coal mining in the Northeast, this will not be an easy transition and will require institutional mechanisms to mitigate risks (Flora et al. 2001). Such mechanisms might include assurances of consistent material supply, creation of incentives targeted at product market development, or reduction of transportation and handling costs.

One fact is immutable—the potential supply of fuels-reduction material far outstrips current processing capacity in those regions of the country where most of the extensive forest thinning is needed (Keegan et al. 2001a, 2001b; Spelter and Alderman 2003). Coupled with the decline in facilities that can efficiently process smaller material located within an economically viable service region, transporting small logs for value-added manufacturing is cost prohibitive. The growing emphasis on small logs in the Western U.S. requires retrofitting some existing manufacturing facilities and constructing new ones closer to areas in need, as well as development of mobile processing options (Becker et al. 2004). This transition also requires improvements in transportation systems, and co-location with related industries to create competitive advantages in raw-material input and processing costs (see, e.g., Braden et al. 1998; Krugman 1991; Shaffer 1989). Furthermore, because of the long-running decline of the forest products industry in some regions of the country, the lack of forestry contractors and workers available to undertake fuels-reduction and -utilization projects will need to be addressed in training and re-employment programs (Moseley 2002).

Product options

Resource characteristics must be appropriately matched with product options for successful community development to evolve. The difficulty is in doing so at a competitive price. Because of low value and high harvest cost relative to imports and other sources of competition, the majority of low-value fuel-reduction material in the West, Upper Midwest, Northeast, and South will, for the moment, need to find niche markets and specific or locale-based applications. However, technological advances and government investment are increasingly allowing small-diameter wood to be used for a greater variety of applications, including dimensional lumber, roundwood construction, and composite and engineered products. A broad range of other products such as flooring, paneling, trusses, moldings, and furniture have also been successfully introduced. Extensive listings, and discussion of research on specific products from small-diameter trees, can be found elsewhere (e.g., LeVan-Green and Livingston 2001; Lynch and Mackes

2002; Spelter et al. 1996; USDA Forest Service 2000). Successful market entry for these products will require product differentiation and the forging of new relationships with distributors and consumers.

Markets for Utilization Products

As the variety and availability of small-diameter wood products expand, the challenge will be to establish competitive and sustainable markets. Small-diameter wood products cannot currently compete on a price basis alone in a commodity situation for many of the possible products. Product differentiation and anticipation of consumer demand, locally as well as globally, is perhaps the most underdeveloped and elusive aspect of small-wood utilization and a key to any expansion of related community-development opportunities. In anticipation of an increased volume of small-diameter trees and fewer large trees, the wood products industry will need to focus increasingly on small-diameter inputs (Wagner et al. 1998). This will not only entail substantial investment in retrofitting existing or constructing new infrastructure where applicable, but adjusting business plans and financial calculations to account for cost changes (Fry et al. 1999). Importantly, existing industries have a long-standing market relationship with wholesalers. A shift in product requires new market segmentation and the forging of new and unproven business relationships (Porter 1980). Market reconfiguration will be particularly difficult where philosophies of business investment and recruitment favor large-scale commodity industries. Traditional industry structures may not be accustomed to the nuances of small-diameter timber and may be reluctant to invest the necessary capital for marginal or less-predictable financial returns. The challenge for communities will be to seek out and provide the institutional support—markets and investment mechanisms—that facilitate utilization choices that contribute to ecosystem health and economic viability, and are socially acceptable and politically responsible (Flora et al. 2001).

It will also be important for communities and producers to approach the utilization of fuel-reduction by-products from the perspective of developing market pull (demand) rather than market push (Rogue Institute for Ecology and Economy 1999). Products developed from small-diameter timber could more closely approach prices of traditionally sourced products as processing technology improves, and also as fuel-reduction products become more broadly accepted and available. Changing the perception of small-diameter wood from that of an expensive ecological problem to an emerging economic asset will be an important step in gaining market access (Rogue Institute for Ecology and Economy 1999). Another way to gain competitive advantage is to concentrate on a particular segment of the market. Knowledge of consumer preferences, market competition, and regional and local demand, each is a means to differentiate product markets (Fry et al. 1999). Biomass for energy production, while capital intensive, could be regionally viable if local utilities were to require increased use of non-fossil-fuel inputs. Product branding for sustainably produced goods or local labeling can also command higher prices.

Sustainable Community Development

Community capacity
An integrated approach to community development links the utilization of fuels-reduction by-products and markets with community characteristics. Substantial investment in building and strengthening community capacity will be necessary for utilization-enhanced economic development. This means that industry development and re-capitalization be closely matched to community goals for wildfire protection and economic development. Careful assessment of supply and other factors will be necessary to ease or avoid boom-bust cycles inherent to the wood products industry (several reviews of this literature are available; see, e.g., Kaufman and Kaufman 1946; Lee 1990; Machlis and Force 1988; Smith et al. 2001). Community capacity will be necessary to mobilize resources (money, knowledge, and leadership), develop relationships among key stakeholders (industry, contractors, consumers, and communities), and anticipate opportunities corresponding to community desires (Flora and Flora 1993; Kusel 2003; Wilkinson 1991).

Community capacity is commonly described as a function of past experiences, activeness, and solidarity that in turn affects a community's ability to mobilize resources (Tilly 1973; Zekeri ett al. 1994). It includes the physical and human capital with which to take action (Doak and Kusel 1996; Kusel 2003; Pretty 2000). Physical capital is defined as the natural resource base and physical infrastructure (Flora and Flora 1993), and human capital as the collection of skills, education, and experiences of residents, as well as leadership qualities and entrepreneurship (Becker 1975; Pretty 2000). Community capacity also relates to individuals' capabilities (Lehtonen 2004; Sen 1987), a necessary component to developing networks of social relations and facilitating coordinated actions. Relationships, critical to engaging opportunities, may be among community residents (see, e.g., Putnam 1993) or with external partners like trade organizations, land management agencies, nonprofit groups, or even consumers (see, e.g.,

Coleman 1988; Flora 1998; Gittell and Vidal 1998). Individual capabilities can also relate to the ability to leverage resources in the form of ideas, information, and financial capital (Flora and Flora 1993; Lehtonen 2004).

Community capacity provides the cache of resources and abilities to draw from to engage opportunities. Sustainable community development takes place—or does not—in the context of community capacity. Therefore, when assessing community assets, residents must ask "the capacity for what?" and match available or potential utilization options with their strengths and abilities.

Community identity

Part of recognizing community capacity is understanding the contribution of previous and existing industries. Those industries and development experiences work to shape the workforce and other capacities for development. Although it is not necessary to provide identical employment opportunities, congruence of new opportunities to traditional livelihoods contributes to a community's acceptance of ideas and individuals' ability to make productive contributions (Castells 1997; Selznick 1992). Community identity and the resulting sense of belonging that accompanies a particular livelihood are necessary to marshal collective action, but, to contribute to this identity, actions must be locally relevant (Wilkinson 1991). These actions in turn reinforce norms of identity that add to the way individuals see themselves and outsiders (Carroll 1995). The realm of possibility for a given community is then influenced by its identity. That is, communities are likely to support development opportunities that complement their history, build on shared experiences, and reinforce community values. Utilization options that fail to some sufficient degree to fulfill community and individual needs may ultimately be unsustainable. Reinforcing community identity is therefore dependent upon the ability to trace natural resource physical constraints, through the technical and logistical elements of product conversion, to social acceptability.

Social Acceptability

For *utilization options* to be sustainable, environmental health and economic viability must be linked to social acceptability. Social acceptability is, logically, a key to sustainability—without sufficient community acceptance it is unlikely that development opportunities will be an integral, desired, and evolving community component. As discussed by both Shindler and Daniel (this volume), support for fuel-reduction strategies and subsequent community-development opportunities hinges on public perception and evaluation of a complex set of trade-offs among uncertain and potentially conflicting values. Among these values are life, property, scenic value, recreational pursuits, watershed protection, and wildlife habitat. For some, the immediate aesthetic value of forests outweighs the unrealized benefits of thinning. For those living in the wildland-urban interface fuel-reduction projects may be perceived as the only way to protect those same aesthetic values. For either, acceptability hinges on how benefits are achieved and at what cost.

Social acceptability is also provisional; that is, it depends on many influences that can change by situation and over time (Shindler et al. 2002). Evaluation of community and individual trade-offs therefore entails a complex array of perceptions of the need for forest restoration, environmental protection, fire-risk reduction, and timber harvesting (Findley et al. 2001). Individuals may have low awareness of fire severity and subsequent risks and as such desire an unaltered landscape (Gardner and Cortner 1987). Even if perceptions of risk are elevated, acceptance for the type of thinning may remain low because the means to reduce fuels are perceived as similar to those used in commercial timber management, which historically may have had negative impacts in a particular community (Daniel et al. 2002). The public might also lack a clear vision of mitigation actions, may be concerned with environmental consequences of thinning, or may desire increased involvement for where and how treatments are conducted. As such, perceptions of fire risk, thinning mechanisms, environmental consequences, and development opportunities all shape how a community collectively evaluates trade-offs and assigns acceptability.

The ability to make choices amid alternatives allows communities to develop strategies to meet quality of life goals but that are also in unison with principles of environmental integrity and economic viability. Decisions and tradeoffs will involve more than simply which trees to cut, but which investment strategies are best for economic development, wildfire protection, and forest health. Moreover, any benefit derived from forest fuel reduction activities must be in concert with sustainable forest practices to maintain trust and transparency and to facilitate broad community acceptance.

Strategies for Investment

Federal legislation, like the Healthy Forest Restoration Act, significantly affects management of national forests, in particular the ability to carry out fuel-reduction projects. One challenge is to understand future linkages among national policies, small-diameter wood markets, and the wood products industry, and to craft initiatives directed at the most appropriate and feasible community-development strategies based on these linkages.

Developing relationships will require investment in community capacity by residents, industry, and government. Investment strategies range from the simple infusion of money to the purchase of harvesting equipment to complex cost-accounting strategies for wildfire suppression, environmental services, and investment in capacity building. Local strategies might include subsides to reduce transportation costs of fuel-reduction by-products or to invest in workforce-training programs. Joint public-private partnerships will also be increasingly important, such as public investment in programs to purchase electricity generated at biomass plants. Here, a key challenge will be defining the role of government in private-enterprise development. Specifically, should public entities deliberately invest in building community and private-industry capacity as a mechanism to restore forests and reduce wildfire risks? And if so, what are the parameters and most effective mechanisms? Free-market principles will be challenged by the desire to protect the public interest in air and water quality, forest health, life, and property. Recognition of the social benefits and value of forest thinning on public lands translates to increased public investment at some scale. However, if small-wood products continue to lack sufficient markets—that is, cost too much or are not successfully differentiated—substantial public investment may be needed to stimulate private investment in thinning and utilization.

Conclusion

Much of the focus of this book, as well as of national discussions on wildfire, has been on the cost of suppression of wildfire and landowner perceptions of and reactions to wildfire, and the institutional arrangements by which wildfire policy is established. In this chapter, we have briefly addressed the issue of wildfire from the perspective of forest-linked communities and the development opportunities presented by forest fuels-reduction projects. An integrated approach was suggested, whereby the characteristics of the forest resource must be matched to efficient processing technologies, to the availability of supply and product markets, and finally to the desires and capacities of forest communities.

The abundance of small-diameter timber, coupled with large areas of altered forest ecosystems, requires new thinking. Vague notions of sustainable community development linked to resource characteristics are not sufficient.

Successful development requires knowledge of sustainability principles, market development, capital attraction, reduction of transaction costs, capacity building, social acceptability, and more. Depending on utilization options, some mix of mechanical, technical, financial, and relational skills will be required to carry out economic-development activities (Flora et al. 2001). The interaction of social, economic, and ecological systems compels us to approach the wildfire situation in a manner that simultaneously improves forest health while strengthening the economic and social fabric of communities (Monserud et al. 2003). Sustainable development in this context hinges foremost on sustainable jobs. Without lasting employment, development will not be stable or cumulative. A transition to development based in some part on small logs will be difficult in areas characterized by suppressed forests, but a return to the boom-bust cycle of the forest products industry is not an attractive or viable option.

The capacity of forest-linked communities to create or take advantage of sustainable-development opportunities is therefore linked to the biophysical dimensions of wildfire just as it is to external factors of national policies and global markets. The factors acting on—and being acted upon—by community members and communities shape development opportunities. Consequently, any community-development effort must take into account all the biophysical and human dimensions discussed in this book to be sustainable and successful in the long-term.

References

Barbour, R. J., D. D. Marshall, and E. C. Lowell. 2003. "Managing for wood quality." In R. A. Monserud, R. W. Haynes, and A. C. Johnson (eds.), *Compatible Forest Management*. Dordrecht, The Netherlands: Kluwer Academic Publishers, 299-336.

Becker, D. R., E. E. Hjerpe, and E. C. Lowell. 2004. Economic assessment of using a mobile MicroMill(R) for processing small diameter ponderosa pine. PNW-GTR-623. Portland, Oregon: USDA Forest Service, Pacific Northwest Research Station.

Becker, G. S. 1962. "Investment in human capital: A theoretical analysis." *The Journal of Political Economy* 70(5): 9-49.

Bédard, P. 2002. "Guidelines to better match resource characteristics, conversion technology, and products." In D. Baumgartner, L. Johnson, and E. DePruit (eds.), Small-diameter timber: Resource management, manufacturing, and markets. Proceedings of the small-diameter timber symposium, February 2002, Spokane, Washington. Pullman: Washington State University, 219-25.

Braden, R., H. Fossum, I. Eastin, J. Dirks, and E. Lowell. 1998. "The role of manufacturing clusters in the Pacific Northwest forest products industry." CINTRAFOR Working Paper #66. Seattle, Washington.

Carroll, M. S. 1995. *Community and the Northwestern Logger: Continuities and Changes in the Era of the Spotted Owl.* (Rural Studies Series of the Rural Sociological Society.) Boulder, Colorado: Westview Press.

Castells, M. 1997. *The Power of Identity*. Malden, Massachusetts: Blackwell Publishers.

Coleman, J. C. 1988. "Social capital in the creation of human capital." *American Journal of Sociology* 94:S95-S120.

Covington, W., and M. Moore. 1994. "Post-settlement changes in natural fire regimes and forest structure: Ecological restoration of old-growth ponderosa pine forests." *Journal of Sustainable Forestry* 2:153-81.

Daniel, T. C., E. Weidemann, and D. Hines. 2002. "Assessing public tradeoffs between fire hazard and scenic beauty in the wildland-urban interface." In P. J. Jakes (compiler), Homeowners, communities, and wildfire: Science findings from the National Fire Plan. Proceedings of the Ninth International Symposium on Society and Management; 2002 June 2-5; Bloomington, Indiana. NC-231. St. Paul, Minnesota: USDA Forest Service, Northcentral Research Station, 36-45.

Doak, S., and J. Kusel. 1996. "Well-being in forest-dependent communities, part II: Social assessment focus." In Sierra Nevada Ecosystem Project: Final Report to Congress, vol. II, Assessments and Scientific Basis for Management Options. Davis: University of California, Centers for Water and Wildland Resources, 375-402.

Erickson, R. G., T. D. Gorman, D. W. Green, and D. Graham. 2000. "Mechanical grading of lumber sawn from small-diameter lodgepole pine, ponderosa pine, and grand fir trees from northern Idaho." *Forest Products Journal* 50(7/8):59-65.

Findley, A. J., M. S. Carroll, and K. A. Blatner. 2001. "Social complexity and the management of small-diameter stands." *Journal of Forestry* 99(12):18-27.

Flora, C. B., and J. L. Flora. 1993. "Entrepreneurial social infrastructure: A necessary ingredient." *Annals of the American Academy of Political and Social Sciences* 539:48-58.

———, G. McIsaac, S. Gasteyer, and M. Kroma. 2001. "Farm-community entrepreneurial partnership in the Midwest." In C. Flora (ed.), *Interactions between Agroecosystems and Rural Communities*. Boca Raton, Florida: CRC Press, 115-30.

Flora, J. L. 1998. "Social capital and communities of place." *Rural Sociology* 63(4):481-506.

Fry, F. L., C. R. Stoner, and L. G. Weinzimmer. 1999. *Strategic Planning for New and Emerging Businesses: A Consulting Approach*. Chicago, Illinois: Dearborn Financial Publishing.

Gardner, P. D., and H. J. Cortner. 1987. "The risk perceptions and policy response toward wildland fire hazards by urban homeowners." *Landscape and Urban Planning* 14:163-72.

Government Accountability Office. 1999. Western national forests: A cohesive strategy is needed to address catastrophic wildfire threats. Report to the Subcommittee on Forests and Forest Health, Committee on Resources, House of Representatives. GAO/RCED-99-65. Washington, D.C.: General Accounting Office.

Gittell, R., and A. Vidal. 1998. *Community Organizing: Building Social Capital as a Development Strategy*. Thousand Oaks, California: SAGE Publications.

Han, H. S., H. W. Lee, and L. R. Johnson. 2004. "Economic feasibility of an integrated harvesting system for small-diameter trees in southwest Idaho." *Forest Products Journal* 54(2):21-27.

Kaufman, H. F., and L. C. Kaufman. 1946. Toward the Stabilization and Enrichment of a Forest Community: The Montana study. Missoula: University of Montana.

Keegan, C. E., A. L. Chase, T. A. Morgan, S. E. Bodmer, D. D. Van Hooser, and M. Mortimer. 2001a. Arizona's forest products industry: A descriptive analysis 1998. The University of Montana, Bureau of Business and Economic Research. Missoula, Montana.

———, K. M. Gebert, A. L. Chase, T. A. Morgan, S. E. Bodmer, and D. D. Van Hooser. 2001b. Montana's forest products industry: A descriptive analysis 1969-2000. The University of Montana, Bureau of Business and Economic Research. Missoula, Montana.

Koch, P. 1996. *Lodgepole Pine in North America*. Vols 1-3. Forest Products Society, Madison, Wisconsin.

Krugman, P. 1991. *Geography and Trade*. Cambridge, Massachusetts: MIT Press.

Kusel, J. 2003. "Assessing well-being in forest-dependent communities." In L. E. Kruger (ed.), Understanding community forest relations. PNW-GTR-566. Portland, Oregon: USDA Forest Service, Pacific Northwest Research Station, 81-103.

Lee, R. G. 1990. "Sustained yield and social order." In R. G. Lee, D. R. Field and W. R. Burch (eds.), *Community and Forestry: Continuities in the Sociology of Natural Resources*. Boulder, Colorado: Westview Press, 85-94.

Lehtonen, M. 2004. "The environmental-social interface of sustainable development: Capabilities, social capital, institutions." *Ecological Economics* 49:199-214.

LeVan-Green, S. L., and J. Livingston. 2001. "Exploring the uses for small-diameter trees." *Forest Products Journal* 51(9):10-21.

Lowell, E. C. and D. W. Green. 2001. "Lumber recovery from small-diameter ponderosa pine from Flagstaff, Arizona." In R. K. Vance, W. W. Covington, C. B. Edminster (eds.), Ponderosa pine ecosystems restoration: Steps toward stewardship. Proceedings RMRS-P-22. Ogden, Utah: USDA Forest Service, Rocky Mountain Research Station, 161-65.

Lynch, D., and K. Mackes. 2002. "Opportunities for making wood products from small-diameter trees in Colorado." RMRS-RP-37. Fort Collins, Colorado: USDA Forest Service, Rocky Mountain Research Station. http://www.fs.fed.us/rm/pubs/rmrs_rp037.pdf.

Machlis, G. E., and J. E. Force. 1988. "Community stability and timber-dependent communities." *Rural Sociology* 53(2):220-34.

Monserud, R. A., R. Haynes, and A. Johnson (eds.), 2003. *Compatible Forest Management*. Dordrecht, The Netherlands: Kluwer Academic Publishers.

Morris, G. 1999. The value of the benefits of U.S. biomass power. NREL/SR-570-27541. Berkeley, California: U.S. Department of Energy, National Renewable Energy Laboratory.

Moseley, C. 2002. A survey of innovative contracting for quality jobs and ecosystem management. PNW-GTR-552. Portland, Oregon: USDA Forest Service, Pacific Northwest Research Station.

Pollet, J., and P. Omi. 2002. "Effect of thinning and prescribed burning on wildfire severity in ponderosa pine forests." *International Journal of Wildland Fire* 10:1-10.

Porter, M. E. 1980. *Competitive Strategy: Techniques for Analyzing Industries and Competitors*. New York: The Free Press.

Pretty, J. 2000. "Towards sustainable food and farming systems in industrialized countries." *International Journal of Agricultural Resources, Governance, and Ecology* 1(1):77-94.

Putnam, R. D. 1993. "The prosperous community: Social capital and public life." *The American Prospect* 13:35-42.

Roberts, B. (ed.) 1982. *Harvesting Small Timber: Waste Not, Want Not.* Dubuque, Iowa: Kendall / Hunt Publishing.

Rogue Institute for Ecology and Economy. 1999. "Small-diameter timber: A survey of the Rogue River Valley's wood products market's capacity to improve the value and utilization of a local forest product." Report produced for the Rogue Institute, Ashland, Oregon.

Selznick, P. 1992. *The Moral Commonwealth: Social Theory and the Promise of Community.* Berkley: University of California Press.

Sen, A. K. 1987. *Commodities and Capabilities.* Oxford, England: Oxford University Press.

Shaffer, R. 1989. "Location theory and community economic development." In R. Shaffer (ed.), *Community Economics: Economic Structure and Change in Smaller Communities.* Ames, Iowa: Iowa State Press, 46-70.

Shindler, B. A., M. Brunson, and G. H. Stankey. 2002. Social acceptability of forest conditions and management practices: A problem analysis. PNW-GTR-537. Portland, Oregon: USDA Forest Service, Pacific Northwest Research Station.

Smith, M. D., R. S. Krannich, and L. M. Hunter. 2001. "Growth, decline, stability, and disruption: A longitudinal analysis of social well-being in four western rural communities." *Rural Sociology* 66(3):425-50.

Spelter, H., R. Wang, and P. Ince. 1996. Economic feasibility of products from inland West small-diameter timber. FPL–GTR–92. Madison, Wisconsin: USDA Forest Service, Forest Products Laboratory.

———, and M. Alderman. 2003. Profile 2003: Softwood sawmills in the United States and Canada. Research Paper. FPL-RP-608. Madison, Wisconsin: USDA Forest Service, Forest Products Laboratory.

Tilly, C. 1973. "Do communities act?" *Sociological Inquiry* 43(3/4):209-40.

USDA Forest Service. 2000. Protecting people and sustaining resources in fire-adapted ecosystems–a cohesive strateg. The Forest Service management response to the General Accounting Office Report, GAO/RCED-99-65.

———. 2003. "A strategic assessment of forest biomass and fuel reduction treatments in western states." USDA Forest Service, Washington, D.C. http://www.fs.fed.us/research/pdf/Western_final.pdf

Voorhies, G., and B. R. Blake. 1981. "Properties affecting drying characteristics of young-growth ponderosa pine." Arizona Forestry Notes, Northern Arizona University, School of Forestry, Note #14, Flagstaff, Arizona.

Wagner, F. G., C. E. Keegan, R. D. Fight, and S. Willits. 1998. "Potential for small-diameter sawtimber utilization by the current sawmill industry in western North America." *Forest Products Journal* 48(9):30-34.

———, C. E. Fiedler, and C. E. Keegan. 2000. "Processing value of small-diameter sawtimber at conventional and high-speed sawmills in the western United States: A comparison." *Western Journal of Applied Forestry* 15(4):208-12.

Wilkinson, K. P. 1991. *The Community in Rural America.* New York: Greenwood.

Willits, S., R. J. Barbour, S. Tesch, J. McNeel, S. Kumar, G. Myers, B. Olson, and A. Mason. 1997. The Colville study: Wood utilization for ecosystem management. Preliminary results of study of a product potential from small-diameter stands. FPL-RP-559. Madison, Wisconsin: USDA Forest Service, Forest Products Laboratory.

Wolfe, R., and C. Moseley. 2000. "Small-diameter log evaluation for value-added structural applications." *Forest Products Journal* 50(10):48-58.

Zekeri, A. A, K. P. Wilkinson, and C. R. Humphrey. 1994. "Past activeness, solidarity, and local development efforts." *Rural Sociology* 59(2):216-35.

Class, Ethnicity, Rural Communities, and the Socioeconomic Impacts of Fire Policy

Cassandra Moseley

Federal fire policies, like all federal land management policies, have the potential to greatly impact public lands communities—those communities located in or near public lands. The federal impact on public-lands communities can be large because, as major landowners, the federal government controls most of the physical resources of a particular area and makes the key decisions about how those resources will be used. Public-lands communities in the Pacific Northwest, for example, are more likely than other rural communities to have low socioeconomic well-being, although not all public-lands communities are poor (Charnley et al. 2006). Federal policies can change ecological conditions of public lands by building roads, harvesting timber, suppressing fire, and designating land as wilderness. These decisions in turn affect the economic opportunities, social and cultural life, and safety of nearby residents. In addition, the federal government has considerable financial and technical resources under its control. Its decisions about the distribution of its resources through the hiring of government employees, acquisition of goods and services from contractors, and selling federal resources such as timber, other forest products such as boughs and mushrooms, grazing allotments, minerals, permits for filming movies, ski resorts, cell phone towers, and recreational concessions have direct financial consequences on rural communities. In Oregon, where the federal government manages more than 50% of the land, federal employment was over 5% of the workforce in 23% of rural counties in 2002 and overall government employment was over 25% of the workforce in 45% of the rural counties (Oregon Employment Department 2004).

From the founding of the USDA Forest Service, local community well-being has been a policy concern both in Congress and the agency. Historically, this concern can be found in the writings of Gifford Pinchot, early payments to counties en lieu of taxes, and the Sustained Yield Forest Management Act of 1944 (Drielsma, Miller & Burch Jr. 1990; Hibbard 1999; Richardson 1980; Schallau 1989; Schallau & Alston 1987). In the 1960s, the Forest Service's computer model to estimate sustained-yield harvest, FORPLAN, included

Cassandra Moseley, Ecosystem Workforce Program, University of Oregon
(cmoseley@uoregon.edu)

parameters in some places to ensure that harvests would not fall below levels needed to support local mills (Hirt 1994). In recent years concern with rural community well-being can be seen in stewardship contracting authorities, the Secure Rural Schools and Community Self-Determination Act of 2000, and annual Forest Service and Bureau of Land Management (BLM) appropriations language that allows the agencies to consider rural community benefit when awarding service contracts for fire hazard reduction and forest and watershed restoration (Moseley and Toth 2004).

Federal fire policy, in particular, impacts public-lands communities heavily because of the ecological impacts of fire exclusion and the significant resources dedicated to fire management each year. Federal fire policy has altered the landscape over time, especially in areas with naturally occurring frequent fire with low and mixed severity (Agee 2002; Arno and Allison-Bunnell 2002). Annually, the Forest Service and other federal land management agencies also allocate funds for fire suppression, preparedness, prevention, and hazard reduction. Spending on these activities has increased in recent years with the National Fire Plan and the Healthy Forest Initiative (McCarthy 2004). Given the increased resources being invested in fire management, it is particularly important to understand the distributive consequences of fire policies, particularly on rural communities. This chapter reviews the limited literature available about the social and economic costs and opportunities over time of fire suppression, prescribed fire, and hazard reduction for rural communities and other minority groups in the United States.

This review reveals that federal wildland-fire policy has shifted several times over the past one hundred years; however, suppression has long been and continues to be a central component. Over time, the ecological and socioeconomic costs of long-term fire suppression are growing. These costs (as well as the benefits) are not spread evenly across the landscape or across demographic groups. Some ecological regions have suffered more change than others; some areas are experiencing increasing numbers of large fires, while others are not. Similarly, some demographic groups are less able than others to prepare for and recover from fire. In particular, poor rural people are particularly vulnerable to fire and yet are likely to be the least able to recover due to a lack of financial resources. Fire suppression and fire-hazard reduction have benefits as well, and these are also not distributed evenly. Government workers and contractors, and contract firefighters all benefit economically from wildfire suppression and from efforts to reduce fire hazard. However, these contract workers—particularly the growing number of Hispanic workers—appear to have poorer working conditions, earn less money, have less training, and be more vulnerable to exploitation than government workers.

Wildland Fire Policy

If there has been one pervasive theme in federal fire policy over the past century, it has been to suppress wildland fire and prevent human-caused fire, whether it was accidental or intentional. According to Pyne (1982), "The history of modern fire protection is basically the story of how one fire regime, that of frontier economies, was replaced by another, that of an industrial state." Even as suppression has remained a central tenet of federal fire policy, the specifics have changed over the past century. Pyne (1981) argues that American fire policy has had four periods, each precipitated by a major fire year and taking advantage of the resources abundant during that time. During each period, the fire problem was understood differently.

During the frontier fire period (1910-1930), which came into to its own after the 1910 fires, the focus was on creating and protecting forests by stopping deliberate burning. Deliberate setting of fires had been a component of Native American and frontier economies (Boyd 1999; Hallan 1975; Lewis 1993; McKinley and Frank 1996; Timbrook et al. 1993). Gifford Pinchot, first chief of the Forest Service, knew that fire played a vital role in some forests and had significant ecological impacts, but he still believed that it was basically destructive and should be prevented everywhere in order to foster forest management (Carle 2002; Pinchot 1899). Grazing permittees and other national forest users were expected to help fight fire when it was burning near them. During the subsequent backcountry fire period (1931-1949), the Forest Service had a wealth of manpower, in the form of Civilian Conservation Corps members, which it deployed in large numbers to fight fires and build trails, roads, and fire breaks to facilitate fire suppression in the backcountry. After World War II (1950-1970), the Forest Service's focus was on mass fire, and it used the abundant surplus military equipment from World War II, Korea, and Vietnam to attack fire from the air. In Pyne's final period (1971 onward), the focus shifted from all-out suppression to a more complex regime of allowing some fires to burn, and even setting them in the wilderness to mimic natural processes. This new period of federal fire policy took advantage of, and funded, growing knowledge of fire behavior and ecology. Arguably, after the 2000 fires, the policy shifted again, this time to protection of structures and lives in the wildland-urban interface through suppression, emphasizing human safety and structural protection; hazard reduction using mechanical treatments and prescribed burning; community fire planning for hazard reduction and coordinated fire suppression; and the restoration of fire-adapted ecosystems. Even though this new framing of the problem of fire was under discussion prior to 2000 (e.g., Bailey 1991; Fischer and Arno 1988; Freedman and Fischer 1980), as with other fire policy shifts, it was a series of large fire years in the early 2000s that led to new political attention to wildland fire, changed policy emphases, and instigated agency reorganization (Pyne 1981).

Many of the policy documents in the early 2000s emphasize preparation for fire suppression, fire hazard reduction in the urban-wildland interface, community-based fire planning, and restoration of fire-adapted ecosystems (e.g. Western Governor's Association 2001; Government Accounting Office 1999, 2002). Over 70% of the National Fire Plan appropriations in the early 2000s, however, was for fire suppression and preparation for fire, with more limited funding for hazard reduction, ecosystem restoration, community-based planning, and development of ways to use the by-products of thinning activities (McCarthy 2004). Given the disparity between the policy documents and spending, it is too soon to accurately describe what the new policy regime will be or its socioeconomic impacts. Nevertheless, given that some of the new fire policies have historical antecedents, the literature about the socioeconomic impacts of fire policy historically and forest management more generally can suggest some of the likely impacts of today's fire policies, particularly fire suppression and hazard reduction, two of the cornerstones of current fire policy.

Fire suppression
The Weeks Act of 1911 and other early legislation allowed the Forest Service to spend money beyond its annual appropriation for fire suppression, and later, for fire preparedness during dry years. With this authority, the Forest Service developed a culture of expansive spending in which almost any amount of money could be used and all fires should be suppressed (Pyne 1981). The costs to the federal budget grew over time and have increased rapidly in recent years. The federal government spent almost $1.7 billion on fire suppression in 2002 and $1.3 billion in 2003 (National Interagency Fire Center 2004b). The institutions of fire suppression have proven difficult to dislodge even though over-suppression and fire exclusion have been clearly recognized problems by the scientific community and the political arena since the 1970s (Arno and Allison-Bunnell 2002).

Ecological change
Fire suppression reduced the number of acres burnt during the middle of the twentieth century. However, beginning in the 1970s, the acreage began to increase. By the 1990s, burnt acres were approaching 1910-1920s levels (Agee 1993, 2002; Arno and Allison-Bunnell 2002; National Interagency Fire Center 2004b). The increase in acres burnt is a byproduct of long-term fire suppression and other management activities that have changed

the vegetation of certain types of ecosystems (Arno 1996). In particular, fire suppression has altered low-severity, high-frequency fire regimes such as those in ponderosa pine, redwood, and Oregon oak, as well as the mixed fire-severity regimes common in the Interior West, making them more vulnerable to stand-replacing fires. Prevention of human-set fire also reduced the reproduction of fire-dependent species such as the long-leaf pine in the South and knobcone pine in the West (Arno and Allison-Bunnell 2002; Carle 2002). Suppression has probably had less-dramatic effects in naturally high-severity fire regimes such as lodgepole pine and coastal Douglas fir regimes, where infrequent stand-replacement fires are the norm. In these regimes, suppression may delay but probably not prevent stand-replacing fire (Agee 1993; Arno and Allison-Bunnell 2002; Hessburg and Agee 2003; Romme and Despain 1989).

Economic and social costs

Fire suppression and prevention have changed ecological processes, which in turn have changed the economic opportunities for people who work on the land. These factors have, for example, reduced grazing lands and meadows, changed the types of non-timber forest products available, and shifted game-animal habitats. Early foresters made this trade-off because they wanted to prevent a timber famine. They believed that fire suppression would ensure forest reproduction through the recruitment of young trees, which they believed fire destroyed (Pinchot 1899; Carle 2002).

Native Americans in many regions of the United States used fire to cultivate desired plant species, increase wildlife habitat, and a number of other activities. Certainly, burning cultures varied considerably, with some tribes undertaking little or no intentional burning and others burning quite frequently (Blackburn and Anderson 1993; Boyd 1999; Lewis 1993; Pyne 1983; Timbrook et al. 1993; see also Reich 2006). Ranchers and farmers in some areas also used fire to clear and maintain pasture and fields (McKinley and Frank 1996; Pyne 1982). The ending of these sorts of burning practices was part of a larger struggle to end Native American and pioneers' control over the West and replace it with an industrial society (Pyne 1982, 1983). Although John Wesley Powell later came to support prescribed burning, he argued, for example, that "protection of forests of the entire Arid Region of the United States is reduced to one single problem—Can these forests be saved from fire?" The chief source of fire, he argued, was Indians. "The fires can, then, be very greatly curtailed by the removal of the Indians" (John Wesley Powell as quoted in Pyne 1982).

Today, prescribed fire is again considered a legitimate management tool, particularly as a part of fire hazard reduction and the restoration of fire-adapted ecosystems. The trade-offs between forestry and other uses are more obvious, as are the consequences of preventing prescribed fire even for forestry. "It is clear that the tragedy of American fire was not that wildfires were suppressed but that controlled fires were no longer set" (Pyne 1982). In some instances, fire suppression may be cost effective, in the short term, for preventing the loss of forest and farmland income (Bennettonet al. 2001) and, in many instances, prescribed fire has been shown to increase immediate income from rangelands and farmlands (Bernardo et al. 1988; Bond and Archibald 2003; Dyer and Smith 2003;). On a larger scale, the hope is that the reintroduction of fire will reduce fire-suppression costs and losses from wildland fire (Graham, McCaffrey & Jain 2004; Western Governor's Association 2001). As with other resource management programs, prescribed burning programs will affect various social and economic groups differently depending on how the burning is structured, because different burn patterns will favor different types of plants and wildlife over time (Bond and Archibald 2003).

Economic and social benefits

Although the institutionalization of fire suppression has cost a great deal, through the federal government and therefore taxpayers, each year for almost a century and changed many North American ecosystems, it has also created considerable economic opportunity for businesses and workers. In addition to their permanent fire-management staff, the federal land management agencies hire temporary seasonal workers and contract with businesses to fight wildland fires. In 2001, for example, with expanded funds from the National Fire Plan, the Forest Service in Oregon and Washington filled 878 new positions and the Fish and Wildlife Service hired 86 fire staff (Moseleyet al. 2002). In addition, the federal land management agencies contract with numerous businesses for fire crews, equipment, food, and other supplies necessary to support suppression.

Individual large fires can create considerable economic opportunity for fire-suppression contractors and government employees. In 2002, for example, the Forest Service spent over $37 million dollars on the Hayman Fire in Colorado and $153 million on the Biscuit Fire on the California-Oregon border (Government Accounting Office 2004; Graham 2003; Quinn 2004) Of the money spent on the Hayman Fire, $6.3 million was spent on federal personnel and $27.8 million on contracted services. In addition, the Forest Service spent almost $24 million on burned-area recovery including $1.8 million on agency personnel and $20 million on contracted services (Graham 2003) on the same area. It is difficult to tell how much of this money went directly to employees in the form of wages and how much was spent on supplies and capital equipment. For fire-crew contracts, the major costs are wages, whereas for other contracts, costs of equipment such as helicopters and supplies such as fuel are likely to be more important.

The increase in fire-suppression spending creates, in absolute terms, more economic opportunity for the fire-suppression industry. But the nature of these opportunities has been changing in recent years. In particular, the federal land management agencies have been making increasing use of fire-suppression contractors. For example, in 1998, the Pacific Northwest had about 88 twenty-person fire crews, about 95% of the twenty-person crews nationwide. By 2003, the Northwest had 293 twenty-person crews (Pulaski 2002, 2003). The increasing use of fire-suppression contractors is in part because of the reduction in personnel working in national forests, which has created a smaller pool of federal employees to draw from to fight fires, especially in the Pacific Northwest (Government Accounting Office 2004). For example, the number of forest-level staff fell in western Oregon and Washington from 6,044 in 1990 to 3,789 in 2001 (Charnley et al. 2006.). In addition, increased fire-suppression contracting is part of a larger government strategy to replace government employees with contracted workers (Executive Office of the President and Office of Management and Budget 2003).

There is some evidence to suggest that contract firefighters have worse working conditions and lower job quality than government employees who fight fire. On the one hand, contract firefighting provides job opportunities for non-citizens, jobs that are not otherwise available to them because federal employees must be U.S. citizens. On the other hand, there is evidence that an increasing number of contract firefighters are Hispanic, some of whom are undocumented. In some instances, firefighters may not be adequately trained or may not speak English adequately to understand directions in an emergency (Moseley 2005; Pulaski 2002, 2003).

Contract fire-crew members are on-call workers paid only when they are called to a fire or to stand by. Seasonal government firefighters are paid throughout their working season regardless of whether they are working on a fire or not; they typically perform other activities when they are not fighting fires. A study of Forest Service National Fire Plan hires in 2002 found that 98% of them were paid above the federal minimum wage for fire-crew contract workers (Moseley, Toth & Cambier 2002). Some fire-suppression contractors obtain non-fire contracts for activities such as thinning to keep employees working between fires. Interviews with Hispanic forest workers in the Pacific Northwest suggest that fire-suppression work is erratic even during the fire season and that some spend considerable time waiting to be called. Moreover, Hispanic contract firefighters see limited opportunities for advancement in forestry services. Both contract and government employees are likely to be paid for food and lodging while fighting fires, although contract workers appear to be paid inconsistently for travel time (Moseley 2006a). Government employees have union representation; there are no collective bargaining agreements for fire-crew contractors. In addition, government employees have formal grievance systems whereas a recent study of Hispanic contract fire-suppression workers suggests that they are likely to believe that there is little recourse if they feel that they have been treated improperly other than to ignore the treatment or quit (Moseley 2006a). They have particularly little recourse if they are undocumented, because complaints may lead to deportation. Although many contractors undoubtedly treat their employees quite well, particularly when they are U.S. citizens, there appears to be more opportunity for abuse of contract workers than government employees, especially when the workers lack legal permission to work in the United States (see also Brown 2000, 2001; Mann 2001).

There has been some question in the political arena about whether rural public-lands communities are getting their fair share of the firefighting opportunities. This has become a particular concern because of the rapid increase in fire-suppression contracting and the decline in federal timber sales and restoration activities not associated with fire, which have historically been viewed as economic-development opportunities for rural communities (Jungwirth 2002; Moseley 2006b; Moseley and Toth 2004; Schallau 1989; Schallau and Alston 1987). For some, fire-suppression activities appear to be among the few remaining economic opportunities on federal lands. One also hears concerns about inadequate use of local firefighting resources whose use might reduce inefficiencies and fire-suppression costs (National Academy of Public Administration 2003).

It may be that direct government employment creates more local employment than contract firefighting; 70% of firefighters the Forest Service hired lived within 150 air miles of their duty station at the time they were hired, although firefighters are sent to distant fires when the need arises. Labor-intensive forestry service contractors often work far from home and rarely hire local people when they do so. For example, on six national forests across the country found that, of the thirty-three fire-suppression contractors in the sample, two always hired locally when working far from home and three sometimes did so; the remainder brought their crews with them (Moseley 2006).

Studies of other types of federal forest management contracting suggest that contractors that perform labor-intensive activities are more likely to work far from home whereas contracts for performing equipment-intensive work are more likely to be awarded to local contractors (Moseley and Shankle 2001; Moseley and Toth 2004; Moseley et al. 2002). Analogously, it may be that federal land management agencies are more likely to use distant fire crews and local fire tender and engine contracts. This is a risky analogy, however, because the contracting mechanisms for fire suppression differ considerably from other types of forestry services. Fire-suppression contracting involves regional or national season-long contracts in which firms wait to be called through a fire-dispatch system, whereas forestry services contracts are typically awarded project-by-project by the particular management unit wanting the contracted services.

Much of the spending on contractors, especially on large fires, is done through regional and national crew contracts. Dispatchers are to exhaust local resources before calling for more distant contractors (Mills & Holtrop 2003). But during the early 2000s, more than 90% of the nation's twenty-person contract fire crews were from Oregon (Pulaski 2003). Under these circumstances, local economic opportunities may be limited whenever fires outstrip government personnel resources. Although systematic studies have not been performed, a cursory review of employment statistics suggests that few employment opportunities were created as a result of the large fires in Montana during 2000 (Byron and McKee 2004; Polizen 2004). It may be, however, that employment impacts, even if positive, were too small to see in aggregated numbers. Although it has not been quantified, the Biscuit Fire did create some local economic benefit in summer 2002, because the Forest Service made considerable use of one of the nation's largest fire crew contractors that had its headquarters nearby. Its resources, including crews, tenders, engines, and a helicopter, were used on the fire (for a discussion of resources deployed on the fire see Galloway 2003). Although Kent et al. (2003) reported the amount of money used on contracted fire-suppression resources on the Hayman Fire in Colorado, they did not consider where the contractors and their employees came from when they evaluated the local economic impact of the fire.

In addition to national contracts, however, Emergency Equipment Rental Agreements and state- and regional-level contracts may create local economic opportunity for people when they are called to stand by when fire danger is high or when an agency is performing prescribed burning or when fires are small. In Lake County, Oregon, for example, a local nonprofit organization coordinated training and equipment inspections to increase the number of local tenders on the regional contract from zero to four in the first year to eight in the second year. This rapidly increased local tender use and created new economic opportunities for the tender owners and their employees (Spencer 2003; Western Forestry Leadership Coalition 2004). More recent changes in equipment specifications, contract requirements, and inspection processes, however, may favor firms with significant capital available to them and make it more difficult for smaller rural firms with limited access to capital (Western Forestry Leadership Coalition 2004).

The literature about the business and employment impacts of fire suppression is thin and it raises as many questions as it answers. But it does suggest that direct government hiring may create more and better-quality local and rural employment opportunities than contracting. Wages, job duration, and worker protections appear to be greater for government workers than for contract workers and government employment may require less rural-community capacity than developing and maintaining local contracting businesses. Direct government employment may also create proportionately more employment opportunities for rural residents, although the data in this area are scant.

Worker and community safety

Another concern with fire suppression and prescribed fire is with worker (firefighter) and community health and safety. Firefighter safety has been a primary concern of federal fire management and a priority of the National Fire Plan (Western Governor's Association 2001). Each year, firefighters are killed in the course of their work, sometimes caught by fire, at other times involved in vehicle and equipment accidents (Fischer and Arno 1988; National Interagency Fire Center 2004a; see also Daniels, this volume). In addition, Reinhardt et al. (2000) have found that among firefighters working on prescribed fire, "up to 14% of the exposures to respiratory irritants . . . and 8% of the exposures to CO [carbon monoxide] were above the limits recommended by occupational health advisory organizations to protect worker health." About 5% of respiratory irritant and 2% of CO exposures also exceeded the limits set by the Occupational Safety and Health Administration (OSHA), which are less stringent. A similar study of firefighter exposure during wildland firefighting found similar exposure rates, about 3% for CO overall, with considerable variation among firefighter tasks; firefighters involved in initial attack and holding the line had greater exposure than mop-up crews (Reinhardt and Ottmar 2000).

Prescribed fire also has impacts on air quality and the health of the general public. The Clean Air Act closely regulates emissions from industrial activities and itinerant pollution sources such as prescribed fire. To comply with the Clean Air Act, federal land management agencies and others must have smoke-management plans that minimize the impacts of smoke on air quality. Although it is an important regulatory concern, evidence suggests that the particulate emissions of prescribed fire are fewer than those of wildfire by perhaps 50%, at least in the interior Columbia River Basin. In addition, because the timing of prescribed fire can be controlled to minimize air-quality impacts, there is more opportunity to limit air-quality degradation than with wildfire (Hessburg and Agee 2003; Huff et al. 1995).

Hazard reduction

If fire suppression has created overstocked stands and increased fire severity in some ecosystems, then the major solution promoted in the policy arena has been fire-hazard reduction, especially in the wildland-urban interface. Thinning of small-diameter trees, the removal of brush, prescribed burning, and the creation of fire breaks have been major focuses of recent legislation and policy documents (Western Governor's Association 2001; McCarthy 2004). There is, however, considerable controversy about the effectiveness of particular hazard-reduction strategies in different ecological circumstances (Agee 2002; Fischer and Arno 1988; Graham et al. 2004; Hessburg and Agee 2003; Martinson et al. 2003).

Regardless of how thinning and other fuels reductions are structured to meet ecological objectives, the way fire-hazard reduction funds are spent will have social and economic consequences. Some might argue that hazard-reduction funding should be targeted at the communities with the highest property values at risk or where the greatest number of homes are located. Others argue that scarce government funds should be spent protecting poor communities because they are most socially and economically vulnerable to fire losses, the least able to pay for fuel reduction on their own lands, and the least likely to be fully insured (ECONorthwest 2001; Lynn and Gerlitz 2005; Morton 2003). One case study in New Mexico found that fire-hazard reduction resources had been directed to wealthier communities, even when the poor and wealthy communities faced similar fire risk (Morton 2003; see also Holmes et al., this volume).

As with fire suppression, fire-hazard reduction has the potential to create economic opportunity for businesses and workers who perform these activities, either as employees of public and private landowners or as contractors and their employees. For example, in 2001, the Forest Service and the BLM in Oregon and Washington spent $39.2 million on fire-hazard-reduction activities, of which $8.2 million was contracted (Government Printing Office 2002; Moseley et al. 2002)

All of the studies of the distribution of fire-hazard reduction and other National Fire Plan contracts have been performed in Oregon, Washington, and Northern California. Typically, labor-intensive contracts are awarded to more distant contractors than equipment-intensive contracts, and contracts for work performed in Washington and eastern Oregon are awarded to more distant contractors than those performed in western Oregon (Kauffman 2001; Moseley et al. 2003; Moseley and Shankle 2001). The appropriations language associated with the National Fire Plan has given the authority to federal land management agencies to consider the local economic benefit when awarding fire-hazard-reduction contracts, which appears to have led to some contracts being awarded to contractors closer to the national forest where the work was performed. However, this did not occur when two isolated rural communities were examined (Moseley and Toth 2004; Moseley et al.. 2003). Because of the labor-intensive nature of much of the thinning and other fire-hazard-reduction activities, rural communities, especially isolated ones, have a difficult time developing and maintaining the capacity to compete against larger, urban-based companies that routinely travel long distances to work on public lands. This is particularly true when the government structures contracts to require large numbers of people over relatively short periods of time.

Conclusions

This literature reveals that fire policy has evolved over time as the American economy has changed from frontier to industrial and post-industrial. With these economic developments and accompanying social changes, the socioeconomic impacts of fire and fire policy have shifted. Even in our current political economy, fire policy has both negative and positive impacts. "The problem of adjusting fire practices to land use has existed for millennia. It is complicated by the fact that, because fire can be as influential by being withheld as by being applied, there is no neutral position possible" (Pyne 1982). These impacts are not distributed evenly across ecotypes, social class, or ethnicity. Long-term fire suppression has changed some ecosystems more than others, even within the fire-dominant ecosystems of the American West. In addition, poor rural communities may be more vulnerable to the losses of wildfire because they are likely to have the fewest resources available to them to reduce fire hazard and to recover from a wildfire without government assistance (ECONorthwest 2001). It is an open question whether our current fire policies are addressing these realities. Similarly, decisions about how to structure the work of fire suppression and hazard reduction have an impact on who receives the economic benefits of these activities. Direct government employment may create better-quality jobs for fire-suppression workers, whereas contract forest work seems to lower job quality and limit benefits to rural communities. Contract fire work incorporates Hispanics into the workforce but some of them are vulnerable to exploitation under the current system and lack the effective worker protections that government employees have.

REFERENCES

Agee, J. K. 1993. *Fire Ecology of Pacific Northwest Forests*. Covelo, California: Island Press.

————. 2002. "The fallacy of passive management." *Conservation Biology in Practice* 3 (1):18-25.

Arno, S. F. 1996. "The seminal importance of fire in ecosystem management—the impetus for this publication." In C. C. Hardy and S. F. Arno (eds.) The use of fire in forest restoration: A general session at the annual meeting of the society for ecological restoration, Seattle, Washington, September 14-16, 1995. Ogden, Utah: USDA Forest Service, Intermountain Research Station.

————, and S. Allison-Bunnell. 2002. *Flames in our Forest: Disaster or Renewal?* Covelo, California: Island Press, 3-5.

Bailey, D. W. 1991. "The wildland-urban interface: Social and political implications in the 1990s." *Fire Management Notes* 52 (1):11-18.

Bennetton, J., P. Cashin, D. Jones, and J. Soligo. 2001. "An economic evaluation of bushfire prevention and suppression." *The Australian Journal of Agricultural and Resource Economics* 42 (2):149-75.

Bernardo, D. J., D. M. Engle, and E. T. M. Collum. 1988. "An economic assessment of risk and returns from prescribed burning on tallgrass prairie." *Journal of Range Management* 41 (2):178-83.

Blackburn, T., and K. Anderson (eds.). 1993. *Before the Wilderness*. Menlo Park, California: Ballena Press.

Bond, W. J., and S. Archibald. 2003. "Confronting complexity: Fire policy in South African savanna parks." *International Journal of Wildland Fire* 12 (3-4):381-89.

Boyd, R. (ed.). 1999. *Indians, Fire, and the Land in the Pacific Northwest*. Corvallis: Oregon State University Press.

Brown, B. 2000. "The multi-ethnic, nontimber forest workforce in the Pacific Northwest: Reconceiving the players in forest management." In D. J. Salazar and D. K. Alper (eds.), *Sustaining the Forests of the Pacific Coast,* Vancouver, Canada: UBC Press, 148-69.

————. 2001. Analysis of challenges facing community forestry: The role of low income forest workers. Wolf Creek, Oregon: Jefferson Center of Education and Research.

Byron, E., and J. McKee. 2004. "Not a big splash." *Helena Independent Record,* May 25.

Carle, D. 2002. *Burning Questions: America's Fight with Nature's Fire*. Westport, Connecticut: Praeger.

Charnley, S., E. Donoghue, C. Stuart, C. Dillingham, L. Buttolph, W. Kay, R. McLain, C. Moseley, R. Phillips, and L. Tobe. 2006. Northwest Forest Plan - The first ten years (1994-2003): Socioeconomic monitoring results, vol. III: Rural communities and economies. PNW-GTR-649. Portland, Oregon: USDA Forest Service, Pacific Northwest Research Station.

Drielsma, J. H., J. A. Miller, and W. R. Burch Jr. 1990. "Sustained yield and community stability in American forestry." In R. G. Lee, D. R. Field, and W. R. Burch Jr. (eds.), *Community and Forestry: Continuities in the Sociology of Natural Resources*. Boulder, Colorado: Westview Press, 55-68.

Dyer, R., and M. S. Smith. 2003. "Ecological and economic assessment of prescribed burning impacts in semi-arid pastoral lands of northern Australia." *International Journal of Wildland Fire* 12 (3-4):403-13.

ECONorthwest. 2001. Wildfire and poverty: An overview of the interactions among wildfires, fire-related programs, and poverty in the western United States. Eugene, Oregon: Center for Watershed and Community Health, Mark O. Hatfield School of Government, Portland State University.

Executive Office of the President, and Office of Management and Budget. 2003. Competitive sourcing: Conducting public-private competition in a reasoned and responsible manner. Washington, D.C.: Executive Office of the President, Office of Management and Budget.

Fischer, W. C., and S. F. Arno. 1988. Protecting people and homes from wildfire in the interior west: Proceedings of the symposium and workshop. Ugdon, Utah: USDA Forest Service, Intermountain Research Station.

Freedman, J. D., and W. C. Fischer. 1980. "Forest home fire hazards." *Western Wildlands* 6 (4):23-26.

Galloway, P. 2003. "Biscuit fire chronology." USDA Forest Service, Siskiyou National Forest. http://www.biscuitfire.com/chronology.htm.

Government Accounting Office. 1999. Western national forests: A cohesive strategy is needed to address catastrophic wildfire threats. Washington, D.C.: Government Accounting Office.

———. 2002. Severe wildland fires: Leadership and accountability needed to reduce risks to communities and resources. Washington, D.C.: Government Accounting Office.

———. 2004. Biscuit fire: Analysis of fire response, resource availability, and personnel certification standards. Washington, D. C.: Government Accounting Office.

Government Printing Office. 2002. National Fire Plan: An interagency accomplishments report for fiscal year 2001, Oregon/Washington. n.p.: Government Printing Office.

Graham, R. T. 2003. Hayman fire case study. Ford Collins, Colorado: USDA Forest Service, Rocky Mountain Research Station.

———, S. McCaffrey, and T. B. Jain. 2004. Science basis for changing forest structure to modify wildfire behavior and severity. Fort Collins, Colorado: USDA Forest Service, Rocky Mountain Research Station.

Hallan, S. (ed). 1975. *Fire and Hearth*. Canberra: Australian Institute of Aboriginal Studies.

Hessburg, P. F., and J. K. Agee. 2003. "An environmental narrative of inland northwest United States forests, 1800-2000." *Forest Ecology and Management* 178:23-59.

Hibbard, M. 1999. "Organic regionalism, corporate liberalism, and federal land management: Creating Pacific Northwest timber towns." *Journal of Planning Education and Research* 19:144-50.

Hirt, P. W. 1994. *A Conspiracy of Optimism: Management of the National Forests since World War Two*. Lincoln: University of Nebraska Press.

Huff, M. H., R. D. Ottmar, E. Alvarado, R. E. Vihnanek, J. F. Lehmkuhl, P. F. Hessburg, and R. L. Everett. 1995. Historical and current forest landscapes in eastern Oregon and Washington. Part II: Linking vegetation characteristics to potential fire behavior and related smoke production. Portland, Oregon: USDA Forest Service, Pacific Northwest Research Station.

Jungwirth, L. 2002. "Who will be the gardeners of Eden?" *Chronicle of Community Spring*:31-34.

Kauffman, M. 2001. An analysis of forest service and BLM contracting in Lake County, Oregon: Fremont national forest and bureau of land management. Lakeview, Oregon: Sustainable Northwest.

Kent, B., K. Gebert, S. McCaffrey, W. Martin, D. Calkin, E. Schuster, I. Martin, H. W. Bender, B. Alward, Y. Jumagal, P. J. Cohn, M. Carroll, D. Williams, and C. Ekarius. 2003. "Social and economic issues of the Hayman fire." In R. T. Graham (ed.), Hayman fire case study. Fort Collins, Colorado: USDA Forest Service, Rocky Mountain Research Station.

Lewis, H. T. 1993. "Patterns of indian burning in California: Ecology and ethnohistory." In T. Blackburn and K. Anderson (eds.), *Before the Wilderness: Environmental Management by Native Californians.* Menlo Park, California: Ballena Press, 55-116.

Lynn, K., and W. Gerlitz. 2005. "Mapping the relationship between wildfire and poverty." Resource Innovations, University of Oregon and National Network of Forest Practioners. http://ri.uoregon.edu/programs/CCE/poverty.html.

Mann, G. 2001. "The state, race, and 'wage slavery' in the forest sector of the Pacific Northwest United States." *Journal of Peasant Studies* 29 (1):61-88.

Martinson, E., P. N. Omi, and W. Sheppard. 2003. "Effects of fuel treatments on fire severity." In R. T. Graham (ed.), Hayman fire case study. Fort Collins, Colorado: USDA Forest Service, Rocky Mountain Research Station.

McCarthy, L. F. 2004. "Snapshot: The state of the national fire plan." The Forest Trust. http://www.theforesttrust.org/images/forestprotection/Snapshot-Master. pdf.

McKinley, G., and D. Frank. 1996. Stories on the land: An environmental history of the Applegate and upper Illinois valleys. Medford, Oregon: USDI Bureau of Land Management, USDA, Rogue River National Forest and Siskiyou National Forest.

Mills, T. J., and J. D. Holtrop. 2003. Letter to regional foresters, station directors, area director, International Institute of Tropical Forestry director, Job Corps, and WO staff re: Clarification of policy for ordering non-local contractors on incidents. Washington, D.C.: USDA Forest Service.

Morton, J. 2003. An evaluation of fuel reduction projects in the eastern Cibola national forest. Santa Fe, Newe Mexico: National Community Forestry Center, Southwest Region.

Moseley, Cassandra. 2006. "Ethnic Differences in Job Quality among Forest Workers on Six National Forests." *Policy Sciences* 3(2): 113-33.

———. 2006a. "Working conditions in Labor-intensive Forestry Jobs in Oregon." EWP Working Paper #14. Eugene, Oregon: Ecosystem Workforce Program, University of Oregon.

———. 2006b. Procurement contracting in the affected counties of the Northwest Forest Plan: Twelve years of change. PNW-GTR-661. Portland, Oregon: USDA Forest Pacific Northwest Research Station.

———, and S. Shankle. 2001. "Who gets the work? National forest contracting in the Pacific Northwest." *Journal of Forestry* 99 (9):32-37.

———, N. Toth, and A. Cambier. 2002. "The business and employment effects of the national fire plan in Oregon and Washington in 2001." EWP Working Paper #6. Eugene, Oregon: Ecosystem Workforce Program, University of Oregon.

———, M. Balaev, and A. Lake. 2003. "Long term trends in contracting and the impact of the national fire plan in northern California." EWP Working Paper #7. Eugene, Oregon: Ecosystem Workforce Program, University of Oregon.

———, and N. Toth. 2004. "Fire hazard reduction and economic opportunity: How are the benefits of the national fire plan distributed?" *Society and Natural Resources* 17 (8):701-16.

National Academy of Public Administration. 2003. Containing wildland fire costs: Utilizing local firefighting forces. Washington, D.C.: National Academy of Public Administration.

National Interagency Fire Center. 2004a. "Historical wildland firefighter fatalities." National Interagency Fire Center. http://www.nifc.gov/reports/index. html.

————. 2004b. "Wildland fire statistics." National Interagency Fire Center. http:// www.nifc.gov/stats/wildlandfirestats.html.

Oregon Employment Department. 2004. "Covered employment and wages." Oregon Labor Market Information System. http://www.qualityinfo.org/olmisj/ CEP.

Pinchot, G. 1899. "The relation of forests and forest fires." *National Geographic Magazine* 10:393-403.

Polizen, P. 2004. Personal communication, May 27.

Pulaski, A. 2002. "State tightens fire crew enforcement." *Oregonian*, September 22, 2002, sec. A01.

————. "Fire crew crackdown proposed." *Oregonian*, January 29, 2003, sec. B01.

Pyne, S. J. 1981. "Fire policy and fire research in the US Forest Service." *Journal of Forest History* 25 (2):64-77.

————. 1982. *Fire in America: A Cultural History of Wildland and Rural Fire.* Princeton, New Jersey: Princeton University Press. Reprinted in paperback 1997. Seattle: University of Washington Press.

————. 1983. "Indian fires." *Natural History* 92 (2):6-11.

Quinn, B. 2004. "Severe season delayed attack on biscuit fire: A GAO investigation report says other 2002 blazes initially took precedence over Josephine county's scattered problems." Oregonian, May 13.

Reinhardt, T. E., and R. D. Ottmar. 2000. Smoke exposure at western wildfires. Portland, Oregon: USDA Forest Service, Pacific Northwest Research Station.

————, R. D. Ottmar, and A. J. S. Hanneman. 2000. Smoke exposure among firefighters at prescribed burns in the Pacific Northwest. Portland, Oregon: USDA Forest Service, Pacific Northwest Research Station.

Richardson, E. 1980. *BLM's Billion-dollar Checkerboard: Managing the O&C Lands.* Santa Cruz, California: Forest History Society.

Romme, W. H., and D. G. Despain. 1989. "Historical perspective on the Yellowstone fires of 1988." *BioScience* 39 (10):695-99.

Schallau, C. H. 1989. "Sustained yield versus community stability." *Journal of Forestry* 87 (9):16-28.

————, and R. M. Alston. 1987. "The commitment to community stability: A policy or shibboleth?" *Environmental Law* 17 (3):429-81.

Spencer, C. 2003. "Federal service contracting in Lake County: Employment opportunities for local businesses, 2001 and 2002." EWP Working Paper #10: Eugene, Oregon: Ecosystem Workforce Program and Lake County Resources Initiative.

Timbrook, J., J. R. Johnson, and D. D. Earle. 1993. "Vegetation burning by the Chumash." In T. Blackburn and K. Anderson (eds.), *Before the Wilderness: Environmental Management by Native Californians.* Menlo Park, California: Ballena Press.

Western Forestry Leadership Coalition. 2004. "Success stories: Oregon: Local resources help fire suppression efforts." Western Forestry Leadership Coalition. http://www.wflccenter.org/success_stories/26.php

Western Governors' Association. 2001. "A collaborative approach for reducing wildland fire risks to communities and the environment." Western Governors' Association. http://www.westgov.org/wga/initiatives/fire/final_fire_rpt.pdf.

Policy and Institutional Arrangements in Federal Wildland Fire Mitigation

Charles Wise and Andrew J. Yoder

This chapter uses an adaptive management framework to assess the evolution of policy and institutional arrangements for wildland-fire management in the United States. This chapter finds that:

(1) Federal natural-resource management agencies, which have historically operated separately and hierarchically, have begun to show recognition of adaptive management.

(2) Although federal agencies have been slow to implement several of the requirements of the 1995 National Fire Policy and the National Fire Plan (NFP), they have begun to jointly develop systems that provide for more comprehensive, data-driven ways to prioritize wildland-fire hazards for management.

(3) Historically, natural-resource management agencies have not evaluated fire-management programs systematically or jointly. Federal policy has been modified to require systematic evaluation, but more informative evaluation awaits completion of comprehensive data systems such as LANDFIRE.

(4) Horizontal coordination of fire-management programs among federal agencies has historically been spotty. Federal agencies have established a headquarters framework for working together but now need to translate this national framework into effective action at the regional and district levels.

(5) Some steps toward greater integration of federal with state and local fire-management efforts have been taken, but collaborative processes must be developed in detail and managed on a sustained basis.

(6) Federal assistance to states and communities to build their capacities to partner with federal agencies in fire management has been limited and scattered.

Charles Wise, School of Public and Environmental Affairs, Indiana University (wise@indiana.edu); Andrew J. Yoder, U.S. District Court, Western District of Texas

Organizational Learning and Adaptive Management

Federal policies early in the twentieth century clearly laid the foundation for extraordinary fire risk in the twenty-first century. The policy that attempted to exclude fire from federal lands started in the 1910-1919 period and the policy that focused on suppressing fires by 10 a.m. the next morning was in force from 1935 to 1982. Such policies increased wildfire risk, resulting in massive wildland fuel accumulations (Government Accountability Office [GAO] 1999; National Commission on Wildfire Disasters 1994; USDA Forest Service 2000). These policies, roundly characterized as failures (Busenberg 2004), resulted when once-successful policies were not revised as they became ineffective and even counterproductive, which can occur in emergency-management settings (Walters 1986). Three characteristics of emergency situations—uncertainty, interaction, and complexity—are particularly relevant to wildland fire because they limit the effectiveness of standard policy formulation and implementation (Comfort 1988; Saveland 1991).

In the wildland-fire context, agencies and managers must respond to uncertain events, which create inherent problems for designing policies and procedures. When uncertainty is the rule, and the magnitude, scope, and timing of the response required by the emergency are complex and unknown, ordinary instruments of planning are inadequate (Comfort 1988; Holling et al. 2000; Johnson 1999). To overcome uncertain environments, managers must develop organizational learning capacity by employing three rational processes: risk assessment, information feedback to decision makers, and adjustment of performance based on current information (Berkes & Folke 2000; Chen et al. 2003; Comfort 1988; Holling 1978; Holling et al. 2000; Walters 1986). In practice, managers employ adaptive management techniques to ensure that decisions are used as an opportunity for organizational learning (Finlayson and McCay 2000; Graham and Kruger 2002; Holling 1978; Walters 1986).

Adaptive management is an iterative process, calling for the integration of science and management, treating policies as experiments from which managers can learn (Graham and Kruger 2002; Holling 1978; Holling et al. 2000; Johnson 1999; Lee 1993; Walters 1986). The adaptive method requires managers to change their approach as new information arrives (Alexander 2002). This mode of management differs from traditional forms of management by emphasizing the importance of feedback in shaping policy, followed by further systematic experimentation and evaluation (Berkes and Folke 2000; Graham and Kruger 2002; McLain and Lee 1996). Adaptive management is premised on the notion that the knowledge available to a manager is always incomplete and that surprise is an inevitable component of implementation (Holling 1978; Holling et al. 2000; Saveland 1989, 1991). In many ways, adaptive management resembles indigenous knowledge systems, or "knowledge-practice-belief complexes," which also stress "learning by doing" (Holling et al. 2000). Implementing adaptive management may require new management approaches to the task of dealing with wildland fire (Graham and Kruger 2002).

The process of adaptive management differs from a number of other, more traditional approaches to making management decisions (Johnson 1999). Adaptive management begins by bringing together interested stakeholders to discuss the problem and any available data and then progresses to developing models of the problem (Johnson 1999). For this reason, adaptive management is thought to be particularly well suited for citizen-agency interactions, which occur in a cyclical pattern of interaction, involving repeat players (Shindler et al. 1999). Adaptive management seeks to bring about decisions that are both "objectively better" because they reflect more information and "subjectively better" because they are more open to public participation (Shindler et al. 1999; Lawrence and Daniels 1996). Fire-management plans and decisions will be "objectively better" if they incorporate factors of the interconnectivity of the soil, water, air processes and functions, and fish and wildlife habitats, and in addition to this interconnectivity pay attention to landscape variability and other disturbance processes such as droughts and floods (DellaSalla et al. 2004).

Once stakeholders have been brought together for discussion and modeling, adaptive managers develop plans to meet goals and generate information to reduce data gaps and uncertainties (Johnson 1999). Management plans are then implemented, along with monitoring plans designed to analyze data and update managers' understanding of how the adopted approach worked in practice (Johnson 1999). At the end of the process, results are monitored in order to evaluate the progress achieved by the management approach taken (Shindler et al. 1999).

Barriers that must be overcome to implement adaptive management include: political interventions (Shindler et al. 1999; Wondolleck and Yaffee 1994); lack of public trust (Shindler et al. 1999); lack of information, including quantifiable data (McLain and Lee 1996; Saveland 1991); disagreements between actors about the "facts" (McLain and Lee 1996); a temptation to hide unfavorable information (McLain and Lee 1996); and cost (McLain and Lee 1996). In the federal government, two departments—Interior and Agriculture—and the five largest land management agencies have responsibility for guiding the implementation of fire policies. These agencies have begun to recognize the value of adaptive management, and the Department of the Interior recently adopted the process, hoping to encourage cooperation among stakeholders and reduce lawsuits filed under the National Environmental Policy Act (69 Fed. Reg. 10866; Berman 2004). In addition, the Quadrennial Fire and Fuel Review Report prepared by an interagency panel for the federal natural-resource management agencies presented a strategic framework for federal agencies that incorporates some adaptive management factors (QFFR Integration Panel 2005). While it is too soon to evaluate the success of these initiatives, adaptive management is a valuable mechanism for incorporating lessons learned in management scenarios (Hobbs 2003).

Planning

Planning is an integral part of the adaptive management process, indispensable to its proper functioning. (De Greene 1982; Shindler et al. 1999) Planning is essential to managing forest lands, and is required by various land management statutes as well as the Government Performance and Results Act (GPRA) (National Academy of Public Administration [NAPA] 2001a; Nelson 1979; Schweitzer et al. 1984). The planning process is critical in determining how fire will be used as a management tool, and must be linked to program management objectives (Coats 1995). The planning process allows managers to specifically define the desired future conditions for wilderness ecosystems, as well as to integrate public health and other considerations into forest and fire management (Stokes 1995). The planning stage is also an important point at which public input is integrated into forest management and it must be approached carefully (Lawrence and Daniels 1996; Murphy 1995). Other recent federal initiatives increase the necessity for large-scale planning. The National Fire Plan has infused over one billion dollars annually into wildland-fire efforts and directs agencies to pursue both improved fire response and vegetative management. The Healthy Forest Restoration Act (16 U.S.C. 6501 et seq.) instructs the Secretary of Agriculture to carry out programs to inventory and monitor forest stands on national forests and (with owner consent) private lands.

Built upon the principles of the 1995 interagency Fire Policy, the National Fire Plan requires that each burnable acre of federal land be covered by a fire-management plan (FMP) that identifies how fires will be managed (GAO 2002b; Stokes 1995). The 1995 policy directs the agencies to conduct fire-management planning on a coordinated, interagency basis using compatible planning processes (GAO 2002b). In fighting wildland fires, agencies rely on FMPs—which contain information on how wildland fires should be addressed—as well as computer planning models that use planning information to identify personnel and equipment needs for safe and effective fire fighting (GAO 2002b). These plans identify the level of risk associated with each burnable acre and set management objectives (GAO2002b; Bunnell 1995).

Despite the requirement in the 1995 Fire Policy, agencies have been slow to establish fire-management plans. By 2001, over half of the land units requiring FMPs were without compliant plans (GAO 2001, 2002b; NAPA 2001a). Reasons for this failure ranged from lack of time, resources, and adequate data to create the plans to lack of accountability on the part of individual land units and inadequate guidance in preparing the plans (GAO 2002b; NAPA 2001a). (However, the remaining plans were scheduled to be completed by December 2004 [GAO 2005].) Further, the land management agencies have been using different computer planning models, leading to divergent approaches that fundamentally fail to meet the 1995 policy's coordination mandate (GAO 2002b). For example, none of the agencies' different models incorporate non-federal lands, ignoring the vital wildland-urban interface that poses direct risks to communities (GAO 2002b). These models also do not consider sources of firefighting resources outside the agencies, failing to reflect the true amount of resources needed. According to agency officials, they have maintained separate plans because of their traditional, agency-specific focus (GAO 2002a).

Federal agencies have now begun the process of replacing individual models with an interagency, landscape-scale fire planning and budget system (Fire Program Analysis) that is expected to provide a uniform system for fire preparedness and management planning by 2007 (GAO 2002b) The agencies also emphasized that neither the 1995 Fire Policy nor the 2001 Fire Policy Review require FMPs to list communities at risk, though they conceded that it was necessary to address suppression needs in the wildland-urban interface (GAO 2002b). In addition, the Departments of Agriculture and Interior are developing a geospacial and modeling system, called LANDFIRE, to identify wildland-fire hazards with more precision and uniformity than the existing hazardous fuels mapping, and to enable comparison of conditions nationwide (U.S. Geological Survey 2004). However, a study by the General Accountability Office pointed out that, while the Healthy Forests Restoration Act's clarification of the priority for protecting communities provided a starting point for identifying and prioritizing funding needs, the federal natural-resource management agencies collectively lack a cohesive strategy and adequate data to allow them to determine the extent and severity of the wildland-fire problem, to target and coordinate their efforts and resources, and to resolve the problem in a timely and cost-effective manner (GAO 2005). To rectify this situation, the agencies need to (1) complete and implement the LANDFIRE system so that the extent and location of wildland-fire threats are more precisely known; (2) update local fire-management plans with more precise LANDFIRE data; and (3) based on these plans, identify various national options and related funding needed to reduce fuels and respond to wildland-fire threats (GAO 2005).

Evaluation

Evaluation is another key component of adaptive management, providing information central to the organizational "learning" process (NAPA 2001a; Newcomer and Sheirer 2001). Evaluation generally is "assessment, through objective measurement and systematic analysis, of the manner and extent to which federal programs achieve intended results" (Center for Improving Government Performance 1999). The Government Performance and Results Act (P.L. 103-62) and other statutes require agencies to integrate program evaluation into their planning and management processes. Evaluation is most effective when citizens and managers collaborate as an assessment team (Shindler et al. 1999). It is also important that evaluators consider how particular actions contribute to larger agency goals, rather than simply labeling them as "successes" or "failures," an approach that departs from the traditional agency orientation, which looks to outcomes more than learning (Schmucker 1996). Thus, performance measures should track progress relative to particular goals, allowing managers to determine the "net" impact over time (NAPA2004). Evaluation is best viewed as an ongoing agency function that provides feedback on policy implementation, making adaptive management possible.

Despite its importance, the 1995 National Fire Policy did not require program evaluation (NAPA 2001a). Noting this omission as a significant oversight, the 2001 revisions concluded that monitoring and oversight of implementation of the 1995 policy was inadequate, there was no capacity to monitor policy implementation on an interagency basis, and managers did not face consequences for failing to implement the policy (U.S. Depts. of Agriculture and Interior 2001; NAPA2001a).

The 2001 revisions to the Fire Policy mandated clear mechanisms for evaluating the policy and its implementation, noting that the agencies did not then have an organizational apparatus for conducting program-evaluation studies (U.S. Depts. of Agriculture and Interior 2001; NAPA 2001a). NAPA and others found that the agencies had not at the time of publication developed the consistent, interagency performance measures required by the Fire Policy that clearly set out intended outcomes (GAO

2001; NAPA 2001a, 2004). Instead, agencies had their own, divergent measures of progress in reducing hazardous fuels and readiness for future wildland fires (GAO 2002b, NAPA 2001a). In part this resulted from a lack of available, uniform data (NAPA 2001a). For instance, the Forest Service measure for fuel reductions included only the total acres for fuel reductions accomplished, which created incentives to treat less-costly acres rather than those that presented the greatest hazards.

Recently, the federal agencies have adopted performance measures that identify the amount of acres moved from high-hazard to low-hazard fuel conditions (GAO 2005). Also, in 2004, the Federal Wildland Fire Leadership Council approved a nationwide monitoring framework for wildland-fire data to monitor the effects of wildland fires so agencies can determine the nature of threats or the likely effectiveness of different actions taken to address them. However, the GAO (2004) found that an implementation plan for the monitoring framework is needed. In addition, studies of data systems have found that agencies can overcome data problems by collecting more data and by making them available to stakeholders (Transportation Research Board 1997). Agencies must collect these data at the community level in order to build a baseline wildfire-hazard inventory that could be used to measure gains from mitigation activities (NAPA 2004; Aplet and Wilmer 2003). However, the agencies have not yet completed the research needed to develop sufficient data to support rigorous evaluation (GAO 2002a). Nonetheless, federal agencies and other stakeholders recognize the real need for national performance assessment (NAPA 2004).

Horizontal Collaboration: Joint Action among Federal Agencies

One of the key findings of the 1995 Federal Wildland Fire Management Policy and Program Review was that wildland fire respects no boundaries and that concerted efforts by federal agencies are required to reduce risks that fire poses to natural resources and communities. The 1995 Fire Policy Report called for uniform federal policies and procedures that would address the risks posed by fire in a uniform manner (U.S. Depts. of Interior and Agriculture 1995). Lack of agency coordination is believed to be one cause of the devastating Cerro Grande fire in New Mexico (Johnson 2000).

However, research by a panel of the National Academy of Public Administration (NAPA) has suggested that this uniformity may be more difficult to achieve than originally thought. NAPA (2001a) noted that "differences among agencies authorizing legislation, missions, regulations, operating practices, and cultures" could affect the agencies' ability to implement the Fire Policy. This sentiment is echoed in literature on organizational politics, which suggests that agencies must share basic goals and interests in order to work together harmoniously (Seidman 1998). Further, effective coordination requires an important, supraorganizational goal guiding agency efforts (Alter and Hage 1993). For integrated actions involving several federal agencies as well as state and local governments, research has shown that a single focal point is critical for success (GAO 2002a). Fortunately, the topic of wildland fire presents a unifying goal that is sufficiently compelling to lead to effective collaboration. However, common goals, while necessary, are not a sufficient component of truly effective collaboration among and between federal agencies.

In the wildland-fire context, agencies must move beyond shared goals and transform their very cultures, integrating fire and resource-management decisions, and involving new partners in managing wildland fire (NAPA 2001b). The difficulty of accomplishing these goals was evidenced by the report of a team chartered in 2000 to review implementation of the 1995 Fire Policy, which concluded that the implementation had been incomplete, "particularly in interagency and interdisciplinary matters" (U.S. Department of Agriculture et al. 2001). Recently, the five federal natural-resource-management agencies formed a Quadrennial Fire and Fuel Review (QFFR) Integration Panel whose report provided for the first time a unified fire-management strategic vision. The report calls for new integrated mission strategies that require the agencies to establish core capabilities in integrate planning, decision making, seamless fuel management, programming, monitoring, ability to respond, community relationships, community education, and training and technical assistance (QFFR Integration Panel 2005).

In its Phase II Report on the implementation of the Federal Wildland Fire Policy, NAPA (2001a) emphasized the complex organizational environment in which federal agencies charged with addressing wildland fire operate. The five federal land management agencies with primary authority to implement national fire policy developed and evolved over the last 125 years, focusing on their individual mandates and guided by diverse agency missions (NAPA 2001a). These factors lead to differing approaches to the problem of wildland fire, and have implications for the interagency collaboration that is essential to developing a truly national policy on wildland fire. In light of these realities, both NAPA and the GAO recommended that the secretaries of the Interior and Agriculture departments establish an interagency fire council to implement the Federal Wildland Fire Policy and other elements of the National Fire Plan, including hazardous fuels reduction (GAO 2002a; NAPA 2001a).

In response to the concern about effective leadership and numerous recommendations for greater collaboration, the departments of Agriculture and the Interior took several steps to move into a broader arena of intergovernmental action. In August 2001, the secretaries joined the Western Governors' Association, National Association of State Foresters, National Association of Counties, and the Intertribal Timber Council in adopting *A Collaborative Approach for Reducing Wildland Fire Risks to Communities and the Environment: A 10-Year Comprehensive Strategy* (NAPA 2004; Western Governors' Association and Dept. of the Interior 2001). The strategy established several guiding principles: Fire-management planning was to be a collaborative effort between all levels of government and interested stakeholders, with primary decision-making power at the local level; mechanical fuels-reduction methods would be preferred; and the economic benefits from these activities would accrue to local communities (Davis 2004). The strategy was followed by completion of the Implementation Plan for the 10-year Comprehensive Strategy (U.S. Depts. of Interior and Agriculture 2002). The Implementation Plan provided a performance-based framework for improving wildland-fire management, meeting the need for ecosystem restoration and rehabilitation, implementing protective measures to reduce risks to communities and ecosystems, and monitoring progress over time (Huber 2005). In November 2004, the Western Governors' Association's Forest Health Advisory Committee issued a report on the implementation of the ten-year strategy and recommended completion of a long-term, federal, cohesive strategy for reducing fuels (Western Governors' Association's Forest Health Advisory Committee 2004).

The secretaries of Agriculture and Interior established the Wildland Fire Leadership Council in April 2002, responding to calls from the GAO and NAPA for more unified and effective leadership. This council, made up of senior officials of Interior and Agriculture, as well as key external constituencies, is charged with providing active, visible interagency leadership and coordination of activities related to wildland-fire management at the Washington headquarters level, and is responsible for interagency coordination of both preparedness and vegetative management. In addition, to coordinate federal agency efforts, it is supposed to work with governors in a partnership intended to reduce wildland-fire risk on an all-lands basis.

Thus, federal agencies have now overcome initial inertia and established the headquarters framework for effective horizontal collaboration, along with a ten-year strategy and implementation plan for working together (NAPA 2004). With national policies, procedures, and an interagency council in place, we may now have the leadership that is needed to hold interagency collaboration together (Agranoff and McGuire 2003; Bardach

1998). However, more questions arise about the need to complete a long-term cohesive national strategy for fuels reduction and how to translate these national efforts into effective actions on the ground by all parties affected by wildland fire.

Vertical Collaboration: Joint Action among Federal, State, and Local Agencies

In light of the ever-increasing dangers posed by wildland fire, successful mitigation requires partnerships involving all levels of government, interest groups, and private citizens (NAPA 2002, 2004). Working with state and local governments as well as private-sector interests is an essential component of an effective federal strategy to reduce the risks associated with wildland fire (McDowell 2003). Only by doing so can policy makers create a truly national fire policy—one that really does approximate a planned, integrated, all-lands approach that is needed to address the wildland-fire problem on a landscape scale.

Most observers agree that a successful, comprehensive wildland-fire policy will emphasize local collaboration along with better information and tools for wildland management (Aplet and Wilmer 2003; NAPA 2004). Comprehensive fire policy requires not only suppressing fires, but also mitigation efforts to decrease the risk of future fires (NAPA 2002, 2004). Fire-hazard mitigation requires managers to address the buildup of fuels in wildlands through methods that include mechanical thinning, prescribed burning, and carefully managed natural fires (NAPA 2004). Given the vast amounts of land at risk of catastrophic fire, the agencies have stressed the importance of treating lands with excess fuels buildup and lands in the wildland-urban interface (GAO 2003b). The Healthy Forest Restoration Act (16 U.S.C.A. Sec.6501-6591, West Supp. 2004) also authorized up to $760 million in annual appropriation for hazardous-fuels reduction projects and directed that at least 50% of the allocation must be used for projects conducted in the wildland-urban interface. In addition, while it provided that National Environmental Policy Act requirements must be met, it reduced the number of alternatives that agencies must consider and in general gave the agencies more autonomy and authority to act without public review and comment (Radmall 2004). As stated in the Act, this greater agency autonomy was designed to alleviate the "maze of procedural and analytical requirements that do little to inform constructive decision-making" (HFRA, H.R. No. 108-96(I)). With regard to these changes, some critics have pointed out, "However, the price of greater managerial discretion and fewer constraints imposed by public participation may also have been lost opportunities for the agency to build upon the broad social consensus among major stakeholders that there is a problem and forge a meaningful and enduring social consensus with those stakeholders about what exactly should be done about it" (Vaughn and Cortner 2005). While the Act may provide greater autonomy to federal agency managers, it will not necessarily foster, in and of itself, the greater local participation in hazard mitigation on all lands that is necessary to bring about vertical collaboration among agencies at various levels of government.

Scholars examining issues of collaboration in the fire context have remarked on the emerging, fire-related federalism established by the National Fire Plan (NFP) (Cheng and Cortner 2003). The NFP and its emphasis on collaboration carries with it many assumptions, one of which is that federal, state, and local governments share the same goals as communities with regard to fire policy (Cheng and Cortner 2003). However, municipalities do not always believe that collaboration is a productive management tool, sometimes viewing it as a necessary evil at best or a burden at worst (Agranoff and McGuire 2003).

Indeed, there are real barriers to and political tensions surrounding the involvement of local people and local resources in decision making on the fire lines (Carroll and Daniels 2003). To some extent, this friction could be the result of age-old power allocations and the historical relationship between federal power and local autonomy. These tensions could also result from the conflicting views on knowledge and experience between federal and local firefighters and managers (Carroll and Daniels 2003). Cortner et al. (1990) have noted that, as the roles of Forest Service and rural firefighters converge with the growth of the wildland-urban interface, questions arise about their respective roles and how to respond to changing circumstances.

There can also be friction between managers and citizens living in or near forest land. Recent expansions of the wildland-urban interface by individuals who do not fully understand the physical and biological relationships of the remote regions into which they are moving (Cortner et al. 1984) reveals a fundamental problem—communities are not doing all they can to minimize risks of wildland fire (Gardner et al. 1987). In part, this stems from communities' and homeowners' reluctance to assume costs of protection for living in a hazardous environment when the costs can simply be passed along to government (Cortner et al. 1990; Gardner et al. 1987). Often, communities at the fringe of the wildland-urban interface prefer to foster development in these areas out of self-interest (Cheng and Cortner 2003). Yet, given the expanding nature and increased risk of fire due to the wildland-urban interface, state and local governments can regulate development and help mitigate fire risks using land use plans, zoning rules, site plan reviews, and building codes (NAPA 2004). Persuading these governments to regulate development in the wildland-urban interface is difficult, in part because of traditional Western tensions between regulation and private property rights (Kenworthy 2002; Platt 1999) This friction is at odds with the goals of the National Fire Plan, which encourages providing assistance and reducing the risks of fire to communities. Clashing incentives can prevent collaboration, or at least slow it down.

These findings show that collaboration does not just happen, but rather must be managed (Agranoff and McGuire 2003). Further, it is a complex developmental process, requiring significant investments of personnel and financial resources (Bardach 1998; Seidman 1998). The rapid devolution of legal power and administrative responsibilities to sub-national units of government over the last few decades has left many localities unprepared and ill-equipped to meet the demands placed on them in the complex intergovernmental system (Honadle and Howitt 1986; McGuire et al. 1994; Reid 1986). Capacity to operate successfully in a collaborative setting is different from capacity to manage a single organization (Agranoff and McGuire 2003). In this environment, there is a need among local communities for increased capacity to partner with federal agencies in addressing wildland-fire risks. In the next section, this topic is discussed in detail, as the focus turns to research on building capacity of state and local governments to effectively partner with federal agencies in addressing wildland fire.

Building State and Local Capacity to Undertake Planned, Integrated All-lands Wildland-fire Programs on a Landscape Scale

With increased emphasis on making wildland firefighting more collaborative, significant progress has been made incorporating state and local agencies and communities into the process (NAPA 2004). Responding to national policy directives, many partnerships between federal, state, and local agencies have been started to address hazard-mitigation issues (NAPA 2004; Wise and Hemenway 2003). However, the capabilities of local governments differ greatly; many do not have fire districts, proactive planning, or land-development controls (NAPA 2001b). Many localities also simply have insufficient staffing resources to meet the growing list of federal rules, requirements, and requests for additional collaboration (McGuire et al. 1994; NAPA 2001b). This reality comports with research looking at issues of scale in management capacity; local governments are frequently thought to have too little capacity because they are simply too small (Mead 1986), because they have inadequate financial resources, leading to unique problems (Brown 1980), or because they lack the political will and skill of larger entities (McGuire et al. 1994). Indeed, rural governments are generally smaller than their municipal counterparts, tend to be less organizationally sophisticated, and employ fewer professional administrators (Reid 1986). Partly as a result of these factors, efforts to build networks have not made progress sufficient to achieve lasting landscape-scale wildfire-hazard mitigation on a national level, and these networks require capacity building at the state and local levels (Wise and Hemenway 2003).

Research on capacity reveals many competing definitions. However, capacity can be adequately defined by the ability to anticipate change, make informed policy decisions and develop programs to implement them, attract, absorb, and manage new resources, and evaluate performance to guide future actions (Honadle 1986). Building this capacity requires significant costs in terms of time, personnel, and resources. One element of the NFP designed to effectuate capacity building is promoting community assistance (National Interagency Fire Center 2001). Assistance to communities to enhance capacity can take many forms, including federal financial support. However, there is also a strong need for training to help local managers participate meaningfully in collaborative efforts (Reid 1986).

Building local capacity often occurs in the form of technical assistance, which can come from any of several sources, including private consultants, state and federal agencies, academic institutions, or volunteers (Brown 1980; Howitt and Kobayashi 1986). Technical assistance—whether actually including technology transfers or not—can result in success, but also in confusion, frustration, and disappointment; individuals and constituencies in the recipient government may see technical assistance as bothersome because it disrupts their traditional ways of doing business (Howitt and Kobayashi 1986). Brown (1980) argues that, in order to adequately address the needs for greater capacity in rural areas, partner organizations should strive to provide local governments with technical assistance through capacity building, which he differentiates from mere assistance by emphasizing capacity building's broader, more community-wide perspective, focused on ongoing educational activities. Honadle (1981) builds upon these themes, arguing for approaches that favor incorporating and institutionalizing capacity into the permanent structure of the target jurisdiction, though he cautions against approaches that adopt uniform approaches to every management problem. The model proposed by this researcher also suggests that capacity building must be done carefully, that large infusions of money or technology are not always optimal responses to low capacity. This lesson is especially important in the wildland-fire context, where increased fire-mitigation funds have been appropriated but not yet applied effectively to reducing overall risk from wildland fire.

In its report on enhancing wildland-fire hazard-mitigation capacity, NAPA (2004) points out the need for improvements in particular state and local capacities, but finds that existing federal programs do not explicitly address this need. Despite calls for landscape-scale planning and coordination across all boundaries, federal funding for these objectives has not followed (NAPA 2004). By emphasizing and helping to build capacity for real hazard mitigation across ownership lines, federal land management agencies can reduce the severity of the impact from wildland fire and attain lasting results.

Federal Financial Assistance for Local Fire Activities

As research on building state and local governments' capacity to implement coordinated, integrated, all-lands wildland-fire policy illustrated, capacity building requires significant investments of time and resources. NAPA has conducted significant research looking at federal aid programs currently available to support state, local, and other non-federal partners in wildland-fire programs (NAPA 2004). Three primary programs provide assistance directly to fire departments: the Forest Service's Volunteer Fire Assistance, Interior's Rural Fire Assistance, and the Federal Emergency Management Agency (FEMA)'s Assistance to Firefighters (NAPA 2004; U.S. Fire Administration 2004). The 2002 Farm Bill authorized a new program—Community and Private Lands Fire Assistance Program—at $35 million per year for assisting landscape-scale planning for hazard reduction (NAPA 2004). FEMA has two programs that provide funding to state and local entities to mitigate fire risks, Hazard Mitigation Grant Program and the Pre-Disaster Mitigation Program. There are many more programs that can potentially help state and local managers. Indeed, GAO (2003b) estimates that there are over six hundred federal grant programs to implement domestic policy. These often overlapping federal grant programs present a highly fragmented network of funding options, which pose unnecessary challenges to local managers seeking federal assistance (NAPA 2004).

Small communities often have trouble raising the matching funds to support federal grants (GAO 2003b). Other administrative difficulties include the bottom-up nature of project applications, which are seldom based on strategically developed mitigation approaches; differences in field structures and annual grant cycles; the unpredictable nature of awards, which makes planning difficult; and the diversity of program requirements (NAPA 2004). The grant programs are also generally small, notwithstanding the twenty or so large grant programs that comprise most of the grant resources (GAO 2003b). As a result, grant funds can be quite meager, particularly in relation to the administrative effort and costs incurred in simply applying for them. The fire department assistance programs administered by the Forest Service and Department of Interior are a perfect example, each limited to less than $20,000. However, the most severe problem with federal grants for fire-mitigation activity is the fragmentation and overlap among the various programs, which leads to problems when local governments seek to identify, obtain, and use federal grants for wildland-fire mitigation (GAO 2003b; NAPA 2004).

Future Research

The foregoing analysis suggests a research agenda on policy and institutional issues:

Identify barriers to adoption of adaptive management for ensuring forest health in the land management agencies, including regulatory, structural, and skill factors.

1. Where adaptive management has begun to be implemented, identify implementation practices that have been effective.

2. Identify the proportion of land management units with fire-management plans. Asses the extent to which completed plans are targeted to a systematic assessment of fire risks and ecological health, and whether an all-lands approach is taken.

3. Assess approaches to evaluation of fire-mitigation programs. Identify the evaluation measures and the use of evaluation in assessing community risk reduction. Assess the integration of evaluation efforts in implementing a national evaluation capability.

4. Research the nature and extent of multiple federal agency participation in community mitigation efforts in wildland-urban interface areas.

5. Examine the capabilities of community area networks to engage in comprehensive all-lands mitigation activities.

This review reveals that the institutional response required to address the United States' wildland-fire problem is one that integrates the efforts of federal, state, local, and private entities on an all-lands basis. It is also one requiring an adaptive management framework incorporating planning and evaluation based on systematically collected scientific data. The adaptive management framework involves widespread participation of stakeholders in the various phases of planning, decision making, implementation, and evaluation. The research reveals that while the federal government's institutional response does not yet represent a cohesive and comprehensive adaptive management approach, indications do exist that some adaptive management components are being considered for incorporation in federal policy, and some are in the process of implementation.

REFERENCES

Agranoff, R., and M. McGuire. 2003. *Collaborative Public Management: New Strategies for Local Government.* Washington, D.C.: Georgetown University Press.

Alexander, D. 2002. *Principles of Emergency Planning and Management.* New York: Oxford University Press.

Alter, C., and J. Hage. 1993. *Organizations Working Together.* Newbury Park, London: SAGE Publications.

Aplet, G. H., and B. Wilmer. 2003. *The Wildland Fire Challenge: Focus on Reliable Data, Community Protection and Ecological Restoration.* Washington, D.C.: The Wilderness Society.

Bardach, E. 1998. *Getting Agencies to Work Together: The Practice and Theory of Managerial Craftsmanship.* Washington, D.C.: Brookings Institution Press.

Berkes, F., and C. Folke. 2000. "Linking social and ecological systems for resilience and sustainability." In F. Berkes and C. Folke (eds.), *Linking Social and Ecological Systems: Management Practices and Social Mechanisms for Building Resilience.* New York: Cambridge University Press.

Berman, D. 2004. "New NEPA manual to encourage cooperation, could reduce lawsuits." Greenwire. March 8. http://www.eenews.net/Greenwire/searcharchive/test_search-display.cgi?q=adaptive+management+interior&file=%2FGreenwire%2Fsearcharchive%2FNewsline%2F2004%2FMar8%2F03080406.htm

Brown, A. 1980. "Technical assistance to rural communities: Stopgap or capacity building?" *Public Administration Review* January/February 1980: 18-23.

Bunnell, D. L. 1995. "Prescribed natural fire planning considerations: Negotiating conflicting goals." In J. K. Brown, R. W. Mutch, C. W. Spoon, and R. H. Wakimoto (tech. coords.) Proceedings: Symposium on fire in wilderness and park management; March 30-April 1, 1993. USDA Forest Service, Intermountain Research Station, General Technical Report INT-GTR-320.

Busenburg, G. J. 2004. "Adaptive policy design for the management of wildfire hazards." *American Behavioral Scientist* 48(3): 314-26.

Carroll, M., and S. Daniels. 2003. "Communities." In H. J. Cortner, D. R. Field, P. Jakes, J. D. Buthman (eds.), *Humans, Fire, and Forests—Social Science Applied to Fire Management.* Flagstaff, Arizona: Ecological Restoration Institute, 18-26.

Center for Improving Government Performance. 1999. *Using Practical Program Evaluation.* Washington, D.C.: National Academy of Public Administration.

Chen, J. Q., T. E. Lee, R. Zhang, and Y. J. Zhang. 2003. "Systems requirements for organizational learning." *Communications of the ACM* 46 (12): 73-78.

Cheng, T., and H. J. Cortner. 2003. "Policy, political, and institutional." In H. J. Cortner, D. R. Field, P. Jakes, J. D. Buthman (eds.), *Humans, Fire, and Forests—Social Science Applied to Fire Management.* Flagstaff, Arizona: Ecological Restoration Institute, 52-58.

Coats, R. 1995. "Agency planning considerations are critical." In J. K. Brown, R. W. Mutch, C. W. Spoon, and R. H. Wakimoto (tech. coords.) Proceedings: Symposium on fire in wilderness and park management; March 30-April 1, 1993. USDA Forest Service, Intermountain Research Station, General Technical Report INT-GTR-320.

Comfort, L. 1988. *Managing Disaster: Strategies and Policy Perspectives.* Durham, North Carolina: Duke Press Policy Studies.

Cortner, H. J., R. M. Swinford, and M. R. Williams. 1990. "Wildland-urban interface emergency responses: What influences them?" *Fire Management Notes* 51(4): 3-8.

———, M. J. Zwolinski, E. H. Carpenter, and J. G. Taylor. 1984. "Public support for fire-management policies." *Journal of Forestry* 82(6): 359-61.

Davis, J., 2004. "The Healthy Forests Initiative; unhealthy policy choices in forest and fire management." *Environmental Law* 34 (3) 1209.

De Greene, K. B. 1982. *The Adaptive Organization: Anticipation and Management of Crisis.* New York: John Wiley & Sons.

Dellasalla, D. A., J. E. Williams, C. D. Williams, and J. E. Franklin. 2004. "Beyond smoke and mirrors: A synthesis of fire policy and science." *Conservation Biology* 18(4): 976-86.

Government Accountability Office (GAO). 1999. Western national forests: A cohesive strategy is needed to address catastrophic wildfire threats. Washington, D.C.: U.S. Government Accountability Office, GAO-RCED-99-65.

———. 2001. The National Fire Plan: Federal agencies are not organized to effectively and efficiently implement the plan. Washington, D.C.: U.S. Government Accountability Office, GAO-01-1022T.

———. 2002a. Severe wildland fires: Leadership and accountability needed to reduce risks to communities and resources. Washington, D.C.: U.S. Government Accountability Office, GAO-02-259.

———. 2002b. Wildland fire management: Improved planning will help agencies better identify fire-fighting preparedness needs. Washington, D.C.: U.S. Government Accountability Office, GAO-02-158.

———. 2003a. Wildland fires: Better information needed on effectiveness of emergency stabilization and rehabilitation treatments. Washington, D.C.: U.S. Government Accountability Office, GAO-03-430.

———. 2003b. Wildland fire management: Additional actions required to better identify and prioritize lands needing fuels reduction. Washington, D.C.: U.S. Government Accountability Office, GAO-03-805.

———. 2004. Forest Service and BLM need better information and a systematic approach for assessing the risks of environmental effects. Washington, D.C.: U.S. Government Accountability Office, GAO-04-705.

———. 2005. Wildland fire management: Important progress has been made, but challenges remain to completing a cohesive strategy. Washington, D.C.: U.S. General Accountability Office, GAO-05-147.

Gardner, P. D., H. J. Cortner, and K. Widaman. 1987. "The risk perceptions and policy response toward wildland fire hazards by urban homeowners." *Landscape and Urban Planning* 14(1987): 163-72.

Graham, A. C., and L. E. Kruger. 2002. Research in adaptive management: Working relations and the research process. Portland, Oregon: USDA Forest Service, Pacific Northwest Research Station. PNW-RP-538.

Hobbs, R. J. 2003. "Ecological management and restoration: Assessment, setting goals, and measuring success." *Ecological Management and Restoration* 4 (February supp.): S2.

Holling, C. S. (ed.). 1978. *Adaptive Environmental Assessment and Management.* London: Whey. Reprinted Caldwell, New Jersey: The Blackburn Press. *date of reprint?*

204 Socioeconomic and Institutional Factors

————, F. Berkes, and C. Folke. 2000. "Science, sustainability, and resource management." In Berkes and Folke (eds.), *Linking Social and Ecological Systems: Management Practices and Social Mechanisms for Building Resilience.* New York: Cambridge University Press.

Honadle, B. W. 1981. "A capacity-building framework: A search for concept and purpose." *Public Administration Review* September/October 1981: 575-80.

————. 1986. "Defining and doing capacity building: Perspectives and experiences." In B. W. Honadle and A. M. Howitt (eds.) *Perspectives on Management Capacity Building.* Albany: State University of New York Press, 9-23.

———— and A. M. Howitt (eds.). 1986. *Perspectives on Management Capacity Building.* Albany: State University of New York Press.

Howitt, A. M., and R. M. Kobayashi. 1986. "Organizational incentives in technical assistance relationships." In B. W. Honadle and A. M. Howitt (eds.), *Perspectives on Management Capacity Building.* Albany: State University of New York Press, 119-38.

Huber, E.. 2005. "Environmental litigation and the Healthy Forests Initiative." *Vermont Law Review* 29 (2) 797.

Johnson, B. L. 1999. "The role of adaptive management as an operational approach for resource management agencies." *Conservation Ecology* 3(2): 8.

Johnson, M. A. 2000. "The Los Alamos Cerro Grande fire: An abject, object lesson." *Natural Hazards Observer* 25(1): 1-3.

Kenworthy, T. 2002. "U.S. fire policy isn't cutting it." *USA Today*, August 22, 2002, sec. A01.

Lawrence, R. L., and S. E. Daniels. 1996. Public involvement in natural resource decisionmaking: Goals, methodology, and evaluation. Corvallis, Oregon: Forest Research Laboratory, Oregon State University.

Lee, K. N. 1993. *Compass and Gyroscope: Integrating Science and Politics for the Environment.* Washington, D.C.: Island Press.

McDowell, B. 2003. "Wildfires create new intergovernmental challenges." *Publius* 33 (3): 45-61.

McGuire, M., B. Rubin, R. Agranoff, and C. Richards. 1994. "Building development capacity in nonmetropolitan communities." *Public Administration Review* 54 (5): 426-33.

McLain, R., and R. G. Lee. 1996. "Adaptive management: Promises and pitfalls." *Environmental Management* 20 (4): 437-48.

Mead, T. D. 1986. "Issues in defining local management capacity." In B. W. Honadle and A. M. Howitt (eds.), *Perspectives on Management Capacity Building.* Albany: State University of New York Press, 24-48.

Murphy, E. M. 1995. "Public involvement in wilderness fire planning and decision making." In J. K. Brown, R. W. Mutch, C. W. Spoon, and R. H. Wakimoto (tech. coords.) Proceedings: Symposium on fire in wilderness and park management; March 30-April 1, 1993. USDA Forest Service, Intermountain Research Station, General Technical Report INT-GTR-320.

National Academy of Public Administration (NAPA). 2001a. Managing wildland fire: Enhancing capacity to implement the federal interagency fire policy. Washington, D.C.: National Academy of Public Administration.

————. 2001b. Conference proceedings: New tools for managing wildland fire. Washington, D.C.: National Academy of Public Administration.

————. 2002. Wildfire suppression: Strategies for containing costs. Washington, D.C.: National Academy of Public Administration.

————. 2004. Containing wildland fire costs: Enhancing hazard mitigation capacity. Washington, D.C.: National Academy of Public Administration.

National Commission on Wildfire Disasters. 1994. Report of the national commission on wildfire disasters. Washington, D.C.: American Forests.

National Interagency Fire Center. 2001. A collaborative approach to reducing wildland fire risks to communities and the environment: A 10-year comprehensive strategy. http://www.nifc.gov/fireinfo/10yrIPfinal.pdf [10-Year Strategy].

Nelson, T.C. 1979. "Fire management policy in the national forests—a new era." *Journal of Forestry* 77 (11): 723.

Newcomer, K. E., and M. A. Sheirer. 2001. Using evaluation to support performance management: A guide for federal executives. Arlington, Virginia: PricewaterhouseCoopers Endowment for the Business of Government.

Platt, R. H. 1999. *Disasters and Democracy.* Washington, D.C.: Island Press.

QFFR Integration Panel 2005. Quadrennial fire and fuel report. http://www.NIFC.gov/nimo/background/qffr_report.pdf

Radmall, L. 2004. "President George W. Bush's forest policy: Healthy Forests Restoration Act of 2003." *Land Resources and Environmental Law* 24(2) 511.

Reid, J. N. 1986. "Building capacity in rural places: Local views on needs." In B. W. Honadle and A. M. Howitt (eds.) *Perspectives on Management Capacity Building.* Albany: State University of New York Press, 66-83.

Saveland, J. M. 1989. "Knowledge-based systems approach to wilderness fire management." PhD diss., Moscow, ID: University of Idaho.

———. 1991. "Adaptive fire policy." In Fire and the environment: Ecological and cultural perspectives. Proceedings of an international symposium; 1990 March 20-24; Knoxville, TN. Gen. Tech. Rep. SE-69. Asheville, North Carolina: USDA Forest Service, Southeastern Forest Experiment Station, 187-91.

Schmucker, E. F. 1996. Adaptive management from FEMAT to ROD to practice. [Unpublished document] on file with USDA Forest Service, Pacific Northwest Research Station, 4043 Roosevelt Way NE, Seattle, Washington 98105.

Schweitzer, D. L., H. J. Cortner, and B. H. Vann. 1984. "Is planning worth it?: An appraisal of RPA and NFMA must be more political than objective." *Journal of Forestry* 82 (7): 404.

Seidman, H. 1998. *Politics, Position, and Power: The Dynamics of Federal Organization,* 5th ed. New York: Oxford University Press.

Shindler, B., K. A. Cheek, and G. J. Stankey. 1999. Monitoring and evaluating citizen-agency interactions: A framework developed for adaptive management. USDA Forest Service, Pacific Northwest Research Station, General Technical Report GTR-452.

Stokes, J. 1995. "Planning for desired future conditions in wilderness." In J. K. Brown, R. W. Mutch, C. W. Spoon, and R. H. Wakimoto (ttech.coords.) Proceedings: Symposium on fire in wilderness and park management; March 30-April 1, 1993. USDA Forest Service, Intermountain Research Station, General Technical Report INT-GTR-320.

Transportation Research Board. 1997. Information Needs to Support State and Local Transportation Decision Making in the 21st Century: Proceedings of a Conference. Washington, D.C.: National Academy Press.

USDA Forest Service. 2000. Protecting people and sustaining resources in fire-adapted ecosystems. http://www.fs.fed.us/publications

U.S. Department of Agriculture and U.S. Department of the Interior. 1995. Federal wildland fire management policy and program review, final report. Dec. 18, 1995 [1995 Report].

———. 2000. Managing the impact of wildfires on communities and the environment. http://www.fireplan.gov

———, Department of Energy, Department of Defense, Department of Commerce, U.S. Environmental Protection Agency, Federal Emergency Management Agency, and National Association of State Foresters. 2001. Review and update of the 1995 federal wildland fire management policy. January [2001 Fire Policy Review].

U.S. Department of the Interior and U.S. Department of Agriculture. 1995. 1995 federal wildland fire management policy and review.

———. 2002. A collaborative approach for reducing wildland fire risks to communities and the environment 10-year comprehensive strategy implementation plan.

U.S. Fire Administration. 2004. Assistance to firefighters Grants Program (AFGP). http://www.usfa.fema.gov/fire-service/grants/afgp/grants.shtm

U.S. Geological Survey. 2004. Landfire: A USDA forest service and department of interior partnership. http://www.landfire.gov

Vaughn, J., and H. J. Cortner. 2005. *George W. Bush's Healthy Forests: Reframing the Environmental Debate*. Boulder, Colorado: University Press of Colorado.

Walters, C. J. 1986. *Adaptive Management of Renewable Resources*. New York: Macmillan; London: Collier Macmillan.

Western Governors' Association and U.S. Department of the Interior. 2001. A collaborative approach to reducing wildland fire risks to communities and the environment: 10-year comprehensive strategy. http://www.fireplan.gov/reports/11-23-en.pdf

Western Governors' Association's Forest Health Advisory Committee, 2004, Report to the western governors on the implementation of the 10-year comprehensive strategy, Denver, Colorado.

Wise, C.R. and K. Hemmenway. 2003. "Community mobilization in an intergovernmental context: The case of community wildland fire management." Presented at the 7th National Public Management Research Conference. Georgetown University, Washington, D.C. Oct. 9-11.

Wondolleck, J. M., and S. L. Yaffee. 1994. Building bridges across agency boundaries: In search of excellence in the United States Forest Service. Ann Arbor, MI: School of Natural Resource and Environment, The University of Michigan.

A Matrix Approach for Understanding People, Fire, and Forests

A. E. Luloff, Donald R. Field, Richard S. Krannich, and Courtney G. Flint

Introduction

Social scientists, biologists, natural resource managers, and the popular press have noted the growing need to draw the public and their respective human communities into the natural resource decision-making equation. It has become common for policy makers to seek out a partnership between professionals and citizens to arrive at stewardship arrangements for the protection and conservation of the nation's public lands—its parks, forests, refuges, and riverways. Moreover, a consistent refrain has been the call for an inclusive, interdisciplinary framework, one that gives equivalent attention to the social-cultural system and the ecological system when addressing natural resource policy, management, and action (Field and Burch 1988; Field et al. 2002; 2003; Grove and Burch 1997; Machlis et al. 1997). It is clear that the events surrounding forest fires over the past five years would benefit from a better understanding of the complex relationships among the social and biophysical systems, human communities, and policies and actions of public land management agencies.

This chapter outlines an interdisciplinary framework that integrates the inherent and complex relationships between people and natural resources and focuses on forest fire, human communities, and public lands issues. We proceed in the following manner. First, we discuss the need for incorporating a broader scientific perspective when considering theoretical parameters that guide research and action in this arena. Theoretical closure is simply premature, given current social and ecological thinking. Instead, we suggest widening our lenses to embrace the complexity of social action on the land in terms of space, time, and scale. Second, we suggest a matrix approach as a means of organizing and synthesizing various studies covering particular

A. E. Luloff, Dept. of Agricultural Economics and Rural Sociology, Pennsylvania State University (ael13@psu.edu); Donald R. Field, Dept. of Forest Ecology and Management, University of Wisconsin - Madison; Richard S. Krannich, Dept. of Sociology, Social Work and Anthropology, Utah State University; Courtney G. Flint, University of Illinois

resource management issues. Use of such an approach would allow resource managers and scientists alike to more effectively identify research gaps or needs. We present an example of a matrix that incorporates key dimensions relevant to addressing human-resource interactions, and draw upon themes and points raised in the preceding chapters to illustrate the application and utility of the matrix. Finally, we conclude with comments on the relevance of our argument for fire planning, management, and policy.

Toward an Interdisciplinary Methodological Strategy: Thinking Outside the Box

As indicated in the foreword, the work appearing in this volume has emerged out of a series of workshops, symposia sessions, and other interactions among a diverse group of social scientists working in various academic and agency contexts. Early discussions among participants revealed a need to develop an organizing framework by which contextual differences across space and time would emerge, and multidisciplinary science and collaborative research would be facilitated. A central goal was to ensure that multiple dimensions of fire at the human-environment interface could be incorporated into and addressed by such a framework. Effort was made to build upon existing research and to address significant gaps that have limited our overall ability to further assist fire-management and decision-making policy.

We believe that a comprehensive methodological strategy that embraces spatial, temporal, and theoretical scales is needed in natural resource-related research work. Studies in these areas must be replicated, both in research design and across physiographic regions. Failure to do this in the absence of common frames for sample selection, study design, and analysis hinders our ability to build cumulative knowledge. We remain convinced that our science, despite great strides in measurement capacity and capability, adaptation and use of hi-tech equipment for sensing and translating important vectors of information, and a growing cadre of well-trained and well-meaning researchers, is not contributing in a cumulative way.

Our approach begins with the recognition that a multidisciplinary framework is needed for studying and interpreting the spatial and temporal patterns associated with landscape changes and their attendant consequences for community and individual land owners. Some have suggested that the nested nature of relationships in increasingly smaller (or larger) geographic spaces helps provide a partial framework (cf., Beckley 1998; Connell et al. 1997). Others point to the use of geographic information systems and/ or the ability to hierarchically layer information from multiple research areas as major breakthroughs (cf., Bradshaw and Muller 1998; Parisi et al. 2003; Pfaff 1999). Still others point to lessons being generated by those doing global climate-change research combining gradient and comparative approaches (Morehouse 2003) or the benefits of using a regional aggregation or mesoscale approach to integrated environmental assessment (Easterling 1997; Kasperson et al. 1995). However, from our perspective, the nestedness of relationships does not vitiate the potential for problems associated with an indiscriminate application of the ideas associated with homology—or the belief that what holds at one level of analysis holds at another (Hannan 1992). Nor does the employment of any tool, regardless of its capabilities and functions, address the thorny issues of how to blend various knowledge systems in meaningful ways.

Since the subject of so many of our studies is identifying and unraveling the relationships among humans, forest, and fire, the question becomes, "How do we best articulate an approach that will allow us to do integrative, multidisciplinary work that is time and space conscious?" Our concerns are clearly with the application of data and lessons so that we can advance the decision-making debate and contribute to good policy formation. The range of issues and concerns being addressed in the twenty-first century suggests a need for some organizing mechanism for social science research associated with forest management. The presence of too many incompatible studies prohibits an accretion of findings. This impediment is directly traceable to the absence of a common framework for conducting this work. Without ability to place management-relevant research results across disciplines and ecological, social, and cultural processes, accretion will not occur. This is precisely why we employ a multidimensional framework that is sensitive to temporal and spatial issues across a range of physiographic regions.

Constructing a Conceptual Model: The Matrix

To help address these issues, and because it is impractical and prohibitively expensive to mount a study of all forest-fire situations in the nation,[1] we have adopted the use of a typological framework to help organize information that can be derived from a more limited array of case studies and other research initiatives. A typology is an abstraction of reality that allows the researcher to maximize similarities while minimizing differences among a set of cases. Typologies facilitate analysis in that representative cases can be identified for in-depth study. They are used to organize data and represent a conceptual model useful for guiding research and developing policy.

The typology of the human/forest intersection that emerged out of the dialogue among those participating in the workshops, symposia, and other interactions that spawned this volume relies on the identification of several key dimensions forming a matrix. The three core axes in this matrix are: (1) The biophysical environment (including such elements as land use and cover; topography; climate dynamics; fuel typologies, fire regimes; wildlife, watershed characteristics and boundaries, and soil characteristics) in the setting where the research is being conducted (Y); (2) the sociodemographic and socioeconomic characteristics (including population and housing characteristics; migration patterns and trends; population distributions and densities; spatial distributions of land use and development patterns; jurisdictional relationships; public- and private-sector organizations and institutions; and economic structure) of the locale where the research is being conducted (Z); and (3) the social and cultural characteristics (including patterns of use; traditions; attitudes; belief and value systems; and perceptions) that characterize the study population (the agents being studied) (X).

Discussion and Illustration

Biophysical environment

It is important to understand the association of the biophysical characteristics of a study area and the underlying social institutions found there. Human action is governed by the interaction of social institutions with the characteristics of the natural environment. This mutuality is central to our interests. The biophysical environment influences the nature of social institutions as they are formed and adapt; these adaptations, in turn, often reshape the biophysical environment. For example, topography is renowned for its ability to shape settlement patterns and neighboring patterns. Forms of extractive resource management, including agriculture, forestry, and mining, have altered the biophysical environment, changing land uses and cover. And social values, interactions, meanings, and symbolic belief systems are routinely reflected in the ways we define "resources" and interact with surrounding landscapes. In our examination of humans, fire, and forests, fire regimes, fuel typology, climate, forest structure, slope, and aspects are particularly relevant for understanding human behavior and community.

Although linkages involving elements of the biophysical dimension are not uniformly addressed in the preceding chapters, there are several points where such relationships are clearly illuminated. For example, Burchfield's chapter notes the relationships of fire to scenic quality and watershed stability, factors that may in turn have important repercussions with respect to development patterns and human population distributions, local economic activity, exposure to health and safety hazards, risk perception and awareness, and shifts in forest use patterns. The chapter by Becker and Viers on utilization

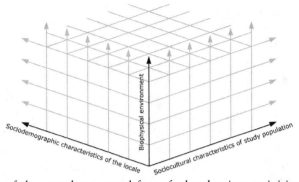

Figure 1: Matrix for social science contributions to fire management

of the wood generated from fuel-reduction activities highlights the need to examine linkages between physical characteristics of the forest resource and the presence of sociodemographic and socioeconomic conditions (markets, industry infrastructure, and labor supply) and sociocultural conditions (social acceptance of fuel-reduction strategies) that will make harvest and use of fuel-reduction by-products feasible. McCaffrey and Kumagai point to the similarities and differences between wildfire and other natural hazards, and how these affect perceptions of risk and risk-management policy options. Daniel's chapter notes that even when focusing on the perspective of the individual actor, it is important to keep in mind that subjective perceptions of wildfire risk are contextualized by and anchored to a biophysical context characterized by climate, topography, vegetation cover, and other features of the landscape. Shindler approaches the biophysical dimension in a different way, arguing that the social acceptability of fuel-reduction practices is likely to be enhanced by carefully linking such actions to specific information about benefits to the ecological resource.

Sociodemographic and socioeconomic characteristics

Social demography refers to the analysis of how social conditions and trends in an area are related to population structures and processes. These factors are tied to fertility, mortality, and migration, but also encompass a far broader range of subject areas that researchers must engage. These include an understanding of the relationships between social and demographic processes, such as population growth trends or the compositional characteristics of local populations, and attributes of social organization and structure that can either facilitate or hinder effective collective response to wildfire or other events. Community capacity dimensions associated with public and private organizations and infrastructure as well as the human capital associated with population size and characteristics can be central factors in areas impacted by fires, and encompass a range of measures that require careful evaluation.

Socioeconomics refers to the relationship between society and economic structures and processes. It focuses on matters related to production, consumption, and distribution, including how dollars circulate through an economy, and reflects the employment, income, industrial infrastructure, and natural resource bases of any area being investigated.

Failure to integrate across subject matters and scales on this dimension of the matrix masks relationships between factors and contributes to poor decision making and policy formation. For example, the association between labor force employment and age structure can be viewed in a context which focuses on levels of resource dependency and retirement status. This relationship has changed the economic base of communities in many fire-prone areas, resulting in parcelization of properties developed to accommodate residential development, increased recreational use, and in-migration, and housing construction in locations characterized as the wildland-urban interface. Such activity has received much recent attention, but little integrated work has been done in this area.

Several chapters in *People, Fire, and Forests* highlight the relevance of sociodemographic and socioeconomic dimensions in attempting to address the linkages between humans and wildfire. For example, the chapter by Holmes and associates describes complexities in measuring costs and losses from wildfires because of sociodemographic and socioeconomic changes that lead to uneven distributional consequences of wildfire hazards across space and time. In contrast, Moseley addresses the economic opportunities created by fire-suppression and hazard-reduction policies, and the inequity of the distribution of these opportunities across communities and ethnicities. For example, residents of rural communities often lose out to urban-based companies in the competition for fire-hazard-reduction contracts, and in this context Hispanics are more likely to work in lower-quality jobs. The chapter by Carroll and Cohn notes that long-time residents of rural areas may be more prepared to deal effectively with wildfire risks than more recently arrived in-migrants from urban settings. Similarly, the chapter by Wise and Yoder notes that many of those who have moved to the wildland-urban interface lack understanding of the physical and biological conditions and relationships of those areas. Wise and Yoder also focus on the relevance of vertical collaboration between local agencies and organizations and state and federal agencies in pursuing successful mitigation of fire hazards. The chapter by Jakes and Nelson incorporates a focus on socioeconomic factors such as the role of local government agencies, businesses, non-governmental organizations, and other institutions in facilitating the social and structural actions needed to achieve community wildland-fire preparedness. Finally, Becker and Viers incorporate a discussion of how community capacity to capitalize on the availability of forest resources derived from fuel-reduction programs is linked to elements of both human capital (including the skills, education, and experiences of residents) and locally accessible financial capital.

Social and cultural characteristics

We all know that the macro-structural characteristics of any geographical area, such as labor force structure, demographic profile, economic infrastructure, and biophysical environment, by themselves reveal little about the ability of local societies to effectively mobilize to protect and/or use their resource endowments. Analyses that focus solely on such factors ignore important social and cultural attributes of people and associated values and behaviors that are reflected in the ability of residents to come together to address issues. Further, the latter characteristics provide insights into use patterns and identify the significance ethnic groups place on the natural resource or area, and their experiences, attitudes, beliefs and values towards these resources. Absent such critical measures, models of relationships of humans, fires, and forests lack an appreciation of context and texture, both critical for designing policy and implementing relevant practices. Understanding fire history in the context of place and culture contributes to an appreciation of how humans have adapted to fire, both in terms of management and action.

Illustrations of the central importance of the sociocultural dimension in understanding the relationships between humans and natural resources can be drawn from several of the chapters in this volume. The chapter by Raish and her associates focuses heavily on the sociocultural dimension, outlining the unique ways in which Native Americans and other cultural/ethnic and racial groups have perceived and utilized both managed fire and wildfire in both historical and contemporary contexts. Burchfield's chapter notes the need to understand the values and perceptions that underlie public views about the benefits of living in the wildland-urban interface as key factors accounting for patterns of population growth and development as well as a general tendency to downplay the risks associated with residence in such areas. He also focuses considerable attention on the ways in which public perceptions and attributions of responsibility can contribute to tensions and conflict with agencies responsible for wildfire mitigation, and to both "galvanizing" and/or "divisive" responses within fire-impacted communities. Becker and Viers' chapter on the utilization of fuel-reduction by-products notes that cultural linkages to traditional livelihoods may allow the reinvigoration of woods-based economic activity to foster strengthened cultural identity. Shindler's chapter on social acceptability highlights the need to adopt policies and programs that are "consistent with prevailing social customs and norms."

Finally, Daniel's chapter situates individual risk perceptions and judgments about wildfire in their broader sociocultural setting and explains how biophysical and sociodemographic and socioeconomic dimensions influence values as well as actions and outcomes.

Summary and Conclusion

Today it is generally accepted that social dimensions of natural resources and biophysical dimensions of the environment must be addressed together if we are to understand and resolve complex resource management issues such as humans, forests, and fire. The matrix approach proposed in this chapter simultaneously embraces sociodemographic and socioeconomic characteristics of a locale, the sociocultural characteristics of place, and the biophysical characteristics of the environment. The matrix also supports our premise that these three sectors of human-resource relationships intersect at varying temporal and spatial scales.

So how are we doing? Does our current knowledge base of people and fire shed light on critical information that can be used to inform public land managers? The authors of each of the chapters included in this volume have canvassed the relevant literature that addresses the complex relationships described above. They were challenged to locate studies where there was an explicit attempt to understand the inherent link between the social and biophysical, where possible using the matrix described above. These authors were charged to synthesize knowledge in their respective fields of study. Each was asked to be reflective in their attempt to organize this material. Finally, each was asked to address a key question: What contributions does our current knowledge provide to public land managers and community leaders for dealing with the complex issue of humans, fire, and forests?

Insights derived from these authors' efforts to summarize and synthesize the existing knowledge about the people-fire relationship clearly support the relevance of the three major dimensions that are at the center of our matrix approach. In varying ways, the chapters highlight the importance of biophysical characteristics of landscapes, sociodemographic and socioeconomic contexts, and sociocultural conditions as key factors in our attempts to understand the interplay between human societies and natural environments. These chapters emphasize the benefits of contextualizing particular research questions in multiple dimensions by allowing the development of common language and integration among multidisciplinary approaches.

At the same time, the chapters are highly variable with respect to their ability to synthesize research findings in a manner that brings all three of the matrix dimensions together at one time. This is, to some degree, a reflection of the varying inclinations of individual authors to adopt the matrix as an organizing framework. However, we believe that it is primarily indicative of a continued tendency for researchers to work within narrowly defined disciplinary perspectives that serve as barriers to a multi-dimensional and multi-scale approach to understanding these complex interactions. In short, the fact that many of the chapters focus primarily on factors associated with just one dimension of the matrix is a reflection of what appears in the research literatures that these authors were asked to synthesize. We are heartened by the fact that, regardless of the degree to which the chapters in this volume embraced the matrix framework, each has important policy and management implications for the three core dimensions of the wildfire experience—the people and places, culture, and landscape.

The insights and syntheses presented herein provide an important foundation for managers and policy makers wishing to become better informed about the multiple ways in which human social organization can affect and be affected by wildfire hazards and events. As a whole, the chapters suggest that the interactions occurring in the cells of the conceptual diagram are highly spatially and temporally dynamic. The matrix framework is not static. Indeed, the interaction across multiple scales and stages of wildfire experience and management is the driving force behind most of the chapters in this volume.

A major contribution of this cumulative work is that it clearly lays out the value of collaborating across disciplines and scales, as well as over time to address the complex realities of wildfire. This integrative framework promotes an appreciation of variation in both the wildfire experience on the ground and in research approaches, and also organizes our efforts to support informed decision making and resource management. At the same time, it is clear that there is a considerable distance to be traveled before our goal of developing the synthesized knowledge base needed to understand the complex relationships among social and biophysical systems, human communities, and public land management policies and actions is realized. Our hope is that this volume stimulates future efforts to move a transdisciplinary agenda forward.

NOTES

1. The federal government has identified over eleven thousand communities as being fire prone. It would be impractical to study all of them, and it is not clear how large a sample would be needed given differences by region, forest ecology, silvicultural practices, ownership, slope, and aspect associated with the country's vast forest resources. Heuristic discussions related to issues affecting fire-prone communities do not contribute to the amelioration of potential problems without first establishing a context for this work. The utilization of a matrix approach for such problems would be a sound first step in such work.

References

Avery, T. E., and H. E. Burkhart. 1994. *Forest Measurements*. New York, New York: McGraw-Hill.

Beckley, T. M. 1998. "The nestedness of forest dependence: A conceptual framework and empirical exploration." *Society and Natural Resources* 11:101-20.

Bradshaw, T. K., and B. Muller. 1998. "Impacts of rapid urban growth on farmland conversion: Application of new regional land use policy models and geographic information systems." *Rural Sociology* 63:1-25.

Connell, J. H., T. P. Hughes, and C .C. Wallace. 1997. "A 30-year study of coral abundance, recruitment, and disturbance at several scales in space and time." *Ecological Monographs* 67:461-88.

Cortner, H. J., D. R. Field, P. Jakes, and J. D. Buthman (eds). 2003. *Humans, Fires, and Forests – Social Science Applied to Fire Management*. Flagstaff, Arizona: Ecological Restoration Institute.

Easterling, W. E. 1997. "Why regional studies are needed in the development of full-scale integrated assessment modeling of global change processes." *Global Environmental Change* 7:337-56.

Field, D. R. and W. R. Burch.1988. *Rural Sociology and the Environment*. Middleton, Wisconsin: Social Ecology Press.

———, A. E. Luloff, and R. S. Krannich. 2002. "Revisiting the origins of and distinctions between natural resource sociology and environmental sociology." *Society and Natural Resources* 15:213-27.

———, P. R. Voss, T. K. Kuczenski, R. Hammer, and V. C. Radeloff. 2003. "Reaffirming social landscape analysis in landscape ecology: A conceptual framework." *Society and Natural Resources* 16:349-61.

Gobster, P. H., R. G. Haight, and D. Shriner. 2000. "Landscape change in the Midwest – an integrated research and development program." *Journal of Forestry* 98:9-14.

Grove, J. M. and W. R. Burch. 1997. "A social ecology approach and applications of urban ecosystem and landscape analysis: a case study of Baltimore, Maryland." *Urban Ecosystem* 1:259-75.

Hannan, M. 1992. *Aggregation and Disaggregation in the Social Sciences*. Lexington, Massachusetts: Lexington Press. 2nd edition.

Kasperson, J. X., R. E. Kasperson, and B. L. Turner. 1995. *Regions at Risk: Comparisons of Threatened Environments*. Tokyo, Japan: United Nations University Press.

Machlis, G. E., J. E. Force, and W. R. Burch, Jr. 1997. "The human ecosystem, part I: the human ecosystem as an organizing concept in ecosystem management." *Society and Natural Resources* 10:347-67.

Morehouse, B. 2003. "Social science applied to studying wildland fire across the gradient." Paper presented at Humans, Fire and Forests: Social Science Applied to Fire Management Conference. Tucson, Arizona.

Parisi, D., M. Taquino, S. M. Grice, and D. A. Gill. 2003. "Promoting environmental democracy using GIS as a means to integrate community into the EPA-BASINS approach." *Society and Natural Resources* 16:205-19.

Pfaff, A. S. P. 1999. "What drives deforestation in the Brazilian Amazon? Evidence from satellite and socioeconomic data." *Environmental Economic Management* 37:26-43.

Biographies of the Contributors

Co-Editors

TERRY C. DANIEL, Environmental Perception Laboratory, Department of Psychology, University of Arizona, Tucson, AZ 85721 (tdaniel@U. Arizona.edu). Dr. Daniel is Professor of Psychology and Natural Resources at the University of Arizona. He has worked for over thirty years in the human-environment field, with an emphasis on environmental perception and values. He is an associate editor for Landscape and Urban Planning, Journal of Environmental Psychology and Society and Natural Resources, and currently serves on the EPA Science Advisory Board Committee on Valuing Ecosystems and Ecosystem Services.

MATTHEW CARROLL, Department of Natural Resource Sciences, Washington State University, Pullman, WA 99164-6410 (carroll@wsu.edu). Dr. Carroll, a natural resource sociologist, has been on the faculty at Washington State University since 1987. Dr. Carroll is author of the book *Community and the Northwestern Logger: Continuities and Changes in the Era of the Spotted Owl* (Westview Press, 1995). He is an associate editor for Society and Natural Resources. He has served on the Rural Sociological Society's National Working Group on Natural Resources and Rural Poverty; chaired the Society of American Forester's National Task Force on Community Stability; and was a consultant to President Clinton's Forest Ecosystem Management Assessment Team (FEMAT) and the Columbia River Basin (CRB) project.

CASSANDRA MOSELEY, Ecosystem Workforce Program, Institute for a Sustainable Environment, University of Oregon, Eugene, OR 97405 (cmoseley@uoregon.edu). Dr. Moseley is the Director of the Ecosystem Workforce Program at the University of Oregon. Her research focuses on community-based forestry in the American West, especially collaboration, federal land management institutions, and forest work. Dr. Moseley received her Ph.D. in Political Science from Yale University.

CAROL B. RAISH, Research Social Scientist, USDA Forest Service, Rocky Mountain Research Station, 333 Broadway SE, Suite 115, Albuquerque, NM 87102-3497 (craish@fs.fed.us). Dr. Raish's research work includes exploring cultural/ethnic variations in fire use and management practices and examining community beliefs and attitudes concerning both managed fire and wildfire among national forest users in the Southwest.

Authors

KAREN L. ABT is a Research Economist with the USDA Forest Service Southern Forest Research Station. Her research interests include non-industrial private forests, timber management, regional economic analysis, and natural resource accounting.

DENNIS BECKER is Assistant Professor of Natural Resource and Environmental Policy at the University of Minnesota. He has worked for more than ten years with natural resource-dependent communities with an emphasis on community development, social impact assessment, and natural resource policy and economics with recent emphasis on strategies to reduce the risks of wildland fire to communities.

HOLLY WISE BENDER is a Principal at Integrated Resource Solutions. Her primary research focuses have been in the area of public land policy, participatory decision making, regulatory analysis, and the integration of marketing and consumer-behavior philosophies into public-land policy issues.

JIM BURCHFIELD is the Associate Dean at the College of Forestry and Conservation at the University of Montana. His major interest centers on how people may reside and interact with forest and grassland settings in a productive, harmonious manner. Dr. Burchfield studies the effectiveness of community-based groups, recently examining the principles of social acceptability of forest management and the effects of wildfires on rural communities.

HANNA CORTNER is President of Cortner and Associates (Flagstaff, Arizona). She has held positions as professor in the Ecological Restoration Institute at Northern Arizona University and in the School of Renewable Natural Resources at the University of Arizona, and has published extensively over the past twenty-five years in the area of fire policy.

PATRICIA J. COHN is a Research Associate at Washington State University. Her research has focused on social assessment in a natural resource context and mill capacity and utilization of small-diameter timber.

DONALD R. FIELD is Professor in the Department of Forest Ecology and Management at the University of Wisconsin–Madison. His current research interests focus on rural landscapes, public lands, and human populations, in particular the changing character of rural communities resulting from in-migration of new and seasonal residents. Dr. Field is cofounder of the International Association of Society and Natural Resources.

COURTNEY G. FLINT is an Assistant Professor at the University of Illinois, where her research interests include community response to large-scale forest ecosystem disturbances and the relationship between risk perception and community action.

ARMANDO GONZÁLEZ-CABÁN is Research Economist with the USDA Forest Service, Pacific Southwest Research Station, Forest Fire Laboratory in Riverside, California. He has worked for over twenty-five years in the fire economics field, with emphasis on the economic effects of wildland fires on natural resources, and the attitudes and values of individuals towards Forest Service fire-management policies.

THOMAS P. HOLMES is a Research Forester with the USDA Forest Service Southern Forest Research Station. His current research is focused on testing new methods and conducting field experiments in the area of non-market valuation; and development of methods and models for investigating sustainable forest management in tropical forests.

ROBERT HUGGETT is an Economist with the USDA Forest Service Southern Forest Research Station. Dr. Huggett's research includes environmental and resource economics, decision making under uncertainty and risk, the economics of wildfire, and natural resource accounting.

PAMELA J. JAKES is a Project Leader and Research Social Scientist with the USDA Forest Service North Central Research Station. Her work focuses on the social and economic dimensions of ecosystem management. Dr. Jakes has been the leader of an influential national program of case studies of the preparedness of communities exposed to wildfire risk.

RICHARD S. KRANNICH is Professor of Sociology and Head of the Department of Sociology, Social Work and Anthropology at Utah State University. His current research interests focus on social change associated with population growth and decline in rural areas affected by economic transition; the social consequences of technological risks and hazards; and the human dimensions of wildlife resource management.

YOSHITAKA KUMAGAI is an Associate Professor, and a Director of Regional Sustainability Research Institute at the Akita International University (AIU) in Japan. Before joining AIU, he had been working at Washington State University and Oregon State University in social science dimensions of natural resource management with an emphasis on understanding causal attribution of wildfire and social impacts of natural disasters, at Washington State University and Oregon State University.

A. E. LULOFF is Professor in the Department of Agricultural Economics and Rural Sociology, at the Pennsylvania State University. His work emphasizes the impacts of sociodemographic shifts on natural and human resource bases; changes in land cover and use, particularly at the rural-urban fringe; and the impact of rural development policy on small and rural communities.

INGRID M. MARTIN is Associate Professor of Marketing at California State University, Long Beach. Her research concentrates on the effect of warnings and risk-related information on individual behavior.

WADE E. MARTIN is Professor of Economics at California State University, Long Beach. His research focuses on environmental and natural resource issues. He received his Ph.D. in economics from the University of New Mexico.

SARA MCCAFFREY is a Research Social Scientist for the USDA Forest Service, North Central Research Station in Evanston, Illinois. She is currently responsible for a National Fire Plan project examining individual reactions to fuel treatments and is co-leader of a national effort to synthesize current scientific knowledge, from both the ecological and social perspectives, that can help inform fuels planners.

KRISTEN C. NELSON is an Assistant Professor of Human Dimensions at the University of Minnesota, in the Department of Forest Resources and the Department of Fisheries, Wildlife, and Conservation Biology. Recently her research focus has included the social mechanisms that influence community impacts on and responses to ecosystem change; water quality and citizen monitoring; community capacity and wildfire preparedness; and homeowner landscape preferences and defensible space.

JEFFREY P. PRESTEMON is a Research Forester with the USDA Forest Service Southern Forest Research Station. Dr. Prestemon's principal study areas are: economic and statistical analysis of forest-based disturbances; international trade; and timber market structure and function.

BRUCE SHINDLER is Associate Professor of Forest Social Science at Oregon State University. His research focuses on human values for natural resources and the relationship between resource agencies and citizens for decision making. Dr. Shindler's studies on forest health and wildland-fire management have been central to ecosystem and adaptive management strategies.

JOEL VIERS is a Research Specialist with the Ecological Restoration Institute at Northern Arizona University where he explores the wide range of economic and social issues related to southwestern pine forest restoration.

CHARLES R. WISE is Professor of Public Affairs in the School of Public and Environmental Affairs at Indiana University. He has worked for over thirty years on environmental and public management topics and served for three years on the National Academmy of Public Administration Panel on Wildland Fire.

ANDREW J. YODER is a graduate of the Indiana University School of Public and Environmental Affairs and the School of Law. He is serving as Law Clerk to the Honorable Royal Furgeson, U.S. District Court, Western District of Texas.

Index